Academics in Action!

Academics in Action!

A MODEL FOR COMMUNITY-ENGAGED
RESEARCH, TEACHING, AND SERVICE

*Sandra L. Barnes, Lauren Brinkley-Rubinstein,
Bernadette Doykos, Nina C. Martin, and Allison McGuire
Editors*

FORDHAM UNIVERSITY PRESS
New York 2016

Copyright © 2016 Fordham University Press

All rights reserved. No part of this publication may be reproduced, stored in a retrieval system, or transmitted in any form or by any means—electronic, mechanical, photocopy, recording, or any other—except for brief quotations in printed reviews, without the prior permission of the publisher.

Fordham University Press has no responsibility for the persistence or accuracy of URLs for external or third-party Internet websites referred to in this publication and does not guarantee that any content on such websites is, or will remain, accurate or appropriate.

Fordham University Press also publishes its books in a variety of electronic formats. Some content that appears in print may not be available in electronic books.

Visit us online at www.fordhampress.com.

Library of Congress Cataloging-in-Publication Data

Names: Barnes, Sandra L., editor.
Title: Academics in action! : a model for community-engaged research, teaching, and service / edited by Sandra L. Barnes, Lauren Brinkley-Rubinstein, Bernadette Doykos, Nina C. Martin, and Allison McGuire.
Description: First edition. | New York : Fordham University Press, [2016] |
Includes bibliographical references and index.
Identifiers: LCCN 2015024178| ISBN 9780823268795 (cloth : alk. paper) | ISBN 9780823268801 (pbk. : alk. paper)
Subjects: LCSH: Action research in education. | Community and school. |
Dewey, John, 1859–1952.
Classification: LCC LB1028.24 .A23 2016 | DDC 370.72—dc23
LC record available at http://lccn.loc.gov/2015024178

Printed in the United States of America

18 17 16   5 4 3 2 1

First edition

Contents

Introduction
Sandra L. Barnes, Lauren Brinkley-Rubinstein, Bernadette Doykos, Nina C. Martin, and Allison McGuire   1

PART I: THEORIES, FRAMEWORKS, AND TWENTY-FIRST CENTURY DEWEYISM

1 John Dewey, Participatory Democracy, and University-Community Partnerships
Robert Innes, Leigh Gilchrist, Susan Friedman, and Kristen Tompkins   27

2 The Ethical Foundations of Human and Organizational Development Programs: The Ethics of Human Development and Community Across the Curriculum
Paul R. Dokecki, Mark McCormack, Hasina Mohyuddin, and Linda Isaacs   49

PART II: IMPLICATIONS AND RESPONSES: *ACADEMICS IN ACTION!*

3 Using Research to Guide Efforts to Prevent and End Homelessness
Marybeth Shinn, Lindsay S. Mayberry, Andrew L. Greer, Benjamin W. Fisher, Jessica Gibbons-Benton, and Vera S. Chatman   75

4 Ecological Research Promoting Positive Youth Development
Carol T. Nixon, Bernadette Doykos, Velma McBride Murry, Maury Nation, Nina C. Martin, Alley Pickren, and Joseph Gardella   98

5 Putting Boyer's Four Types of Scholarship into Practice: A Community Research and Action Perspective on Public Health
Lauren Brinkley-Rubinstein, Vera S. Chatman, Laurel Lunn, Abbey Mann, and Craig Anne Heflinger   124

6 Conducting Research on Comprehensive Community
Development Initiatives: Balancing Methodological Rigor
and Community Responsiveness
*Kimberly D. Bess, Bernadette Doykos, Joanna D. Geller,
Krista L. Craven, and Maury Nation*   142

PART III: ACADEMIC STRUCTURES THAT FOSTER SYNERGY,
COLLABORATION, AND COURSES

7 The Field School in Intercultural Education as a Model for
International Service-Learning and Collaborative
Action-Research Training
*Holly L. Karakos, Benjamin W. Fisher, Joanna Geller, Laurel Lunn,
Neal A. Palmer, Douglas D. Perkins, Nikolay Mihaylov,
William L. Partridge, and Sharon Shields*   167

8 Creating a Mosaic of Religious Values and Narratives:
Participant-Researcher Roles of an Interfaith Research
Group Seeking to Understand Interfaith Organizations
*Hasina Mohyuddin, Mark McCormack, Paul R. Dokecki,
and Linda Isaacs*   191

9 Internship: Situated Learning in the Department of Human
and Organizational Development
*Heather L. Smith, Victoria J. Davis, Marybeth Shinn,
and Stephanie Zuckerman*   213

10 Can Synergy Across Theory, Pedagogy, and Practice Guide
Professional Education? The Community Development and
Action and Human Development Counseling Graduate Experiences
*Andrew Finch, Oluchi Nwosu, Gina Frieden, Emily Hennessey,
Craig Anne Heflinger, Allison McGuire, Sarah V. Suiter,
Emily Burchfield, Nina C. Martin, Linda Isaacs, Lauren
Brinkley-Rubenstein, Paul Speer, Abbey Mann, Sharon Shields,
Neal Palmer, Bethany Pittman, and Sandra L. Barnes*   238

Conclusion: Academics in Action—Bridging Principles
and Practice!   260

About the Editors   273
Index   275

Academics in Action!

Introduction

SANDRA L. BARNES, LAUREN BRINKLEY-RUBINSTEIN, BERNADETTE DOYKOS, NINA C. MARTIN, AND ALLISON MCGUIRE

> Ideas are worthless except as they pass into actions which rearrange and reconstruct in some way, be it little or large, the world in which we live.
>
> —John Dewey, 1929[1]

Town versus gown—publish or perish. The academy is often described as an ivory tower, isolated from the community around it. This edited volume[2] describes a more integrated model for the academy wherein students and faculty work with communities, learn from them, and bring to bear findings from theory and research on generating solutions for solving community problems. Because social problems are not the provenance of any one discipline, the model is inherently interdisciplinary, wherein theory and action span multiple ecological levels from individuals and small groups to organizations and social structures. The communities of engagement range from local neighborhoods and schools to arenas of national policy and international development. These forms of engagement require carefully crafted institutional structures and intentionally monitored processes for support. This volume offers examples of community-engaged theory, scholarship, teaching, and action and describes the nuanced structures that foster and support their development within a research university. Examples are drawn from the Department of Human and Organizational Development (HOD) at Vanderbilt University's

---

1. From *Reason and Teaching* by Israel Scheffler (1973). New York: Routledge Press, p. 154.

2. This volume reflects the editorial efforts of a first editor (Sandra L. Barnes) and a team of second editors. The four-person group of second editors (Allison McGuire, Nina C. Martin, Bernadette Doykos, and Lauren Brinkley-Rubinstein) made equal contributions toward the completion of this volume.

Peabody College of Education and Human Development.[3] In HOD, programs from undergraduate service learning and internships, to masters programs in applied human services, to doctoral training in community research and action embody the vision of *Academics in Action!*

This multidisciplinary, mixed-methodological endeavor includes academic, applied, and instructional collaborative work between faculty and students. Because each chapter includes the unique perspectives of research faculty, practitioners, and graduate students, this edited volume reflects academic cooperation at its best. In the chapters that follow, the authors examine the distinct theoretical frameworks, action-oriented research, traditional academic studies nuanced to reflect specific societal concerns, policy studies, and descriptions of programs and initiatives that make research more relevant to students, faculty, and the communities they serve. This text documents: a specific philosophy of education that fosters and supports engagement; the potentially transformative nature of academic work for students, faculty, and the broader society; and, some of the implications and challenges of action-oriented efforts in light of dynamics such as income inequality, racism, and global capitalism. We posit that embedding participatory action-oriented endeavors strategically in teaching, research, and community service provides real-world examples to counter "town versus gown" tendencies for long-term beneficence inside and outside academia. Moreover, the chapters that follow document how authentic partnerships between the academy and the community result in more relevant and meaningful research and practices.

This edited volume examines the following questions: What constitutes community-engaged research, teaching, and service? How does it take place at and across institutional, group, and individual levels? What are some contemporary examples? What are some of the theoretical lenses, research methodologies, and teaching tools most amenable to such academic endeavors? How can community members, students, and researchers work together to thoughtfully and proactively respond to social problems? How can researchers self-reflect to concertedly cham-

---

3. HOD was formally begun in 2000. Bob Newbrough and Paul Dokecki wrote the rationale for the department. Other persons involved were Sharon Shields, Robert Innes, Gina Frieden, Brian Griffin, and Vera Chatman. Howard Sandler was the first HOD chair. Readers should visit the HOD website for details on how the HOD department was conceptualized, organized, and developed.

pion projects and teaching/learning processes that encourage increased citizenship and critical thinking for themselves and among their colleagues, students, and community members? Responses to these types of questions will help illuminate the possibilities, benefits, and challenges associated with action-oriented work.

We continue in the tradition of nineteenth-century theorist, philosopher, academician, and educational reformer John Dewey (1902, 1910, 1938, 1954, 1981), drawing on varied paradigmatic perspectives, analytical approaches, and informational sources to examine the interrelatedness between academic discourses and the real world. Moreover, because Dewey's stance engenders intellectual curiosity and appreciation for diverse educational perspectives, inquiries here are also undergirded by other scholarly paradigms such as critical race theory (Bonilla-Silva, 2006; Feagin, 2006, 2010), ecological theory of human development (Bronfenbrenner, 1977, 1986), organizational theory (Senge, 2006; Yang, Watkins, & Marsick, 2004), feminist theory (Collins, 2000, 2009, 2010; Ostrander, 1999; Scott, 2005), and reflective-generative practice (Dokecki, 1996; Schön, 1983, 1995). Thoughtfully incorporating other paradigms and ideas enables us to extend Dewey's framework to holistically understand and respond to varied social issues.

Additionally, we consider theoretical and empirical work from disciplines such as social psychology, cultural studies, sociology, psychology, ecology, political science, policy studies, scholarship of teaching and learning, and environmental studies and the relevance of systemic disparities for meaningful community engagement and practices. Synthesis across these and other teaching and learning models provides the collaborative, interactive approaches on which interdisciplinary studies are based. *Academics in Action!* also includes work from a cross-section of noted researchers, instructors, practitioners, and counselors in the social sciences and humanities as well as graduate students who are already making singular contributions as scholar-activists. Chapters illustrate the reciprocal relationship between research, teaching, and praxis as members of academia and the communities they serve strive collaboratively to "make sense" of the complex society we all must negotiate.

Engaging in Relevant Research, Teaching, and Community Action

The model for community-engaged research, teaching, and service emphasized here does not suggest that other disciplines are not actively engaged in responding to social problems and working with students in transformative ways. Rather, the present volume documents specific instances of some of the benefits and hurdles of community-based endeavors. Our goal is to chronicle teaching, research, and community action that influences people both inside and outside the classroom as well as to present dimensions of a participatory model that set such efforts into action. Each chapter illustrates how research, teaching, and community service can be professionally and personally impactful and explains why these three traditional facets of academic life do not have to be mutually exclusive but rather combine to make a more comprehensive, fulfilling academic, student, and community experience. Chapters provide ideas, strategies, and best practices for readers interested in pursuing similar research, teaching, and service—regardless of their institutional or departmental resource level. Although we concede that accomplishing such objectives may seem daunting in light of the diverse spaces from which community members, students, and academics may emerge, we believe that HOD has proven successful in balancing the competing priorities of academia and community engagement.

The primary mission of HOD is to understand organizations and the people who constitute them, prioritizing a community experience alongside rigorous curriculum for students and scholarship on the part of the faculty and staff. The traditional "town/gown" separation has been examined in research, especially in regard to its impact on community-based research (Bruning, McGrew, & Cooper, 2006; Mayfield, 2001; McWilliam, Desai, & Greig, 1997). Studies show that extensive institutional support is required to provide meaningful academic experiences and high-quality community-based research (Ayala, 2009). Simply espousing such a mission is insufficient, due in part to the varied backgrounds and experiences of students, faculty, and communities. For example, despite increasing diversity in post-secondary education, students from wealthy families are more likely to enroll in elite, private universities (Bowen, Kurzweil, & Tobin, 2005). Faculty may come from similar backgrounds or end up in comparable socioeconomic positions as a result of educational attainment. The privilege of such students and faculty can result in lived experiences and perspectives that differ dramatically from communities they may engage.

Common characteristics of privilege include significantly higher household incomes and wealth accumulation, extensive social networks, and other forms of familial capital and their associated accoutrements (Bourdieu, 1984; Oliver and Shapiro 1997). Moreover, in 2005, CEOs of large U.S. companies earned an average annual compensation of $18.9 million—more than 400 times as much as the average factory worker (Strauss and Hansen, 2006). In contrast, 2011 U.S. Census statistics show that 46.2 million people in the United States live in poverty. Furthermore, a disproportionate percentage of racial minorities are poor. Minority students graduate from high school and college at considerably lower rates than their white counterparts (*Journal of Blacks in Higher Education*, 2008). Economic, social, and political disparities have been correlated with the feminization and juvenilization of poverty, chronic unemployment, food deprivation, and homelessness, as well as lack of affordable, accessible, and available childcare, healthcare, and low-cost housing. Furthermore, globally, almost 16,000 children die each day from hunger-related causes—about one every five seconds (Barnes, 2005; Bread for the World, 2010; Fellmeth, 2005; Hays, 2003; Lykens & Jargowsky, 2002; National Center for Child Poverty, 2002). Despite notable strides to improve the life chances and quality of life of disenfranchised people, much work still needs to be done to reduce and eliminate the gap between the most well off and their struggling counterparts both here and abroad.

This sobering information might suggest an untenable chasm between many of the *students* we engage, *faculty* who teach, and the *communities* we serve. Our imperative is to bridge this divide in a manner that taps into often hidden inter-group expertise; challenges each of us to think and act in more inclusive ways; and, simultaneously, maximizes the singular experiences each group brings to the encounter. In this academic space, these often disparate individuals and groups are introduced and challenged to impact each other's lives and experiences in ways that will be mutually beneficial to them and society in general. Practices to educate and build inter-group community require a unique set of teaching and learning skills to challenge students and faculty to question some of their long-standing assumptions and personal stereotypes and acknowledge the proficiencies and value found in multicultural spaces. Similarly, these efforts require uncovering and building social capital among groups that have been directly or indirectly disempowered. We contend that these types of intra- and inter-group transformations necessitate action-oriented, interdisciplinary teaching, research, and community engagement. One must be willing to simultaneously center the disparate experiences and expectations of some of the *most privileged* and the *most historically oppressed* groups—and to accept the challenge of grappling with the often-troubling complexities of this task. This, too, represents contemporary applications of Deweyism in an interdisciplinary context.

Academics in Action! adds to existing literature in several ways. First, it details the theoretical perspectives, processes, and implications of community-based research, teaching, and service. It also informs the applied arena by profiling studies and instruction specifically geared toward faculty engagement, student transformation, and the need to address pressing social problems. Furthermore, this volume provides an important avenue for considering some of the strengths and challenges associated with collaborative, interdisciplinary research and teaching. Finally, as a model of what a department engaged in such endeavors "looks like," it may help encourage and foster similar efforts in other settings. Common threads across each chapter include: contemporary efforts to adopt and adapt aspects of Deweyism to address societal concerns; approaches that inform theory with praxis; practical information and best practices for readers to replicate and implement; and, examples of how interdisciplinary work can inform teaching, research, and community action. To our knowledge, no other current edited volume examines this subject specifically from the varied perspectives of noted scholars in the discipline, burgeoning researchers, graduate students, undergraduate students, and community activists. Our ultimate objective is to inform and inspire readers interested in similar pursuits to collaborate to transform spaces inside and outside academia.

A Summary of Interdisciplinary Inquiry and Action in the Department of Human and Organizational Development

The initial impetus for this project occurred in 2006, as a cadre of professors struggled to identify how to make teaching and research more socially relevant. They conceded that students could no longer be taught, communities entered and exited, or research performed in isolation. Intentional synergy would have to be forged to interconnect these goals most effectively; and these transforming efforts would have to be documented and systematized. Although the project was reluctantly tabled, its initial energy and excitement remained and has been refueled as a result of a plethora of discussions, discourses, and debates as the department grew and became more heterogeneous. A clear consensus emerged that the project be continued with an expanded vision and nuanced objectives. Results are intriguing and sometimes controversial, yet each chapter challenges readers to move beyond myopic, often entrenched, approaches to teaching, research, and community involvement.

An interdisciplinary (also referred to as multidisciplinary in some arenas) approach assumes that multiple theoretical perspectives, methodologies, and analytical strategies are required to most thoughtfully investigate social phenomena. It also posits equal validity across these approaches and queries of interest. However, this stance was not always the case. During the late nineteenth century and much of the twentieth century, professional educators commonly espoused a "one best system" mindset that focused on a single line of inquiry. However, in light of social change such as the globalization of world economies, computer and information revolutions, increasing human diversity, and a growing challenge to recognize and respond to inequality worldwide, a "one best system" approach is being challenged by academicians and practitioners and supplanted by alternative paradigms. Pressing contemporary societal challenges experienced in virtually all dimensions of social life demand the development of sound, culturally informed and culturally sensitive social practices that enhance human development through educational processes operating in a wide variety of community settings. The multifaceted nature of our interdisciplinary work means that the voices and needs of students and communities in which we partner are considered simultaneously. *Interdisciplinarity* enables us to respond to a myriad of issues in society.

Dewey (1910, 1954, 1981) maintained that learning in a truly democratic society would be interactive, collaborative, and evolving. To him, democracy is a result of learning from each other to address individual and collective problems. Furthermore, a democratic society emerges when people realize their interconnectedness through discourse, engagement, and shared participation. These latter two ideals reflect the essence of citizenship that higher education is challenged to inculcate. Students, faculty, and staff are challenged to acknowledge their civic role in solving common problems that impact people at the local, national, and international level. Dewey envisioned education as a space for dialogue and collaboration; he developed a philosophy and pedagogy to support this objective. It suggests that to assume public responsibility and assert public interests, a person must acquire public-oriented consciousness, language, ways of thinking, and habits of action—all are critical teaching and learning objectives of an interdisciplinary model that is coupled with a commitment for excellence. Simply put, interdisciplinary inquiry requires: (1) a problem orientation approach across disciplines; (2) knowledge and usage of varied theories and theoretical perspectives; (3) a decision to develop knowledge and professional practices; (4) acknowledgement of the value and inherent knowledge and experiences of persons and communities with which we partner; and, (5) a commitment to analyzing the value and ethical issues implicit in transformation efforts for individuals, groups, organizations, and the larger society.

Many studies in higher education seem to have reached an impasse in identifying, documenting, and analyzing factors that are directly and indirectly shaping the state of education in a global society. Scholars and teachers are confronted with increasingly more complicated issues, such as continued performance disparities between minority youth and their white peers in both pre-college and collegiate settings, chronic underfunding in public schools, challenges responding to the diverse socialization needs of immigrants, appropriate training strategies to ensure U.S. global competitiveness, and effective community capacity building among the poor (Collins, 2009; Davis, 2004; Delpit, 2006; Dewey, 1916). The inability to systemically address chronic educational challenges in general, and inequities, in particular, stands in contrast with Dewey's (1916) model of providing teaching and learning enterprises in a democracy. Anecdotes describe the benefits of multicultural inquiry informed by community-engaged research and teaching. Yet fewer studies have empirically documented multicultural educational initiatives that originate in community settings; holistic, instructional innovations that are emerging globally; and processes based on the unique circumstances and strengths of diverse populations. These types of complexities as well as related, emerging unknowns suggest the need for the type of paradigmatic emphasis espoused by Dewey and used in HOD.

This volume posits the need for the use of Dewey's model in teaching and research in higher education. Applying a community-based model to academic inquiry and instruction in higher education is also in the spirit of efforts by other Deweyan innovators such as Jurgen Habermas, Alain Locke, Martin Luther King, Cornel West, and Patricia Hill Collins. The chapters in this volume provide direct evidence of the academic and practical benefits of such a model to more comprehensively and thoughtfully perform research, teaching, and community service. Moreover, the volume illustrates how this same educational model can be effectively used in a variety of academic disciplines to systematically study various topics and answer questions that are emerging in the ever-changing landscape of higher education. As evident in HOD, multidisciplinary collaboration, community-based studies, and reflective teaching and mentoring constitute a broad-based model that can help make significant inroads in diverse arenas. Furthermore, chapters in this volume show how strategically embedding community-based research and teaching with Deweyism provide a crucial mechanism to help facilitate the emergence of a more democratic society that engenders educational equality, empowerment, and innovations for students, teachers, and community members alike.

Like Dewey, HOD is interested in the development of both the individual person and the collective. Accordingly, our interdisciplinarity is oriented toward research, both in the university and in the community, about learning environments that produce accessible and useable knowledge about positive development and life-span developmental processes, especially adult learning. Methodologically, this commitment requires reflective-generative practice and human science perspectives that entail a problem orientation and the selection of appropriate methods from the full range of those available for systematic inquiry. Like Peabody College of Education and Human Development, HOD[4]

---

4. In 1979, Peabody College became Vanderbilt University's College of Education and Human Development. Following the merger, Peabody faculty members were challenged to integrate their scholarly activities centered on social change into the orientation of Vanderbilt as a major research university. In addition to continuing to address societal problems in education and human development, now part of a Research I Institution, the college incorporates more traditional behavioral science into its research, development,

contends that education encompasses all socialization functions in a community and serves as the basis for both individual and community development. The intellectual focus of HOD reflects life-span development (including adult development) through the enhancement of life-long learning and the development of caring and competent learning communities.[5] Community service and service learning are integral to the HOD program. Students are introduced to socially problematic situations at the beginning of their program and are challenged to pursue their interests. Such an imperative is expected to inform future decisions such that students consider themselves citizens and community servants—no matter whether they pursue roles as business leaders, homemakers, teachers, lawyers, bankers, scientists, or doctors. Similarly, social development concepts paralleling human development are used to guide the work for community development and social service policy. Evaluation of interventions is a crucial aspect of the work in the department, as well, to continue to accumulate knowledge of what works and what does not.

Our efforts to interrelate the substantive streams of life-span human development and community development mean focusing scholarship on civil society at two broad levels. First, the level of the individual implies that persons are socialized (with an emphasis on well-being and positive development throughout the life span) as responsible civic members integrated into the public life of the community and helped to maximize their potential. Second, the level of collectivities focuses on the development of communities through a social learning process that emphasizes diversity, social justice, social participation, and empowerment. We contend that through enhancement of the individual and the collective, society can be transformed.

---

and training as it simultaneously maintains its historical broad-based understanding of education that extends beyond traditional teaching and learning processes and expectations.

5. Faculty endeavor to develop, and help students learn to apply, conceptual and methodological approaches that contribute to the redesign, reconstruction, and evaluation of a wide variety of social institutions in pursuit of enhanced human development and the creation of social capital. In addition to a focus on social institutions, faculty prepare students to facilitate the development of individuals in various social contexts, thereby allowing students to learn to enhance development on both an individual and societal level.

Participatory Research: Synergizing Old and New Meanings and Methods

This volume is not the first to focus on the nexus between research, teaching, and service as a lens for participatory work. Nor is it the first endeavor to center interdisciplinarity during intellectual collaboration in an intentional way. For example, in *Collaborative Research: University and Community Partnership*, Sullivan and Kelly (2001) describe team-based research among public health researchers, interdisciplinary scholars, community-based organizers, and local residents. In addition to identifying some of the epistemological pitfalls of research that excludes involvement by community members and the insight that could result, its case studies, essays, and experiential commentary by participants illustrate the clear benefits of the participatory research process. Moreover, the authors document the research and evaluation process, paying specific attention to project milestones in which collaboration between research partners was crucial to making decisions most appropriate for the specific context and community issue. Similarly, Gershon's (2009) *The Collaborative Turn Working Together in Qualitative Research* pushes the envelope on what should be considered collaborative qualitative research. Faculty-student interdisciplinary projects from a myriad of teaching and research backgrounds provide examples of how ethics, narrative analyses, reflexivity, storytelling, and revisioned ethnographic approaches can bridge traditional academic and applied efforts, move qualitative studies in new directions, and respond to contemporary social challenges.

More recently, the *Action Research Guidebook: A Four-Stage Process for Educators and School Teams* by Richard Sagor (2010) positions action research as the preferred model for informed academic work in education. The guidebook focuses on collaborative action research and the empowerment of public school educators. Sagor stresses the importance and value of collaborative research teams that include school leaders and traditional scholars united to develop projects based on specific needs in their respective sites. For Sagor, cultivating successful school performance for students, teachers, and administrators alike requires creative problem solving by *educational architects* willing to use research practices in innovative ways. His step-by-step guide to implementing an action research project from inception to analysis and implementation of results represents a seminal instructional piece, particularly for new entrants in the action research arena. Similarly, in *Doing Collaborative Research in Psychology*, Detweiler and Detweiler-Bedell (2012) offer a model to facilitate research conducted by undergraduates. It, too, emphasizes team-based inquiry in the discipline of psychology, focused largely on how faculty and graduate students can help undergraduates perform research. In sum, Sagor (2010) provides a model for collaborative research to transform public schools, Detweiler and Detweiler-Bedell (2012) promote participatory action among psychologists, Sullivan and Kelly (2001) work similarly in the public health arena, and Gershon (2009) successfully re-imagines how qualitative methods can be employed to address current societal problems.

In their own unique way, each of these volumes emphasizes the social nature of relevant research and the pitfalls when research that is expected to impact the community occurs in isolation. Each volume substantiates the necessity of the current work. Since the publication of these texts, significant societal and interdisciplinary changes have continued to occur that challenge academics to establish and/or heighten and strengthen partnerships among students, community leaders, and researchers. Both the challenges described by previous works and the contextual changes that have developed since their publication support the importance of this volume. We continue this same tradition while paying close attention to creative synergies across: diverse disciplines; theories and praxis; classrooms, communities, and other social institutions; and local, regional, national, and global contexts. In doing so, we endeavor ultimately to position collaborative research as a model that energizes the best of existing and emergent approaches to participatory work and its important place in the academy.

Exploring the Practice and Processes of Academic Work That Works

In addition to the Introduction and Conclusion, the ten chapters in this volume are grouped into three broad themes: (1) theories and new frameworks; (2) implications and responses; and (3) academic structures that foster synergy and collaboration. We focus on these three themes because we believe it is important to consider the influence of paradigms, structural forces inside and outside academia, as well as results, outcomes, and possible push-back on participatory academic work. Moreover, each chapter includes a table titled, "Getting Started!" designed to help readers initiate their own action-oriented efforts. The first two chapters illustrate the centrality of theoretical models and perspectives that foster community-based academic inquiry as well as highlight how paradigms linked to social justice and community service can undergird college-based programmatic efforts, particularly as experienced by students, faculty, and community partners.

In Chapter 1, "John Dewey, Participatory Democracy and University-Community Partnerships," Robert Innes, Leigh Gilchrist, Susan Friedman, and Kristen Tompkins position the paradigmatic views and practices of John Dewey as a provocative model for academic investigations. They entertain the question: How is a nineteenth-century theorist and philosopher germane today? They contend that the interdisciplinary field of learning science that has emerged over the last twenty years has been guided by a constructivist view of learning that traces its philosophical roots to John Dewey. However, they suggest that the transformative impact of learning science has been the least impactful in the collegiate teaching arena. This chapter examines the implications of learning science research for meeting educational goals related to tolerance for diversity, civic responsibility, and concern for the common good. Chapter 2, "The Ethical Foundations of Human and Organizational Development Programs: The Ethics of Human Development and Community Across the Curriculum," challenges readers to consider the place of ethics in collaborative teaching and research. Informed by the *ethics of human development and community*, Paul Dokecki, Mark McCormack, Hasina Mohyuddin, and Linda Isaacs present a reflective-generative ethical approach to teaching; develop the approach based on student and colleague interactions; and cultivate a rationale for the centrality of ethics across college curricula.

In Part II, chapters focus on a specific social problem to illustrate how collaborative, participatory efforts can contribute to existing literature as well as help combat societal challenges and enhance the quality of life of disenfranchised groups. They also represent exemplars of community-based research despite the demands of traditional academic expectations. In Chapter 3, "Using Research to Guide Efforts to Prevent and End Homelessness," Marybeth Shinn, Lindsay Mayberry, Andrew Greer,

Benjamin Fisher, Jessica Gibbons-Benton, and Vera Chatman use research to create change around housing and homelessness. Rather than provide a traditional research report, the authors describe the nature of projects in which they have engaged, processes, implementation strategies, research challenges, and outcomes. Projects referenced include work with the housing fund on a neighborhood stabilization grant, research based on a large randomized trial to examine what works for homeless families, and a targeting model for prevention services. Outcomes provide best practices and suggestions for persons interested in combating homelessness proactively and partnering with others with similar objectives. Next, according to Carol Nixon, Bernadette Doykos, Velma Murry, Maury Nation, Nina C. Martin, Alley Pickren, and Joseph Gardella in "Ecological Research Promoting Positive Youth Development" (Chapter 4), many programs that aim to promote youth development have focused on youths' skills and their peers as targets of intervention. An interdisciplinary consensus exists that ecological context greatly affects children's social, emotional, and academic development. Existing research is limited in how it addresses the dynamics of interaction between social context and youth development interventions. Their chapter addresses this limitation by examining important family, school, and community factors that interact with youth development intervention. Moreover, it describes research sponsored by HOD that intentionally addresses ecological factors as part of family- and school-based interventions that are conducted in urban and rural environments.

Just as educational inequities can be countered collaboratively, Chapter 5, "Putting Boyer's Four Types of Scholarship into Practice: A Community Research and Action Perspective on Public Health" by Lauren Brinkley-Rubenstein, Vera Chatman, Laurel Lunn, Abbey Mann, and Craig Anne Heflinger challenges traditional approaches to health that stress biomedical solutions and preventive tactics. The authors contend that a multidisciplinary perspective on health and well-being is needed to understand how social, contextual, and structural elements affect individual and community health. Their chapter considers how social determinants of health can provide an avenue for the incorporation of a health curriculum into social justice–oriented, interdisciplinary research. The final chapter of this section examines the role of academic partners in applying for and implementing a Promise Neighborhoods federal grant.

In Chapter 6, "Conducting Research on Comprehensive Community Development Initiatives: Balancing Methodological Rigor and Community Responsiveness," Kimberly Bess, Bernadette Doykos, Joanna Geller, Krista Craven, and Maury Nation make a compelling argument that Community-Based Participatory Research (CBPR) offers the opportunity for university-affiliated researchers to deconstruct the ivory tower of academia and academic research. They contend that through its innovative methods, collaborative work bridges the gap between "researcher" and "subject" by engaging community partners as essential and equitable contributors, while maintaining high standards of rigor due to the demands of the government administered grant supporting the work. The authors offer a case study of the planning and execution of a Community Needs Assessment to highlight obstacles including barriers to engaging community members, Institutional Review Board challenges, and the competing needs of community partners and institutional procedures and expectations.

Part III concentrates on academic structures that foster synergy and collaboration. In this section, authors present specific programmatic and empirical evidence of the beneficence of collaborative teaching, research, and community involvement both in the United States and abroad. Details are also presented about HOD's professional master's programs in Human Development Counseling (HDC) and Community Development and Action (CDA) as well as the doctoral program in Community Research and Action (CRA). Chapter 7, "The Field School in Intercultural Education as a Model for International Service-Learning and Collaborative Action-Research Training" by Holly L. Karakos, Benjamin W. Fisher, Joanna Geller, Laurel Lunn, Neal A. Palmer, Douglas D. Perkins, Nikolay Mihaylov, William L. Partridge, and Sharon Shields, documents a contemporary innovation to internationalize interdisciplinarity. The Field School trains future professionals and scholars in international, collaborative community-based action-research and provides benefits to host countries and educational partners. It involves faculty; graduate *and* undergraduate students from Vanderbilt University and universities in less-developed host countries such as Ecuador, Argentina, China, and South Africa; as well as local development, health, and education agencies. By engaging in supervised research in cultures very different from their own, both students and local partners learn to: be more culturally sensitive;

develop collaborative research skills needed for interdisciplinary teamwork; understand diverse development policies and political dynamics and their impact; and strengthen human and organizational capacity for generating community ties.

Action-oriented academic work would be remiss without considering how participatory models fare when implemented in religious spaces. In Chapter 8, "Creating a Mosaic of Religious Values and Narratives: Participant-Researcher Roles of an Interfaith Research Group Seeking to Understand Interfaith Organizations," Hasina Mohyuddin, Mark McCormack, Paul Dokecki, and Linda Isaacs describe and self-reflectively analyze ongoing efforts to determine how several local and national community groups have formed to address interfaith conflict, especially where Muslims are involved. Their mixed-methodological research includes participant-observations, narratives, and questionnaire results. The team also engages in self-study as an interfaith group. In doing so, they consider how religiosity potentially nuances collaborative efforts. What are other ways participatory teaching and research can impact the lives of undergraduate students? Heather Smith, Victoria Davis, Marybeth Shinn, and Stephanie Zuckerman provide insight into this query in Chapter 9, "Internship: Situated Learning in the Department of Human and Organizational Development." They illustrate how a supervised field experience should be a critical component for learning and development in a community-based department. The chapter examines the unique internship requirement for students designed to enable them to apply foundational community development principles and coursework as well as build professional skill sets in meaningful settings to address authentic problems and opportunities. The chapter illustrates the "nuts and bolts" of action-oriented community training using organizational profiles, participant experiences, and comments from faculty and students involved in the process.

In Chapter 10, "Can Synergy Across Theory, Pedagogy, and Practice Guide Professional Education? The Community Development and Action and Human Development Counseling Graduate Experiences," a large team of students and faculty address the theoretical and pragmatic aspects underlying two professional master's degree programs situated in HOD called Community Development and Action (CDA) and Human Development Counseling (HDC) as well as capture the experiences and voices of program participants (Andrew Finch, Oluchi Nwosu, Gina Frieden, Emily Hennessey, Craig Anne Heflinger, Allison McGuire, Sarah Suiter, Emily Burchfield, Nina C. Martin, Linda Isaacs, Lauren Brinkley-Rubenstein, Paul Speer, Abbey Mann, Sharon Shields, Neal Palmer, Bethany Pittman, and Sandra L. Barnes). The CDA program is designed for the professional preparation of leaders in community and human service organizations, where students develop the knowledge and skills necessary to facilitate community and organizational change. By marrying theory and praxis, the authors illustrate a contemporary example of how faculty, courses, disciplines, and institutional requirements can be combined strategically in graduate teaching/learning spaces. The chapter also considers the unique contributions in the human development counseling program and its efforts to engender interest and participation in social justice endeavors via the counseling experience. The HDC program trains prevention specialists and counselors cognizant of the complexities of human development who can then translate theoretical knowledge into effective counseling programs and practice. Findings from this chapter also illustrate how counseling and consulting can foster human development that moves beyond traditional ways of meeting human needs. Comments by tenured, tenure-track faculty, practice faculty, and graduate students illuminate some of the motivations, challenges, and trajectories that result in a commitment to collaborative research, instruction, and community engagement. Moreover, readers are able to connect to an online Internet site for videos of students, faculty, and community members who participated in this volume and/or continue to participate in HOD.

The volume conclusion highlights overarching objectives and themes, summarizes outcomes that emerged, and suggests potential future research. It also provides commentary on approaches to cultivate similar multidisciplinary, multi-teamed, and multi-methodological approaches to research, teaching, and community service in other academic settings. Final remarks include best practices and challenges to consider when embarking upon interdisciplinary, action-oriented work. It also includes a broad framework on Deweyism as a meaningful rubric in the twenty-first century that challenges individuals to undertake *transdisciplinary* work. Overall, each chapter is designed to inform and invigorate readers about how the academic endeavor can be a point of departure to engage in a myriad of research, programs, and activities inside and outside classroom walls. Moreover, the mosaic of intellectual and practical approaches included here illustrates how queries and concerns can be addressed from a variety of perspectives and methods and serve ultimately to educate and enlighten readers about the joys and challenges of collaborative research and community engagement.

Internet URLs for Video Interviews

Want to know more about HOD and the chapters in this volume? Follow the URLs given here to view the documentary *Academics in Action! A Model for Community-Engaged Research, Teaching, and Service* as well as shorter video interviews with faculty, community partners, and students. Chapters in which respondents contributed are provided after each person's name.

Academics in Action! A Model for Community-Engaged Research, Teaching, and Service—Documentary (http://vu.edu/hod1a)

FACULTY

Camilla Benbow, Dean of Peabody College of Education and Human Development (http://vu.edu/hod6a)

Sandra L. Barnes, Professor, Department of Human and Organizational Development and the Divinity School (coeditor, documentary and video organizer, Chapter 10, http://vu.edu/hod10)

Paul Dokecki, Professor Emeritus, Department of Human and Organizational Development (Chapters 2 and 8, http://vu.edu/hod9a)

Gina Friedan, Assistant Professor of the Practice, Department of Human and Organizational Development (Chapter 10, http://vu.edu/hod7a)

Robert Innes, Professor Emeritus, Department of Human and Organizational Development (Chapter 1, http://vu.edu/hod5a)

Doug Perkins, Professor, Department of Human and Organizational Development (Chapter 7, http://vu.edu/hod14)

Sharon Shields, Associate Dean for Professional Education, Office of the Dean; Professor of the Practice and Associate Dean, Department of Human and Organizational Development (Chapters 7 and 10, http://vu.edu/hod11)

Marybeth Shinn, Professor and Chair, Department of Human and Organizational Development (Chapters 3 and 9, http://vu.edu/hod2a)

Heather Smith, Assistant Professor of the Practice, Department of Human and Organizational Development (Chapter 9, http://vu.edu/hod8a)

STUDENT MONTAGE (HTTP://VU.EDU/HOD15)

Magaela Bethune, Ph.D. student, Community Research and Action

Lauren Brinkley-Rubinstein, Ph.D. student, Community Research and Action (coeditor, Chapters 5 and 10)

Caleb Chadwick, M.Ed. student, Human Development Counseling

Bernadette Doykos, Ph.D. student, Community Research and Action (coeditor, Chapters 4 and 6)

Holly Karakos, Ph.D. student, Community Research and Action (Chapter 7)

Mark McCormack, Ph.D. student, Community Research and Action (Chapter 8)

Caitlin Nossett, M.Ed. student, Community Development and Action

Oluchi Nwosu, Ph.D. student, Community Research and Action (Chapter 10)

Ashley Smith, M.Ed. student, Human Development Counseling

Jay Tift, M.Ed. student, Human Development Counseling

COMMUNITY PARTNER: MARTHA O'BRYAN CENTER (HTTP://VU.EDU/HOD13)

Kimberly Bess, Assistant Professor, Department of Human and Organizational Development (Chapter 6),

Robin Veenstra-VanderWeele, Director, Martha O'Bryan Center

Cheryl Horton, Martha O'Bryan Center staff person

COMMUNITY PARTNER: WATT HARDISON ELEMENTARY SCHOOL (HTTP://VU.EDU/HOD12)

Susie Turner (Principal), Sylvia Bradshaw (5th grade teacher), Arin Dahlhauser (physical education teacher), Katie Mitchell (4th grade teacher), Ashleigh Hines (first year teacher), Sarah Mitchell (Coordinated School Health Coordinator, Sumner County

Schools), Carol Nixon (Vanderbilt University, HOD task force member, Chapter 4), Sharon Shields (Vanderbilt University, HOD task force member)

COMMUNITY PARTNER: OASIS CENTER SHELTER (HTTP://VU.EDU/HOD4A)

Ben Kinghorn (Director), Karwan Abdulkader (Crisis Specialist and M.Ed. graduate of HDC)

References

Barnes, S. (2005). *The cost of being poor: A comparative study of life in poor urban neighborhoods in Gary, Indiana*. New York: State University Press of New York.

Bonilla-Silva, E. (2006). *Racism without racists: Color-blind racism and the persistence of racial inequality in the United States*. Lanham, MD: Rowman & Littlefield Publishers.

Bourdieu, P. (1984). *Distinction: A social critique of the judgment of taste*. Cambridge, MA: Harvard University Press.

Bronfenbrenner, U. (1977). Toward an experimental ecology of human development. *American Psychologist, 32*(7), 513–31.

Bronfenbrenner, U. (1986). Ecology of the family as a context for human development: Research perspectives. *Developmental Psychology, 22*(6), 723–42.

Collins, P. H. (2000). *Black feminist thought: Knowledge, consciousness and the politics of empowerment* (2nd edition). New York: Routledge.

Collins, P. H. (2009). *Another kind of public education: Race, schools, the media and democratic possibilities*. Boston, MA: Beacon Press.

Collins, P. H. (2010). "Toward a new vision: Race, class, and gender as categories of analysis and connection." In M. S. Kimmel & A. Ferber (Eds.), *Privilege: A Reader* (pp. 233–50). Boulder, CO: Westview Press.

Davis, D. (2004). "Merry-go-round: A return to segregation and the implications for creating democratic schools." *Urban Education, 39*(4), 394–407.

Delpit, L. (2006). *Other people's children: Cultural conflict in the classroom*. New York: The New Press.

Detweiler, J., & Detweiler-Bedell, B. (2012). *Doing collaborative research in psychology*. Thousand Oaks, CA: Sage Publications.

Dewey, J. (1981). *The philosophy of John Dewey (2 volumes in 1)*. Chicago: University of Chicago Press.

Dewey, J. (1902). *The child and the curriculum*. Chicago: University of Chicago Press.

Dewey, J. (1910). *How we think*. Lexington, MA: D.C. Heath Press.
Dewey, J. (1916). *Democracy and education*. New York: Simon & Schuster.
Dewey, J. (1929). *The quest for certainty*. New York: Minton.
Dewey, J. (1938). *Experience and education*. New York: Touchstone Books.
Dewey, J. (1954). *Public and its problems*. Athens, OH: Swallow Press.
Feagin, J. R. (2006). *Systemic racism: A theory of oppression*. New York: Routledge.
Feagin, J. R. (2010). *The white racial frame: Centuries of racial framing and counter-framing*. New York: Routledge.
Fellmeth, R. (2005). Child poverty in the United States. *Human Rights: Journal of the Section of Individual Rights and Responsibilities, 32*(1), 2–19.
Gershon, W. (2009) *The collaborative turn working together in qualitative research*. Rotterdam, Netherlands: Sense Publishers.
Hays, S. (2003). *Flat broke with children: Women in the age of welfare reform*. New York: Oxford University Press.
The Journal of Blacks in Higher Education. (2008). "Black student college graduation rates inch higher, but a large racial gap persists." Retrieved March 15, 2008 from http://www.jbhe.com/preview/winter07preview.html.
Lykens, K., & Jargowsky, P. (2002). Medicaid matters: Children's health and Medicaid eligibility expansions. *Journal of Policy Analysis and Management, 21*(2), 219–38.
National Center for Child Poverty. (2002). *Child poverty fact sheet: March 2002*. Columbia University. http://cpmcnet.columbia.edu/dept/nccp/ycpf.html.
Oliver, M., & Shapiro, T. (1997). *Black wealth/white wealth*. New York: Routledge.
Ostrander, S. (1999). Gender and race in a pro-feminist, progressive, mixed-gendered, mixed-race organization. *Gender and Society, 13*(5), 628–42.
Sagor, R. (2010). *Action research guidebook: A four-stage process for educators and school teams*. Thousand Oaks, CA: Sage Publications.
Scott, E. K. (2005). Beyond tokenism: The making of racially diverse feminist organizations. *Social Problems, 52*(2), 232–54.
Senge, P. (2006). *The fifth discipline: The art and practice of the learning organization*. New York: Doubleday.
Strauss, G., & Hansen, B. (2006). CEO pay soars in 2005 as a select group breaks the $100 million mark. *USA Today*, April 11, 2006. Retrieved at www.usatoday.com/money/companies/management/2006-04-09-ceo.
Sullivan, M., & Kelly, J. (2001). *Collaborative research: University and community partnership*. Washington: American Public Health Association.
Yang, B., Watkins, K. E., & Marsick, V. J. (2004). The construct of the learning organization: Dimensions, measurement and validation. *Human Resources Development Quarterly, 15*(1), 31–55.

Part I: Theories, Frameworks, and Twenty-First Century Deweyism

Although valuable for the sake of scholarly inquiry, academicians are increasingly challenged to make their research applicable and accessible outside the classroom. Moreover, more institutions of higher learning are realizing the untapped sources of knowledge in the public domain. Educational and social reform involves combining the potential and acumen found in both academic and public spaces to solve problems. This practice of collaborative capacity building is a hallmark feature of John Dewey (1916, 1927/1954, 1938). This premise reflects an indomitable approach for instruction and thoughtful inquiry. Several imperatives frame this understanding: (1) theoretical and praxis are not mutually exclusive domains but rather can and should inform each other; (2) theory can provide intellectual *momentum* to transport scholarship beyond journal outlets, classroom chalkboards, and school assignments; (3) familiarity with various theoretical frameworks expands our ability to understand and potentially address social problems; (4) an increasingly multicultural society requires us to acquire new skills and methods of engagement; and (5) individuals should question explanations and solutions that are not informed by some thoughtful, broader view of social issues. Together, these imperatives mean that intellectual scaffolding must be expected and encouraged to more effectively engage in academic work that is action- and community-oriented, practical, and culturally sensitive.

Informing theory with practice is not a new phenomenon; Dewey also espoused this approach (Dewey, 1916, 1927/1954, 1938). In the present volume, we endeavor to use Dewey's principles of participatory democracy, lifelong learning, and experiential and constructivist learning, and extend his ideology by adopting and adapting it to respond to students' developmental needs as classroom learners and global citizens and to tackle both chronic and new social challenges in communities. "Extending Deweyism" means acknowledging the timeless value of his broad tenets as well as being willing to modify them for best use in a society that is now international in its economic, political, cultural, and social scope. Reductionism and simplistic approaches, explanations, and decisions will no longer suffice. Researchers, teachers, practitioners, and students alike must be able to acquire, understand, and employ an array of skills, ideas, and paradigms to successfully negotiate society as global citizens.

Part I of this volume examines two theoretical frameworks that broadly inform the intellectual focus in the department of Human and Organizational Development (HOD) and, we contend, should be considered when attempting action-oriented research, teaching, and service. Each model emphasizes the importance of theory that intentionally engages praxis to promote individual, group, and community betterment. Each chapter presents fundamental assumptions associated with reflexive academic work that has strong implications outside the ivory tower and illustrates the relationship between the intangible world of thoughts, ideas, and meaning-making and the tangible realities of human development, human interactions, conflict, and community. The chapters challenge readers to become critical thinkers to develop synergy around various theoretical paradigms that can be employed to transform academics into action; they also lay the foundation for subsequent examples of the contemporary usage of Deweyism. Moreover, the theories described in these chapters undergird and inform the empirical studies in Part II as well as the departmental structures and processes detailed in Part III of this volume.

In Chapter 1, "John Dewey, Participatory Democracy, and University-Community Partnerships," Deweyism is positioned as a paradigmatic lens to guide human development, teaching, and learning practices, as well as university-community engagement. This chapter provides a unique perspective on the possibilities associated with community-based work that thoughtfully reflects theory and practice.[1] According to its authors, effective university-community partnerships are historically undergirded by the philosophy of John Dewey. Moreover, the authors make a strong case that a quest for lifelong learning should permeate academe *and* the larger society. The chapter details Dewey's premise that citizens are interested and

---

[1]. The lead author, Robert Innes, is one of the HOD founders and a longtime Dewey advocate.

capable of actively participating in processes to address issues for the common good. Embracing this premise means that intellectual approaches tied to action research, problem-based learning, participatory research, and service learning become effective tools in educating and challenging society members toward proactive community engagement. The chapter provides the broad theoretical framework for the entire volume as well as key dimensions of Deweyism that are adopted and adapted in subsequent chapters.

Chapter 2, "The Ethical Foundations of Human and Organizational Development Programs: The Ethics of Human Development and Community Across the Curriculum," illustrates the importance of ethical practices in teaching, research, and community service. According to these writers,[2] professional ethics should permeate the efforts of students, researchers, practitioners, and anyone who embraces social justice tenets. Just as Deweyism informs HOD, so do aspirations for moral professional practices that focus on human betterment. Like Dewey, the writers of this chapter contend that interventions and programs intended to enhance society and contribute to the common good must be ethically centered. This chapter also describes approaches to counter unhealthy power dynamics, both individual and systemic, in favor of power that fuels collaboration and community. For the authors, practitioners, by definition, are ethically centered persons trained to foster individual, group, and community development. Such persons are self-reflective, culturally sensitive, intellectually prepared, and psychologically and emotionally willing to meet the task of community engagement head on! According to this theoretical framework, participating in efforts to benefit the common good will require personal traits such as courage, honesty, caring, community-mindedness, and a justice-orientation—all informed by the professional and practical training to make sound decisions. And during this lifelong process, the ethics of human development become contemporary expressions of Dewey in real time.

Both chapters in this section are theoretical in nature. They document several ideologies historic to HOD and that we believe to be critical at the foundation of any academic enterprise that is committed to social justice

---

2. The lead author, Paul Dokecki, was one of the initial members of HOD and central to the development of its PhD program, Community Research in Action (CRA).

in research and action. They also suggest the existence and necessity of other departmental frames of reference expected in an interdisciplinary space. Yet neither chapter positions theory as a panacea or suggests that a paradigmatic focus alone constitutes academics in action. Instead, both illustrate how theory and practice must inform each other for community engagement for the common good to occur. The theoretical lenses for participatory work that are described in Part I speak to the centrality of: interdisciplinary inquiry; values that engender community action and self-reflection; multicultural appreciation; on-going intellectual and professional development; relationship-building between community partners and academe; and ultimately, proactive engagement to achieve transformation for individuals, groups, organizations, and society at large.

References

Dewey, J. (1916). *Democracy and education*. New York: Simon & Schuster.
Dewey, J. (1927/1954). *The public and its problems*. Chicago: The Swallow Press.
Dewey, J. (1938). *Education and experience*. New York: Touchstone, Simon & Schuster.

1 John Dewey, Participatory Democracy, and University-Community Partnerships

ROBERT INNES, LEIGH GILCHRIST,
SUSAN FRIEDMAN, AND KRISTEN TOMPKINS

> ... if I were asked to name the most needed of all reforms in the spirit of education, I should say: "Cease conceiving of education as mere preparation for life, and make it the full meaning of the present life."
>
> —John Dewey, 1893

> It is no longer the case that historically marginalized groups are simply excluded from good schools, jobs, neighborhoods, and the like. Rather, the terms of their inclusion—the rules that regulate their participation—have grown in importance.
>
> —Patricia Hill Collins, 2009

Introduction

Occupy Wall Street Live-Streams Chicago March (Associated Press 2013)
Tea Party Plans to Abandon GOP Stars (ABSNews.com 2013)
Occupy Wall Street Protestors Regroup After Eviction (The Guardian 2013)
"Five Years Later, an Evolving Tea Party Movement Wades into the 2014 Elections" (Fox News 2013)

The preceding headlines were taken from recent news reports about two contemporary examples of participatory democracy. Whether one agrees or disagrees with the Occupy Wall Street or Tea Party movements,[1]

---

1. Occupy Wall Street (OWS) is a protest movement that began in the fall of 2011 in Zuccotti Park in New York City's Wall Street financial district. OWS protested economic and social inequality, greed, corruption and perceived corporate influence in government via sit-ins and petitions. The Tea Party movement (TPM) is a political

they represent examples of grassroots collective responses to societal change and concerns. Moreover, they inform the current chapter on the nature and scope of historic forms of participatory democracy and their implications for university-community partnerships. This chapter focuses on the philosophical and theoretical underpinnings of universities as they endeavor to accomplish three global missions: teaching and learning, research and scholarship, and service to communities and society. It also considers some of the challenges universities face as they try to achieve synergy across these three missions and explores approaches to accomplish this broad objective based on the legacy of John Dewey. Additionally, the potential barriers to reaching this goal are contextualized within broader questions about the viability of participatory democracy, communicative action, and dialogic communication in a multicultural, postmodern society. We posit that the foundation for the rationale for many models for achieving productive university-community partnerships (for example, problem-based learning, action research, service learning, and participatory research) map back to the philosophy of John Dewey.

Dewey's Philosophy as the Foundation for Higher Education Reform

Consistent with his role as one of the three founders of the school of philosophy known as American Pragmatism (with Charles Peirce and William James), John Dewey's (1859–1952) philosophy has been useful as a guide to the development of theory and practice in a broad range of academic fields such as education, political science, psychology, and the arts. He was a political activist who lent his support to a range of progressive causes such as women's suffrage and world peace. He sustained a lifelong commitment to addressing a broad range of societal problems through active participation in both educational and social reform. Dewey's commitment to education reform and active involvement in addressing local community and societal problems began with his establishment of a laboratory school at The University of Chicago to test his theories of learn-

---

movement focused on reducing the federal budget deficit and national debt through reduced government spending and taxes. Its name is derived from the Boston Tea Party of 1773, a historic colonial protest. Some critics suggest that the TPM may not see social justice beyond its anger over government's power and Barack Obama's presidency. Each is ideologically disparate, yet engages in similar forms of political and social protest.

ing. This commitment continued throughout his 70-year career, especially in efforts to bring the spheres of academic and public life into active dialogue for cooperative problem solving.

Participatory Democracy

In the early twentieth century, Dewey wrote *The Public and Its Problems* (1927/1954) to respond to critics who questioned the efficacy of participatory democracy. He "had faith in the capacity of human beings for intelligent judgment and action if proper conditions are furnished" (Dewey, 1939, p. 2). Yet Dewey recognized a problem highlighted by his chief critic, Walter Lippmann (1925/1993), that is all too familiar in the political climate in the twenty-first century: that "powerful special interests" actively manipulate public opinion to their own ends. Lippmann's solution was to create an elite technocracy made up of objective experts, specialists, and government bureaucrats. In contrast, Dewey advocated for the improvement of education to expand the capacity of people in face-to-face communities to engage in meaningful dialogue and problem solving. The core of Dewey's democratic ideal was to foster productive communication that would help communities reach consensus solutions for the common good. A basic principle of participatory democracy as expressed in *The Public and Its Problems* is that "all those who are affected by social institutions must have a share in producing and managing them" (Dewey, 1927/1954, pp. 15–16). For Dewey (1916), "democracy is more than a form of government; it is primarily a mode of associated living, of conjoint community experience" (p. 87). He believed that such participation is "necessary both for the general welfare and for the fullest development of individuals, and that such a principle should be applied not only in the political sphere as we understand it but in the spheres of family and child-raising, in school, in business and in religion" (quoted in Hayden & Flacks, 2002, p. 18).

Throughout his long career in academic and public life, Dewey was linked to organizations that sought to promote participatory democracy and actively supported dialog between grassroots movements with diverse political positions to find common ground. For example, he was a leader and longtime active member of the League for Industrial Democracy, a branch of the AFL-CIO designed to educate college students about the labor movement. The League for Industrial Democracy was the parent organization of the Students for Democratic Society (SDS) founded in 1962 based on the principle of participatory democracy (Hayden, 1962/2005). In its early days, SDS can be compared to both the Tea Party and the Occupy Wall Street movements: Both collective efforts are calling for participatory democracy. Interestingly, if Dewey were alive today, he might try to promote an active dialogue between these two movements to reach a consensus that would have real power to confront the entrenched special interests. Thus participatory democracy at its best still challenges conflicting parties to attempt to engage each other in proactive, productive, and respectful ways to meet objectives.

Dewey's Perspective on Teaching and Learning

Before discussing the potential for using Dewey's philosophy as a guide to reshape the university, it is important to outline his basic view of how learners acquire useful knowledge. Dewey represented one pole in an ongoing debate about teaching and learning in American schools. His view contrasted with the traditional model of "essentialism" that defined learning in terms of "what everyone should know" to be a well-educated person. In contrast, his teaching model emphasized experiential learning through cooperative problem-solving. Over the past twenty years, Dewey's perspective has reemerged within the new interdisciplinary field of learning science and constructivist perspectives of teaching and learning.

Holders of constructivist views of learning believe that knowledge is *constructed* by learners rather than *transmitted* to learners through methods such as lecturing. This perspective was also represented in later educational reforms in the critical pedagogy of Paulo Freire (1970). Freire characterized traditional teaching as depositing knowledge in students' heads "banking style." Most constructivist theories trace their philosophical roots to John Dewey (for example, Bransford, Brown, & Cocking, 1999; Cobb 1994). Models that focus on constructing "useful knowledge" have been changing teaching practices from elementary school classrooms to corporate training programs, but this revolution has had the least impact on teaching in universities. Even less attention has been given to the implications of learning science research for meeting educational goals related to qualities of character, appreciation for diversity, political consciousness, and concern for the common good.

Professors tend to identify themselves with their roles as scientists and scholars in their academic disciplines (Kember, 1997) and typically view teaching as "transmitting" their disciplinary knowledge to students through lectures and demonstrations (Boulton-Lewis et al., 2001). The chief task of curriculum development in the transmission or banking model of teaching is to decide what content should be transferred to students. However, constructivist approaches provide an alternative to the transmission model that governs most university teaching. An oversimplified characterization of this shift in perspective is a move away from receiving and memorizing toward thinking and doing. Constructivist and problem-based learning models dating back to Dewey have characterized the transmission model as producing "inert knowledge" rather than useful knowledge (Dewey, 1916; Whitehead, 1967/1929). Critics of the transmission model assert that, although students may memorize information long enough to pass an exam, they will not be able to use that knowledge to solve future problems unless that knowledge is acquired in a context and under conditions that are similar to the context and conditions in which it will be used. In this view, if citizenship and civic responsibility are learned as academic content that is *memorized for the test*, it will be inert and irrelevant to students' lives. Constructivist approaches to teaching and learning call for a vastly different approach to defining curriculum. Dewey and constructivists recommend changing the orientation of education from transmitting knowledge to creating environments where students can create their own knowledge (Brown, Collins & Druid, 1989). Following John Dewey, constructivists begin by identifying the kinds of problems students will confront in their personal and professional lives. For example, in courses, this identification may be accomplished through participation in simulations that require students to address "real world" problems and reflection papers that connect course concepts to problems experienced in problem-solving groups. The primary goal is to give students useful knowledge and skills to solve those problems and to arm them with the skills and motivation to be lifelong learners. Accordingly, students cannot develop civic responsibility and political consciousness by learning *about* community issues; they have to engage in genuine dialog with real people in real communities to help them address real community problems. Simply put—thinking, doing, and learning should be an exciting, collaborative, participatory process.

An important difference between constructivist and transmission models is that constructivists believe that all types of learning (content knowledge, values, and skills) are best learned in active learning communities addressing authentic problems. Within the constructivist model, efforts to promote civic responsibility are intimately involved with the acquisition of other types of knowledge. Both meaningful content knowledge and civic responsibility are products of participation in learning communities characterized by certain forms of association and communication. This insight led to the development of service-learning programs that link academic content to community service. Problem-based learning, a model derived from Dewey's perspective on learning, has been most popular in the professional disciplines, especially in the health sciences and medicine (Hmelo-Silver, 2004; Woodward-Kron & Remedios, 2007). Hmelo-Silver (2004) defines problem-based learning as "focused, experiential learning organized around the investigation, explanation, and resolution of meaningful problems" (p. 236).

For Dewey (1916), useful knowledge included ideas that are both abstract and connected to the context of the learning environment. Useful knowledge includes generalizable concepts broad enough to be effective tools for problem solving in a range of practical situations. Learners are armed with tools that enhance their adaptability (which, by Dewey's definition, makes them more intelligent). Reflection is an essential ingredient of an educative experience in any constructivist curriculum, whether it is classroom- or field-based. Moreover, Dewey (1938) posited that reflection is the central process for organizing concepts into a meaningful structure that is integrated within experience. Developing the capacity for reflective practice (thinking about why we are acting the way we are) and metacognition (thinking about our thinking) are essential to the development of civic responsibility. This idea is further articulated by Schön (1983) as the "reflective practitioner." Dewey's focus on reflective practice (praxis) highlights the difference between some forms of volunteer work and service learning because the latter endeavor involves reflection using abstract concepts to deepen understanding and generalization.

Dewey's Naturalistic and Community Perspectives

Dewey is revered as a primary source of philosophical support for developing a society built on a strong sense of community and characterized by a genuine concern for the common good. He was a champion of the school's role in ensuring the survival of democratic institutions. A key to avoid distorting Dewey's philosophy of education is to understand his strong orientation toward seeing the individual as firmly embedded in the community. In Dewey's philosophy, the individual retains the power to take action, but the person is considered highly contextualized within his or her culture and community. Dewey's primary goal of education (growth and increased adaptive capacity) is measured on the level of the "face-to-face" community rather than from the perspective of radical individualism. In other words, the broader goal is for both individuals and communities to function adaptively. From this perspective, adaptation promotes the common good because it takes place at the community level. The individual's learning is not considered growth if it isolates him or her from open communication and participation in community life or reduces the adaptive capacity of the community as a whole.

Although Dewey's (1925/1958) analysis of the nature of experience is the cornerstone of his philosophy, its foundation is his naturalistic worldview. This naturalistic orientation connected him to the real world and its problems and led naturally to an ecological perspective that defined his primary goal of education noted above. Dewey believed that people have a unique capacity to address their problems by conducting systematic inquiry to acquire knowledge and improve their adaptive capacity. This ability would enable them to develop in the face of uncontrollable changes in their environments and even to alter their environments intentionally. Dewey's instrumental orientation is most important because it anchors meaning in a problem context. Within this framework, thinking is an activity in the world that is no less natural than any other human activity. The activities of the mind are *in* the world and not separate from it (McCarthy & Sears, 2000). This orientation toward problem-solving views knowledge and behavior in terms of its consequences. Intelligence is behavior (including both thinking and doing) that leads to more effective adaptation. Dewey's particular project was to make practice more intelligent (Eldridge, 1998). A core principle of Dewey's (1938) instrumentalism suggests that knowledge is the result of inquiry motivated by a problem that causes discomfort. This perspective indicates that we cannot hope to develop citizenship skills in students unless they are confronted with problems that *disturb* their equilibrium. Growth demands that students confront ideas and cultures that are very different from their own.

Although the term "diversity" typically refers to heterogeneity in terms of race, ethnicity, gender, age, religion, sexual preference, and/or national origin, it is necessary to extend this important concept to include broad arrays of belief systems, ideas, cultures, and ideological frames of reference. And in a multicultural society, diversity can function either as a hindrance or a facilitator of productive problem solving. For Dewey (1916), diversity is pedagogical; it can facilitate learning because different perspectives are required for creative problem solving. He believed that the most important role of democracy as a form of association is to increase communication and that diversity is the key to creative dialogue. Thus, creating situations in which different kinds of people are engaged in face-to-face, undistorted communication is an *indispensable* feature of an educative experience. We need communication between diverse people because we need to hear ideas that disrupt our ways of seeing things (Garrison, 1996). That said, it is clear that these are difficult ideals to realize in situations where groups of people with diverse views and cultural backgrounds attempt to reach consensus (for example, dialogue between members of the Occupy Wall Street and Tea Party movements). For Dewey, a well-constructed classroom is a place to practice these difficult skills in a setting that provides the necessary support for this challenging goal. He and constructivist learning theorists see little value in community service that simply "exposes" students to other cultural perspectives. Exposing students to diversity outside the context of real relationships and genuine communication would not produce useful knowledge or promote problem solving. Achieving authentic mutual understanding across cultural boundaries requires that students engage in a genuine two-way dialogic communication. Promoting this form of communication is the most important and difficult challenge in establishing genuine learning communities both in the classroom and in the community. Furthermore, globalizing the process has become essential.

The Role of Inquiry and the Problematic Situation

Because inquiry is a social activity, the primary characteristic of an educative experience is that it presents learners with a problematic situation that stimulates inquiry. Such inquiry begins when an indeterminate situation attracts the learner's attention because it is considered problematic. Inquiry leads to growth, which is the goal of education, because *the problem* defines the meaningful unit of experience. Moreover, instruction must create situations that demand problem solving through systematic inquiry. The problematic situations must be embedded in a larger enterprise and learning emerges from work conducted in an ecologically valid context. Ultimately, the inquiry process should increase the learner's ability to take meaningful action in the future. Problem-based instruction, cooperative learning, and service learning provide good examples of current methods of instruction consistent with this philosophy (Bruffee, 1999). Within this frame of reference, learning *is* developing new and more productive ways of participating in social practices (Cobb & Bowers, 1999).

Yet Brown & Duguid (1996) suggest that what people learn has to be understood in relationship to their prior knowledge. This is a key insight with very important implications for teaching and learning in community settings. For example, if students have an idea about the answer to a question before they take a course or are involved in a community-based learning experience, they are very likely to return to their original theory after they complete the experience, especially if they are not actively involved in correcting misconceptions and constructing new understandings. Students are not blank slates; changing their preexisting ideas often presents educators with a difficult challenge. One of the most important implications of this principle for community-based learning is that what students "see" in unfamiliar community settings and/or cultures is highly influenced by what they *expect* to see. Research on stereotype confirmation processes indicates that preconceptions about other groups are easily "confirmed" and difficult to change (Biernat & Ma, 2005; Rothbart & Park, 1986). Offsetting these tendencies is complicated because learners are often unaware of their biases and their expectations can become self-fulfilling prophesies (Chen & Bargh, 1997). Translating "academics to action" means cultivating learning spaces that challenge students to build community in the midst of diversity.

Participatory Research

Participatory research is a community-based action-research model that is consistent with Dewey's philosophical perspective. In this model, participants (for example, researchers, students, and community members) define problems, gather information, and develop solutions together. This approach does not deny the usefulness of expertise for understanding and finding solutions to complex problems. However, the communication between *experts* and novices is dialectical rather than focused on one-directional advice from experts to community members. It respects different types of expertise and the necessity of developing mutual respect between participants with different types of experiences and expertise. Community members are experts about the issues that face them and researchers have expertise about a variety of abstract concepts and procedures that might be useful for addressing community problems once they are contextualized within the community's experience. Ideally, members of each group are *legitimate peripheral participants* in the other groups' life worlds who gain increasing appreciation for each others' perspectives (Lave & Wagner, 1991).

The key difference between participatory research and conventional research practices does not lie in the specific research methods used but in the sharing of *power* between researchers and community members throughout the stages of the research process (Cornwell & Jewkers, 1995). A range of definitions of participatory research exists. A definition formulated by Miles Horton (1990) that emphasizes empowering communities fits well with the philosophy of the HOD Department:

> Participatory Research is defined by different people in different ways, but there are some universal characteristics. It is an investigation and an analysis of a problem by a group of people whose lives are directly affected by that problem. Ideally, their investigation will lead to action. Participatory research differs from the more conventional kind done by experts, usually identified with universities, in that it doesn't take decision making away from the people. Instead of becoming dependent on experts, the people become experts themselves. (p. 208)

We know that it is difficult to maintain a balance of power between constituent groups, especially in the context of cultural differences. For instance, years ago, one of the authors of this chapter invited a community activist from a rural Tennessee community involved in participatory research around pollution of local rivers to make a presentation in one of his courses. The activist introduced himself to the students by saying, "This will be a presentation by someone who 'talks funny.' I've come to invite you to visit my community where you 'talk funny.'" The problem "funny talking" researchers face when they seek access to a community for participatory research is that just explaining the ideal of dialogic communication sounds very strange, especially in the language we are used to using. In many cases, both the university-based participants and the participants from the local community can agree to a standard, such as, "Everybody should be allowed to speak their mind and say why they think that way, and everyone else should listen carefully until they really understand where the speaker is coming from." But experience and a plethora of research evidence indicate that this form of communication is very difficult to achieve.

Participatory Democracy, Dialogic Communication, and Social Justice

Dewey's concept of participatory democracy is the overarching idea that links the models for learning, research, and community development highlighted in this chapter. The central feature of this model is open communication that is free of coercion. Dewey wanted classrooms to be communities characterized by the forms of association that define the heart of democratic community life. We refer to this form of open, reciprocal, transactional communication as dialogic discourse and communicative action. A primary concern related to the functions of effective learning communities is the systematic marginalization of certain groups of people. For example, in Lave's apprenticeship model (Lave & Wenger, 1991), apprentices are considered *legitimate peripheral participants*. As apprentices move toward acquiring expertise, their participation becomes more central and meaningful. In the context of education, one might expect a similar progression as new members join a learning community. But this process of increasing meaningful participation is often stunted because systems of power and oppression that exist in the larger society are imported into the group (Hawkins, 2000). Typically, groups that are marginalized in the larger society continue to be marginalized in learning communities and develop a pattern of *sustained peripheral participation*. The fact that the same diversity that is essential for meaningful learning and finding effective solutions to difficult problems promotes exclusion of much of the most relevant knowledge needed for adaptive solutions creates a paradox that is very difficult to resolve.

Since the positive outcomes of dialogic communication depend on active participation by all, evidence of lack of participation is a serious challenge to the efficacy of constructivist pedagogies (for example, problem-based learning) and models of community problem solving based on participatory democracy (for example, participatory research). Research on participation indicates that there are also many personal and cultural reasons for lack of participation (Remedios, Clarke & Hawthorne, 2012). These include personal styles (for example, silent but active participants) (Chalmers & Violet, 1997) and cultural preferences (for example, low participation by Asian students) (Khoo, 2003), as well as lack of cultural literacy across cultural boundaries (Schirato & Yell, 2000). Communication across cultural barriers is complicated by the fact that the rules that govern the structure of dialogues (for example, cues for when it is proper to speak) are usually culturally embedded. These factors indicate that it is important to provide problem-solving groups with training, process facilitation, and alternative avenues of participation (for example, asynchronous online communication) (Remedios, Clarke & Hawthorne, 2012).

Informed by the broad definition of diversity presented earlier, Dewey (1927/1954) thought that democratic principles of association and open communication are "equivalent to breaking down the barriers of class, race, and national territory which keep men from perceiving the full import of their activity" (Middle Works 9:93). Race, gender and religion are important dimensions of diversity in our culture because they define the boundaries between people that have been problematized in this culture. They also typically form the patterns of inclusion and exclusion that function as barriers to open communication in our classrooms and communities. Issues of social justice and diversity are central to both a functioning democracy and the classroom because they describe the way people should relate to each other and live together if they want to promote the positive growth of entire communities and society overall.

Dialogic Communication in Learning Communities

When a process of communicative action that helps students construct knowledge can be incorporated as a core activity in constructivist curricula, it helps create a method for building a pedagogy of social justice. The concept of *communities of inquiry* is central to Dewey's educational philosophy. Without a method for reconstructing Dewey that resonates with the other elements of the model, the social justice theme is "tacked on" as content. Social justice becomes isolated as a simple concept that will be transmitted to the students through lecturing rather than lived in community. Yet if the problem-solving process within a constructivist curriculum model is coordinated by communicative action, mutual understanding can be organically integrated into the lived experience of classroom and community-based experiences.

Dewey's (1927/1954) focus on the importance of participatory democracy and his careful attempts to clarify what democratic "modes of association" are involved reflected his awareness that our natural tendency to form communities may be too fragile to survive without support from strong democratic institutions. Such institutions are mediating structures that shape human behavior in ways that promote social justice and the common good. For Dewey, a viable democracy is the necessary context for a society that enhances the development of its members. A strong link exists between the way Dewey conceptualized democracy and the types of classrooms he designed. For example, classrooms in early "progressive" schools were characterized by groups engaged in dialogue to solve meaningful problems cooperatively, similar to today's constructivist classrooms (Eldridge, 1998). These spaces were based on the premise that people will not move toward a concern for the common good unless they develop a strong sense of community, and communities cannot be broadened to include more and more marginalized people without open communicative practice. Therefore, to develop adaptive people and an adaptive democratic society, education should be built on purposeful social cooperation. Dewey's mission of giving equal participation to all was carried forward by social reformers such as Paulo Freire (1970) and Miles Horton (1990). These reformers recognized that the hidden motivation for keeping knowledge inert in traditional pedagogy is to prevent it from being used to promote social justice.

A number of models for ideal classroom dialogue exist. For example, because it focuses on the importance of basing assertions on evidence, Accountable Talk is a model for dialogic communication that matches with the values of the university. Michaels, O'Connor, and Resnick (2008) describe Accountable Talk as an "ideal discussion-based classroom community [where] students have the right to speak and the obligation to explicate their reasoning, providing warranted evidence for their claims so that others understand and critique their arguments" (pp. 284–85). Accountable Talk has three broad features. It is accountable to the community of practice in the classroom, the body of knowledge in the field, and to accepted standards of reasoning. According to these same scholars, "the classroom culture assumes that all students have equal access to the floor and to academic content, and that all students have comparable discourse experience to make their voices heard and recognized as offering reasoned and cogent contributions" (p. 285). Since the linguistic demands of problem-based, dialogic models are high (Woodward-Kron & Remedios, 2007), these models are difficult to implement successfully without extensive training and support. When implemented successfully, however, they have the added advantage of developing students' thinking strategies, problem-solving skills, and dialogic communication skills in addition to content knowledge (Hmelo-Silver, 2004).

Research on dialogic communication supports the link between dialogic discourse and the development of useful learning (Blanton, 2002; Nystrand, 1997). Unfortunately, changing the culture of schooling to establish a norm for this type of communication has been very challenging. Most attempts at generating dialogic discourse in the classroom have had only minimal success (Blanton, 2002; Innes, 2007; Kittleson & Southerland, 2004; Staarman, Krol, & vander Meijden, 2005). By the time they reach a university, most students have experienced twelve years of being acculturated to an environment where teachers tell them the "right answers" and expect to have those answers repeated back to them. Despite its benefits, students and teachers are not conditioned to engaging in open two-way communication, sharing their own thoughts, and solving unstructured problems (Boaler, 1999; Capon & Kuhn, 2004). Yet evidence indicates that students involved in cooperative learning are more actively engaged, more highly motivated, and more intellectually challenged than students involved in large group instruction (Csikszentmihayi & Schneider, 2000).

Just as Dewey defined democracy as a mode of association, students' experience with open dialogue can build essential democratic citizenship skills. Unless educational institutions can develop the skills needed to communicate across cultural boundaries, education's potential for advancing the cause of social justice will be neutralized. If education is to play a role in developing a more democratic society that functions effectively and utilizes the talents of an increasingly diverse population, it has to play a role in increasing communication and understanding across cultural boundaries. This objective can be accomplished only by creating open communication that at least partially transcends the structural boundaries of the dominant culture. Furthermore, this communication must take place within the context of a learning community that is actively addressing authentic community problems. The advantage of linking the classroom to the community is that it disrupts the culture of the traditional classroom that has been resistant to change.

Moving from the Classroom to the Community

Reshaping the culture of the classroom and the community is a daunting task, especially in the current political climate of distrust and polarization. We have witnessed a multiracial, multicultural President, a disciple of John Dewey, try and fail to establish productive dialogue with Congress (Khimm, 2013; Whitaker, 2013). Furthermore, studies show that institutions, especially the public schools, that Dewey considered essential to a functioning democracy, are rapidly disintegrating (Collins, 2009; Davis, 2004; Delpit, 2006). If we accept Dewey's assertion that real change in both schools and communities requires adopting participatory democracy as a "way of life" rather than as content in the curriculum, we must find ways of making basic transformations in the culture of schooling and community development to enhance the development of dialogic discourse. We are challenged to concertedly move his message into the twenty-first century.

The current culture of the classroom tends to be dictated by the academic lecture, which is characterized by one-way communication from teacher to students. The prevailing discourse genre in different communities may dictate one-way communication from authority figures to the community or one-way communication from the authorities in the community to university representatives. However, this need not be the norm. Altering the established communication patterns is especially challenging in the increasingly globalized environment where local communities are often collections of diasporic people. These barriers to communication and ultimately to community building are also evident in attempts to create cooperative dialogues among the range of academic disciplines necessary to address complex real-world problems (Roth, 2008). Moreover, embracing and implementing such transformative change will be largely driven by the educational ideologies of academic leadership rather than institutional resources.

KEEPING DEWEYISM ALIVE!

This chapter has challenged readers to thoughtfully incorporate Dewey's educational model in various facets of teaching, research, and community service. We pose several questions. How can we keep Deweyism and its emphasis on participatory democracy and research as well as democratic citizenship alive? How can we accomplish this goal given our many constraints related to time, finances, and human resources? The "Getting Started!" table provides suggestions for readers to begin to incorporate this paradigm in their courses and projects. Each suggestion directly relates to concepts and themes presented in this chapter; most suggestions are cost effective and can be implemented short-term such that Deweyism as an ideology can be espoused and practiced professionally and personally.

Conclusion

This chapter has presented core elements connected to Dewey's ideal of participatory democracy. We are now challenged to dream of the possibility that the university could lead a new movement toward participatory democracy. Benson and Harkavy (2007) presented two contrasting scenarios and alternatives of the future role of universities in the twenty-first century. The positive image of the future is described as follows:

Chapter 1: Getting Started!
John Dewey, Participatory Democracy and University-Community Partnerships

Action Item 1: *Add Dewey to reading lists.*
Dewey mainstays such as The Public and Its Problems (1954), Democracy and Education (Chapters 1–4) (1916), and Experience and Education (1938) will help students grasp the ideology and foundational concepts as well as prepare them as you incorporate Dewey in class, assignments, or research projects. Making Dewey an assigned reading in a class or project is possibly the easiest way to translate his theory into practice. More creative approaches include providing individuals with a set of excerpts from Dewey's work and challenging them to select those that best address a course topic or research question and to justify their selections.

Action Item 2: *Update the syllabus.*
Incorporate Deweyism directly by placing excerpts from his work in the class syllabus, including a service learning component, adding group discussions, and replacing traditional lectures with dialogic experiences.

Action Item 3: *Expose individuals to key concepts and themes early.*
Introduce concepts such as participatory democracy, constructionism, participatory research, and democratic citizenship to help prepare students, other faculty, and community members to apply Dewey's model, preferably during the first week of class or at the start of a research project. As the course/project progresses, challenge students to use these concepts to potentially create new knowledge and learn to apply them professionally and personally. Introduce readings that connect Dewey's theories to contemporary issues in education. A specific contemporary interpretation of Dewey's democratic theory will enhance the student's understanding of the implications of his work for contemporary life. For example, readers should consider Garrison's (1996) "A Deweyan theory of democratic listening (*Educational Theory 464*, 429–51) as well as the relevance of Freire's pedagogy to service-learning found in Deans's (1999) "Paulo Freire's critical pedagogy in relation to John Dewey's pragmatism" (*Michigan Journal of Community Service Learning*, 6, 5–29).

Action Item 4: *Increase experiential learning.*
Help students engage in cooperative problem solving and open communication by providing actual case studies and real-world problems they must work together to investigate, explain, and attempt to solve. Challenge them to develop multiple remedies, assess possible constraints, and consider their personal views about each case.

Action Item 5: *Encourage interdisciplinary reading.*
Add required readings from various disciplines and also challenge individuals to thoughtfully reference and include such readings and examples as they engage in experiential learning. Be sure to include work from diverse authors based on factors such as age, race, class, gender, sexual orientation, and international origin. Writing by Freire, Collins, Schön, Bonilla-Silva, and Innes are great places to start.

> In our scenario's optimistic version, the twenty-first century becomes the global Democratic Century—the century in which the irrepressible information and communication (ICT) revolution powerfully contributes to the worldwide democratization, civic engagement, and action-oriented social responsibility of universities. In turn, socially responsible and engaged, participatory action-oriented, democratic universities powerfully contribute to the worldwide democratization of cosmopolitan communities and societies committed to the worldwide abolition of poverty and racism. (pp. 169–70)

The negative image stands in contrast:

> The twenty-first century becomes the global Commodification-of-Everything Century in which the irrepressible ICT revolution powerfully broadens, deepens, and accelerates the commodification of universities. In turn, thoroughly commodified universities, tightly controlled and operated by Social Darwinist technocratic entrepreneurs in academic clothing, powerfully accelerate the commodification of societies and the worldwide intensification of poverty, inequality, and racism . . . Updated for our pessimistic twenty-first century scenario, it envisions a world in which Social Darwinist capitalism has completely triumphed. In that commodified world, universities, like all other institutions, function as amoral, "nakedly" for-profit corporations that produce and sell commodities (broadly conceived to include all types of services and cultures) . . . Or, as Eric Fromm subsequently summarized the Manifesto's dehumanization thesis, in *Escape from Freedom*: in a fully capitalist world, "Man does not only sell commodities, he sells himself and feels himself to be a commodity." (p. 170)

The careful reader will recognize an unresolved paradox in citing two conflicting perspectives in the exploration of participatory democracy and dialogic discourse. This paradox is precisely the one that must be resolved to overcome the barriers we confront when we endeavor to create open dialogic discourse in classrooms and communities. Research indicates that the nature of the intervention required to resolve this problem has eluded practitioners inside and outside academia. It is clear that a successful solution will be a very labor-intensive effort involving innovative methods of analysis and training to develop new insights and communication skills. Our task is further complicated by the fact that trends toward the commodification of higher education will inevitably involve cost-cutting that will create competition between the three missions of the university listed in the introduction to this chapter. For example, the higher status afforded to research in today's universities will likely provide resistance to dedicating additional resources to teaching and community development. These trends are expected to create additional resistance to education reform, especially at the undergraduate level. This somewhat sobering prediction returns us to another quixotic adventure that parallels the task of bringing the members of the Occupy Movement and the Tea Party Movement into productive dialog leading to consensus. Furthermore, the reality of these two participatory collectives reminds us that Dewey's framework may be more difficult to realize than expected and group motives may vary dramatically. But despite challenges, like these groups, we are committed to championing participatory democracy now and in the future.

References

Benson, L., & Harkavy, I. (2007). Saving the soul of the university: What is to be done? In L. Benson, I. Harkavy & J. Puckett (Eds.) *Dewey's dream; Universities and democracies in an age of educational reform* (169–209). Philadelphia: Temple University Press.

Biernat, M., & Ma, J. E. (2005). Stereotypes and the confirmability of trait concepts, *Personality and Social Psychology, 31*(4), 483–95.

Blanton, M. L. (2002). Using an undergraduate geometry course to challenge pre-service teachers' notions of discourse. *Journal of Mathematics Teacher Education, 5*(2), 117–52.

Boaler, J. (1999). Participation, knowledge and beliefs: A community perspective on mathematics learning. *Educational Studies in Mathematics, 40*, 259–81.

Boulton-Lewis, G. M., Smith, D. J. H., Mcrindle, A. R., Burnett, P. C., & Campbell, K. J. (2001). Secondary teachers' conceptions of teaching and learning. *Learning and Instruction, 11*, 35–51.

Bransford, J. D., Brown, A. L., & Cocking, R. C. (Eds.) (1999). *How People Learn: Brain, Mind, Experience and School*. Washington, DC: National Academy Press.

Brown, A. L., Collins, A., & Druid, P. (1989). Situated cognition and the culture of learning. *Educational Researcher, 18*(1), 32–42.

Brown, John S., & Duguid, P. (1996). Practice at the periphery: A reply to Steven Tripp. In H. McLellan (Ed.), *Situated learning perspectives* (169–73). Englewood, N.J.: Educational Technologies Publications.

Brufee, Kenneth A. (1999). *Collaborative learning: Higher education, interdependence, and the authority of knowledge.* (2nd ed.) Baltimore: The Johns Hopkins University Press.

Capon, N., & Kuhn, D. (2004). What's so good about problem-based learning? *Cognition and Instruction, 22*(1), 61–79.

Chalmers, D., & Violet, S. (1997). Common misconceptions about students from South-Asia studying in Australia. *Higher Education Research and Development, 16*(1), 87–98.

Chen, M., & Bargh, J.A. (1997). Nonconscious behavioral confirmation processes: The self-fulfilling consequences of automatic stereotype activation. *Journal of Experimental Social Psychology, 33*, 541–60.

Cobb, P. (1994). Where is the mind: Constructivist and sociocultural perspectives on mathematical development. *Educational Researcher, 23*(7), 13–20.

Cobb, P., & Bowers J. (1999). Cognitive and situated learning perspectives in theory and practice. *Educational Researcher, 28*(2), 4–15.

Collins, P. H. (2009). *Another kind of public education: Race, schools, the media and Democratic possibilities.* Boston, MA: Beacon Press.

Cornwell, A., & Jewkes (1995). What is participatory research? *Social Science & Medicine, 41*(12), 1667–76.

Csikszentmihayi, M., & Schneider, B. (2000). *Becoming adult: How teenagers prepare for the world of work.* New York: Basic Books.

Davis, Donna. (2004). Merry-go-round: A return to segregation and the implications for creating democratic schools. *Urban Education, 39*(4), 394–407.

Delpit, Lisa. (2006). *Other people's children: Cultural conflict in the classroom.* New York: The New Press.

Dewey, J. (1916). *Democracy and education.* New York: Simon & Schuster.

Dewey, J. (1925/1958). *Experience and Nature.* New York: Dover.

Dewey, J. (1927/1954). *The public and its problems.* Chicago: The Swallow Press.

Dewey, J. (1938). *Education and experience.* New York: Touchstone, Simon & Schuster.

Dewey, J. (1939). Creative democracy—The task before us, address given at a dinner in honor of John Dewey, New York, October 20, 1939. (Cited in Fielding, M., & Moss, P. (2012). *Radical democratic education.* Presentation at the American Sociological Association, August 17, 2012, Denver, Colorado.).

Dewey, J. (1893). Self-realization as the moral ideal. *The Philosophical Review, 2*(6), 652–64.

Eldridge, M. (1998). *Transforming experience: John Dewey's cultural instrumentalism.* Nashville: Vanderbilt University Press.

Freire, P. (1970). *Pedagogy of the oppressed.* New York: Herder & Herder.

Garrison, J. (1996). A Deweyan theory of democratic listening. *Educational Theory*, Fall 1996, 46(4), 429–51.

Hawkins, M. (2000). The reassertion of traditional authority in constructivist pedagogy. *Teaching Education*, 11(3) 279–96.

Hayden, T. (1962/2005). *The Port Huron Statement*. New York: Thunder's Mouth Press.

Hayden, T., & Flacks, D. (2002). The Port Huron Statement at 40. *The Nation*, August 5, 2002. 18–21.

Hmelo-Silver, C. (2004). Problem-based learning: What and how do students learn? *Educational Psychology Review*, 16(3), 235–66.

Horton, M. (1990). *The Long Hall*. New York: Doubleday.

Innes, R. (2007). Dialogic communication in collaborative problem solving groups. *International Journal for the Scholarship of Teaching and Learning*, 1(1), 1–19.

Kember, D. (1997). A reconceptualization of the research in to university academics conceptions of teaching. *Learning and Instruction*, 7(3), 255–75.

Khimm, Suzy. (2013). "Economy: without congress, all Obama can do is talk." *MSNBC*. Retrieved from http://tv.msnbc.com/2013/07/23/economy-without-congress-all-obama-can-do-is-talk/.

Khoo, H. (2003). Implementation of problem-based learning in Asian medical schools and students' perception of their experience. *Medical Education* 37, 401–9.

Kittleson, J. M., & Southerland, S. A. (2004). The role of discourse in group knowledge Construction: A case study of Engineering students. *Journal of Research in Science Teaching*, 41(3), 267–93.

Lave, J., & Wenger, E. (1991). *Situated learning: Legitimate peripheral participation*. Cambridge, England: Cambridge University Press.

Lippmann, W. (1993/1925). *The phantom public*. New Brunswick, NJ: Transactions.

McCarthy, C. L., & Sears, E. (2000). *Deweyan pragmatism and the quest for true belief. Educational Theory*, 50(2), 213–27.

Michaels, S., O'Connor, C., & Resnick, L. B. (2008). Deliberative discourse idealized and realized: Accountable talk in the classroom and in civic life. *Studies in Philosophy and Education*, 27(4), 283–76.

Nystrand, M. (1997). *Open dialogue: Understanding the dynamics of language and learning in English classrooms*. New York: Teachers College Press.

Remedios, L., Clark, D., & Hawthorne, L. (2012). The silent participant in small group collaborative learning contexts. *Active Learning in Higher Education*, 9(3), 201–16.

Roth, W. (2008). Bricolage, metissage, hybridity, diaspora: Concepts for thinking science education in the 21st century. *Cultural Studies in Science Education*, 3(4), 891–916.

Rothbart, M., & Park, B. (1986). On the confirmability and disconfirmability of trait concepts. *Journal of Personality and Social Psychology, 50*, 131–42.

Schirato, A., & Yell, S. (2000). *Communication and cultural literacy: An introduction.* St. Leonards, NSW: Allen and Unwin.

Schön, D. (1983). *The reflective practitioner: How professionals think in action.* New York: Basic Books.

Staarman, J. K., Krol, K., & van der Meijden, H. (2005). Peer interaction in three collaborative learning environments. *Journal of Classroom Interaction, 40*(1), 29–39.

Woodward-Kron, R., & Remedios, L. (2007). Classroom discourse in problem-based learning classrooms in the health sciences. *Australian Review of Applied Linguistics, 30*(1), 1–18.

Whitaker, Morgan. (2013). "Meet the repealicans—Obamacare battles continue in congress." Retrieved from http://tv.msnbc.com/2013/07/30/meet-the-repealicans-obamacare-battles-continue-in-congress/.

Whitehead, A. (1967/1929). *The aims of education and other essays.* The Free Press: New York.

2 The Ethical Foundations of Human and Organizational Development Programs
The Ethics of Human Development and Community Across the Curriculum

PAUL R. DOKECKI, MARK McCORMACK, HASINA MOHYUDDIN, AND LINDA ISAACS

The heart of reflective morality is reflection, and reflection is sure to result in criticism of some matters generally accepted and in proposals for variation in what is currently regarded as right . . . Every act has potential moral significance, because it is, through its consequences, part of a larger whole of behavior.

—John Dewey[1]

Action is the sole medium of the expression of ethics.

—Jane Addams (1902)

The ethical theory presented in this chapter, the *Ethics of Human Development and Community* (EHDC), is a direct inheritor of the legacy of Nicholas Hobbs, who, among his many accomplishments, developed the first code of ethics for the field of psychology.[2] Hobbs was the founder of the modern era of psychology and disability studies at Peabody College. In the early 1950s, he encouraged Peabody faculty members and students to develop an approach to research that served the common good—in effect, research as an extension of Dewey's notion of democracy and in pursuit of the Caring and Competent Society, with an emphasis on human rights and social justice (Hobbs, Dokecki, Hoover-Dempsey, Moroney, Shayne, & Weeks, 1984). The EHDC theory is a product of HOD and

---

1. As cited in Boydston, J. A. (ed.), 1985/2008, p. 213, and John Dewey, 1960, p. 11.
2. This chapter draws on the work of Dokecki (1996) and on Dokecki's contributions to Moroney, Dokecki, Gates, Haynes, Newbrough, and Nottingham, J. (1998).

reflects the Peabody motto, "We make a difference." We offer an ethical approach incorporating a general theory of professional ethics (rather than relying on any particular professional ethical code) whose purpose is to help students make difficult choices in a world rife with political and ideological controversy and social injustice. In this chapter, we present the reflective-generative ethical approach at the heart of this model and explicate ways in which it may be used in varied teaching/learning spaces.

What Is New or Different When Thinking About Ethics?

Our framework of thinking about ethics for human development in HOD is an extension of Deweyism. Thus, it is not new, yet it is unique in two important ways. First, our orientation toward practice-research-practice (in which we draw on both universal and situated ethics) is still a minority position (Browning, 1991). While the participatory action research model is not unique to HOD or Peabody College, it is central to our teaching and practice and is not widely accepted in the social sciences at large. The question facing all would-be participatory researchers is, how ought we to conduct our research in an ethical manner? It continues to be a source of tension within academia, and the model of EHDC addresses this current tension with the concept of the reflective-generative practitioner.

Second, our model addresses the current tensions between a postmodern way of viewing the world in academia on the one hand, while many individuals experience and make sense of their lived experiences using a modernist perspective on the other. To the extent that academia is moving toward a postmodern framework (suggesting there are no universals, and there is no overarching narrative that encompasses the human experience), this theory provides a way to assert there are some universal ethical principles, but it meets the postmodern value of the lived individual human experience by integrating this experience within the context of bottom-up principles. We posit that the "both/and" perspective of our ethical framework provides a way for community practitioners to guide their actions in the community: We can keep one foot in the waters of postmodern theory with another firmly rooted in the ground of the lived experiences of those with whom we conduct research.

You Can Run, but You Can't Hide from Ethics

One of central tenets of the EHDC is that professionals must understand that their vocation is ethical to the core—both in their interventions and in their systematic inquiry. Therefore, ethics is at the heart of the HOD department. Despite the ethical nature of professional practice, however, many professions are in crisis. The crisis is one of legitimacy and of self- and public confidence, shared by the professions with most of society's major institutions such as government, religion, education, and corporate business (Bellah, 1985). This crisis has its own dynamics with prominent methodological and ethical features. Methodologically, the professions' approaches to generating usable knowledge have typically been limited to practical tasks and have been inadequate in solving the confusing problems professionals face. As Schön (1987) suggested:

> In the varied topography of professional practice, there is a high, hard ground overlooking a swamp. On the high ground, manageable problems lend themselves to solutions through the application of research-based theory and technique. In the swampy lowland, messy, confusing problems defy technical solution. The irony of this situation is that the problems of the high ground tend to be relatively unimportant to individuals or society at large, however great their technical interest may be, while in the swamp lie the problems of greatest human concern. (p. 3)

Many professionals seem to have lost touch with the major reason for their practice, their ethical center, which, we argue, is to foster the human development of their clients and thereby enhance community and contribute to the common good. At the heart of both these dimensions of the crisis of the professions—the client and the community—are issues of power.

Power

As we move through the second decade of the new millennium, we are busily fulfilling many of the prophecies Fromm (1955) made in *The Sane Society*, a deeply ironic title for a book analyzing the *insane* society we have been creating in the modern world. According to its premise, many of us have been behaving like machines, like robots, dehumanizing each other in our selfish, narcissistic, egotistical, overly competitive, not sufficiently cooperative, and characteristically masculine (macho) pursuit of power. Our society not only tolerates but also seems to invite the abuse of power. Although professionals, on behalf of their clients and the common good, should be leading the effort against the abuse of power, they often fall prey to the temptation to use the power inherent in their roles primarily for their own good and only incidentally or accidentally for the good of others.

A universal feature of client-professional relationships is a power differential; a client enters a relationship with a professional experiencing a need that the professional is believed competent to address. The situation entails a *necessary* status differential, based on the professional's presumed training, experience, skills, and special knowledge. Unless the professional is believed to know something the client doesn't, there is no reason for the client-professional relationship in the first place. Because knowledge is power, the knowledge differential is also a power differential. Professional power, argued Lebacqz (1985), is "legitimated and institutionalized power" (p. 113). Professionals not only have the power to fix a problem, but they also largely define its reality. Thus, there is potential for distortion depending upon the way professionals use their reality-defining power. The professional person's power may be used manipulatively in coercive fashion, where the intent is to give priority to her or his needs over those of the client, or caringly, where the intent is the mutual promotion of human development and community and thereby the common good. Figure 2-1 depicts this dual understanding of power at the heart of the EHDC. It assumes that a central human motive is the need to exercise more and more power. The vertical arrow suggests that power as self-efficacy exists on a continuum where a person has very little power (bottom of the arrow) to a great deal of power (top of the arrow). The kind of power we strive to develop, however, is two-fold, depending on whether we relate to others as objects (coercive power) or as persons (synergic power).

Coercive power is used by professional "experts" to exercise control over their clients. In doing so, they often make the client dependent and powerless (Craig & Craig, 1973). It reduces their belief in their own self-efficacy. If we approach clients from this unfortunately typical use of power, we will rarely participate in their empowerment. In contrast, synergic power

ETHICAL FOUNDATIONS 53

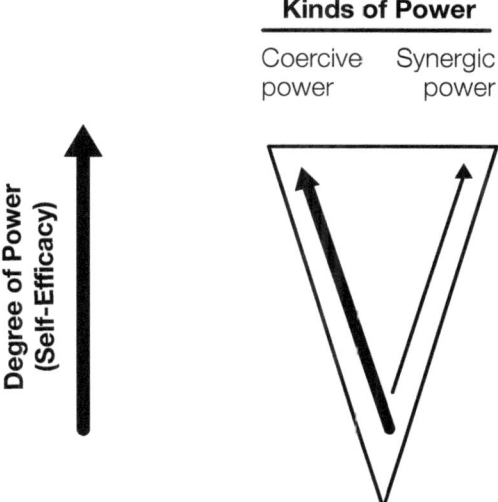

FIGURE 2-1. The tragi-comic triangle of power (based on Craig and Craig, 1973)

suggests a very different view of professional power. It is "the capacity of an individual to increase the satisfaction of all participants by intentionally generating increased energy and creativity, all of which is used to co-create a more rewarding present and future" (Craig & Craig, 1971, p. 62). Synergic power grows from trust and prudence; it is caring. Its ultimate goal is to enhance people's: sense of autonomy and interdependence, which grows out of working together; view of themselves as capable of affecting their own and others' destiny; and view of others as capable of working together. One crucial result of synergic power is its ability to simultaneously enhance the development of the initiator as she or he enhances the development of others. Synergic power counters the traditional view of the professional as a controlling expert. It is this type of power that caring professionals would employ as *reflective-generative practitioners* to promote clients' human development.

Figure 2-1 depicts power as varying along two dimensions: *degree* of power (from less to more self-efficacy) and *kind* of power (from coercive to synergic power). As depicted by the two arrows inside the triangle in Figure 2-1, competing tendencies exist within the human personality. The thick arrow, which we call "Freud's arrow," corresponds to the powerful

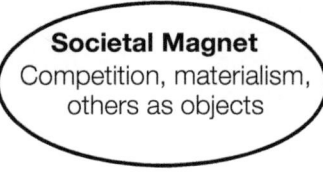

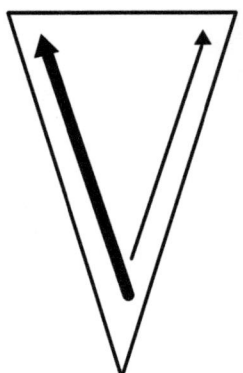

FIGURE 2-2. The task of ethical human development

selfish, egotistical, and narcissistic forces or drives that impel us to have our own way at all costs and to use others as means to our own ends. Here the use of power is often the abuse of power. The thin arrow corresponds to the more selfless and altruistic personal forces, difficult to follow because of Freud's powerful and compelling demons, that impel us to treat others as persons in their own right and whose human development we can and should enhance by our actions. Then there are the societal tendencies, constituting the *societal magnet* in Figure 2-2, which tend to reward those who compete and win by being able to bend others to their will and coerce them to do their bidding. When this magnet turns on, persons in the triangle are like iron filings drawn to it and thereby further motivated to exercise coercive power. The ethical task of being synergic, therefore, is doubly difficult but not impossible to master, which highlights the power and challenge of the tragic dimensions of the human situation.

For professionals willing to take on the challenging and difficult task of being synergically powerful, the EHDC suggests, as depicted in Figure 2-2, that *two ethical tasks* exist: (1) developing oneself humanly, and (2) changing one's society. The concept of synergic power also relates to the societal distribution of power. Professionals must "seek to share power and redistribute it" (Lebacqz, 1985, p. 131), yet a complex tragicomic paradox exists in notions such as empowerment and liberation. If professionals assume that their role is to empower or liberate clients, they may be operating paternalistically. The professional's use of power, therefore, must involve synergic efforts, wherein the client and the professional achieve levels of human development greater than either one alone could reach. Professionals, however, are tragicomic and thereby are never able to be fully synergic in their exercise of power.

What would the social world look like if the professional's use of synergic power was helpful in overcoming the societal obstacles to enhancing the human development of people, their community, and the common good? The pursuit of this question is the focus of our work. A brief answer comes from Judith Green (1999). Based on an approach she calls *prophetic pragmatism* (an extension of the thinking of John Dewey, Jurgen Habermas, Alain Locke, Martin Luther King, Cornel West, and other democratic social thinkers), deep democracy within beloved communities that would result in societal transformation must include at least these main aspects:

Respect for human rights understood as common humane values
Democratic cultural revitalization
Lifelong education within collaborative processes of rebuilding the public square
Political re-inhabitation (participatory democracy)
Shared community efficacy and commitment to mutual flourishing
Economic relocation (economics in service of human development)
Shared commitment to ecosystem health
Shared memories and hopes
A web of caring within a consciously shared community life. (p. 217)

This list must be supplemented by a theory for the practice of human development professionals that would facilitate bringing about deep democracy, to which we now turn.

Professions as Practices

One of the basic considerations in EHDC is that a tragicomic dual relationship is at the heart of professional practice. As depicted in Figure 2-3,

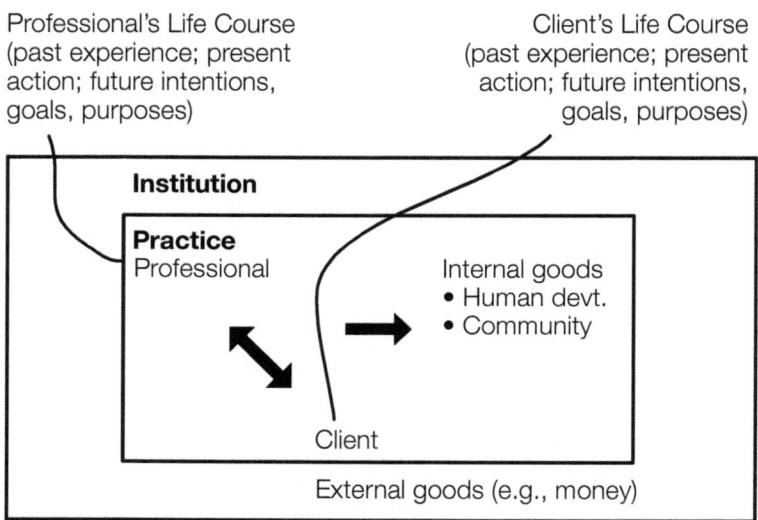

FIGURE 2-3. Professions as practices

this relationship entails a tension between the pursuit of *goods internal* to a professional practice (human development and community) and *goods external* to it (other goods, such as money and self-gratification, selfishly pursued by the professional, often through the coercive or exploitative use of professional power). What does it mean to view the professions as practices? A *practitioner* is broadly defined as one who performs or carries out something, often a profession or occupation. The associated noun is *practice*, one definition being the "exercise of an occupation or a profession," as in the practice of law, medicine, social work, teaching, or psychotherapy. A practitioner is a professional person who engages in a practice to do good—in the context of our present discussion, to promote human development and community.

More generally and philosophically, says MacIntyre (1981), a practice is defined as:

> [A]ny coherent and complex form of socially established human activity through which goods internal to that form of activity are realized in the course of trying to achieve those standards of excellence which are appropriate to, and partially definitive of, that form of activity, with the result that human powers to achieve excellence, and human conceptions of the ends and goods involved, are systematically extended. (p. 175)

From this view, kicking a football, bricklaying, playing a musical scale, and interpreting a dream are not practices, while the game of football, architecture, jazz, and psychotherapy meet this definition. A professional practice entails a complex set of actions and dispositions (knowledge, skills, competencies, and values) that are coherently organized. It is socially established, having its origin in the life of the community. Moreover, it is structured and can be evaluated according to generally and traditionally accepted standards of excellence. At any given time, professional community members can and do make judgments of what constitutes good and bad, competent and incompetent, ethical and unethical. Such judgments are far from relative and arbitrary, emanating as they do from the history and tradition of the practice and embodied in those who have achieved the status of recognized authorities or masters in a field. These authorities are among the persons who socialize new members into the practice through teaching, serving as role models and mentors, and arbitrating current practice.

A practice is defined or has meaning as a practice in terms of the ends or goods it is socially established to achieve and its codified and systematic means for achieving these goods. We may call these goods, after MacIntyre (1981), *goods internal to a practice* (see Figure 2-3). The achievement of internal goods contributes to the overall good of the community, benefiting all affiliated partners. The excellence and ethics of a practice are judged relative to the goods practitioners achieve and how they achieve them, within the context of the practice community itself. In the realm of sports, for example, relative to the history and traditions of basketball, both in the way he plays the game and in his already remarkable achievements in the game per se, LeBron James deserves the accolade, excellent performer. The same could be said of an excellent jazz musician, such as Wynton Marsalis, or lawyer, such as Thurgood Marshall. However, the enormous sums of money LeBron James receives for engaging in the practice of basketball constitute goods that are not internal to the practice. The phenomenon of money being paid to practitioners introduces MacIntyre's companion concept, *goods external to a practice* (refer again to Figure 2-3). These goods are characteristically competed for; there are winners and losers. Competition for external goods and many other factors beyond a practice inevitably penetrate and influence the pursuit of goods internal to it, creating a tragicomic situation. Practices occur amidst complex social contexts, resulting, at times, in mixed motives. Some form of blending of internal and external concerns, or of resolving the tension between them, is necessary to achieve the kind excellent and ethical professional practice that promotes human development and community.

Goods internal to a professional practice are pursued primarily during face-to-face transactions between client and professional and entail professional *persons* treating clients as *persons*, exercising synergic power and caring for them in pursuit of mutual human development and community. The client and professional transact in the professional situation to enhance the client's (and thereby the professional's) human development and community, which are the goods internal to professional practice. As depicted in Figure 2-3, each is a personal agent with a particular tragicomic narrative. This narrative is comprised of: (1) *past* experiences (and attendant psychodynamics) concerning significant events and people; (2) *present* actions, motivations, priorities, and projects; and (3) *future* intentions, goals, and purposes. Life narratives can be understood through a combination of methods (Polkinghorne, 1988), including psychoanalytic-like archaeological exploration of the past, phenomenological analysis of present experience, and teleological probing of transcendent future life directions. When such a narrative is well developed, it has meaning and may be termed a *generative narrative*. Generativity is an achievement, an ongoing developmental task, and the culmination of the developmental process, which leads people to be capable of making progress ethically and meaningfully, albeit tragicomically.

Generativity has two coordinates—time and space. *Temporally*, generative persons live in a world in which past, present, and future are dynamically interrelated. We live in a constantly moving present infused with traditions, memories, and influences from the past, which is oriented intentionally toward a future filled with possibilities. Over time, a life characterized by caring will come to a reasonable degree of certainty complemented by faith in the order of things, intelligibility with an appreciation for life's tragicomic mystery, a feeling of satisfaction with life, and a psychological sense of community. *Spatially*, we live in a complex ecosystem where an appreciation for the interdependence of persons and their interdependence with other species and with the physical environment should characterize our lives. Thus, we are generative when we tragicomically construct and enact a narrative that manifests an appreciation (1) that we come from prior generations, are "in place" in our present lives, and have a duty to generations yet unborn, and (2) that we have a responsibility for the quality of the environment we occupy.

Competent and effective professional actions relative to the client's generative narrative constitute the hallmark or regulative ideal of excellent and ethical reflective-generative practice. Immature personality development may lead professionals to be tempted to emphasize their own rather than the client's agenda, to pursue goods external to their practice rather than to enhance the client's human development and community. Selfishness, egotism, or narcissism may, therefore, come unduly to influence the client-professional transaction and cause external goods to be given priority over internal ones. Professionals may freely intend to put their needs ahead of their clients' needs and thereby exploit them, use them as means to their own ends, or they may inadvertently do so because of psychopathological factors. In either case, society expects professionals to be mature enough to be ethical and not to succumb to these self-centered concerns. Ethical practice requires the practitioner to have a mature generative narrative, to have strength of character, to be *virtuous* in the tragicomic life world. To speak of virtue in professional ethics is to emphasize the enduring habits or characteristics developed over time that come to distinguish the overall nature of a professional person's life.

Virtue Ethics

An ethical reflective-generative professional must ask not only "What am I to do?" but also "Who am I?" The questions from this virtue ethics perspective become: What should the reflective-generative practitioner be like? What should be the professional's life story? Virtue ethics goes to the core of what reflective-generative practitioners must bring with them into professional situations, in the form of personal characteristics and virtues, to promote human development and community. Codes of professional ethics serve several purposes, perhaps the most important one being to provide an ideal of professional life (Lebacqz, 1985). This ideal typically suggests that professionals should be fair with clients, competent and honest in their dealings with them, and not take advantage of them. Professionals must interact with their clients in ways that do not replicate power inequalities suffered in the external culture (Freire, 1970). These characteristics point toward the virtues of justice, courage, and honesty, which are central to professional life (Bok, 1978).

Elaboration of the nature of caring is in order. Required is a nurturing and supportive community to meet the many challenges facing those who choose to care in a sustained and meaningful fashion. Community here should be understood as a social grouping that promotes human development. However, the concept of "community" is not inherently positive; one that hinders human development would be an anti-community. When you care, in Mayeroff's (1971) view, you enact a common pattern in which you are with and experience another person both as part of you and apart from you and needing to develop humanly. Thus, in caring, both the cared for person and the person caring grow and develop. Moreover, caring enables you to grow, *if you intend your caring actions primarily to benefit the person for whom you are caring.* This seems paradoxical, but it is essential to understanding caring's truly interdependent nature and to avoiding exploitative, dependency-inducing, or codependent relationships.

Building the Concept of Caring and Generativity into an Academic Program

We can best illustrate the connection between caring and narrative in professional life and explicate a framework for implementing this ethical theory in other settings by describing a demanding but ultimately much appreciated, assignment required in ethics courses at all levels in HOD. Students are asked to read and analyze Mayeroff's *On Caring* and use it as a personal and professional lens.

Students reflect on their lives in light of these ideas (they may, of course, reject Mayeroff's formulation and offer an alternative of their own that helps them make sense of who they are as emerging professionals). They write a personal narrative making sense of their lives in three parts: (1) *Past*—What key people and experiences in their lives to date have led them to be committed to caring as human development professionals? (2) *Present*—How do they see the university and their current major as embodying (or not) the ideal of caring? (3) *Future*—Can they discern how caring might be relevant to their future lives, both personal and professional, and what obstacles to being a caring person they might encounter in their particular professional worlds (helping services, public policy, law, business, and the like)? To what extent are they prepared to be caring, culturally competent community change agents (Schmidt & Finkbeiner, 2006)? In effect, they are asked to make explicit the narrative structure of their emerging lives as reflective-generative practitioners. They reflect on the origins and future of their character and virtue. Understanding one's own orientation toward ethical decision-making and community practice is a critical first step in developing community change agents. The next critical piece is ensuring that professionals are equipped to continue to learn from their experiences, rather than become stale and stuck in outdated models of thinking about their world. The framework for developing this skill is reflection.

Reflective Practice

Caring for clients in today's world requires a fundamental professional role reassessment, one that Donald Schön (1971) described by contrasting two very different models of professional roles: technical rationality (Model I) and reflective practice (Model II). Tables 2-1 and 2-2 illustrate these models. The major professional role in technical rationality is problem solving. Technically rational professionals give little attention to the value-laden task of problem setting. A danger clearly inherent in this technically rational approach to caregiving is arbitrarily molding the practice situation to conform to a more decontextualized professional knowledge base. The Model I professional assumes the role of the expert, the one who knows all. Professionals have all the power and all the answers; their role is to "fix" or cure the client.

In contrast, reflective practice entails reframing both the professional's and the client's role expectations. Reflective practice calls for complementarity. The client and the professional enter a partnership in which caregiving entails caring and joint exploration of the situation. The professional has expertise yet realizes that this knowledge is incomplete without the unique perspective of the client. As a reflective practitioner, the Model II professional enters into a reflective and caring relationship with the client that involves exploring multiple perspectives and sharing responsibility for both problem setting and problem solving. The contrasting professional perspectives in Table 2-1 suggest the need for significant

Table 2-1. Contrasting Professional Perspectives

Technically Rational Expert (Model I)	Reflective Practitioner (Model II)
I am presumed to know, and must claim to do so, regardless of my own uncertainty.	I am presumed to know, but I am not the only one in the situation to have relevant knowledge. My uncertainties may be a source of learning for me and for them.
Keep my distance from the client, and hold onto the expert role. Give the client a sense of my expertise, but convey a feeling of warmth and sympathy as a "sweetener." Look for deference and status in the client's response to my professional persona.	Seek out connections to the client's thoughts and feelings. Allow his respect for my knowledge to emerge from his discovery of it in the situation. Look for the sense of freedom and of real connection to the client, as a consequence of no longer needing to maintain a professional façade.

Schön (1983, p. 300)

Table 2-2. Contrasting Client Perspectives

Technically Rational Expert (Model I)	Reflective Practitioner (Model II)
I put myself into the professional's hands and, in doing this, I gain a sense of security based on faith.	I join with the professional in making sense of my case, and in doing this I gain a sense of increased involvement and action.
I have the comfort of being in good hands. I need only comply with his advice and all will be well.	I can exercise some control over the situation. I am not wholly dependent on him; he is also dependent on information and action that only I can undertake.
I am pleased to be served by the best person available.	I am pleased to be able to test my judgments about his competence. I enjoy the excitement of discovery about his knowledge, about the phenomenon of his practice, and about myself.

Schön (1983, p. 302)

change. Technical rationality's all-knowing, objectively distant, and status-conscious professional role would be shifted to reflective practice's appreciation for the limits of one's knowledge, a caring relation with the client as a person at both intellectual and emotional levels, and more genuine, less status directed relationships. For professional practice to become caring, many professionals must move from Model I to Model II. Tables 2-1 and 2-2, adapted from Schön, depict the changes in outlook required for such change. Changed modes of professional and public education will also be necessary to bring about this more caring professional role. Many clients may be intimidated by reflective practitioners if they expect to encounter the "all knowing" practitioner. What happens when we combine reflective practice with the concept of generativity? What then, is reflective-generative practice?

Reflective-Generative Practice

Reflective practice requires changes in both the professional's and the client's role expectations. It calls for the client and the professional to enter a partnership of shared responsibility involving joint exploration of their situation—reflection-in-action. The process requires *double vision*: The reflective practitioner as inquirer, according to Schön, must "(1) impose an order of his own on the situation [vision #1], (2) take responsibility for the order he imposes, (3) hold himself open, at the same time he imposes order, to the situation's 'back talk' [vision #2]" (p. 163). When we bring visions 1 and 2 together, it is akin to the complementary perspectives provided by our two eyes when they yield a clear, three-dimensional image.

The professional is ethically obligated both to inquire and to be ethical in her or his inquiry. The reflective practitioner is an intervention agent and inquirer who intends to enhance human development and community, and thereby the common good, through the *close interplay of knowledge use and knowledge generation*. The reflective practitioner intends to avoid the dualism of practice and theory. Recall Lewin's famous dictum that nothing is as practical as a good theory (Marrow, 1969). Theory here is reflection inspired by the challenges of practice. Rather than operating within positivism-empiricism's methodology of technical rationality, which insists that practice is legitimate when and only when it derives from scientifically tested theoretical knowledge, the reflective practitioner sees inquiry as transactionally arising from the very practice of intervention. Knowledge is practical; practice yields knowledge. The logic is one of practice-theory-practice (Browning, 1991). Generativity is a developmental achievement, the culmination of the human developmental process (Browning, 1973).

Toward a Decision-Making Framework for the EHDC

Figure 2-4 presents a schematic for decision-making in the EHDC. Before proceeding, we must make a crucial distinction between actual duties and prima facie duties. We have, for example, a prima facie duty to tell the truth (Bok, 1978), but may decide to lie to deceive someone who intends to harm our child. Truth telling, however, is thereby in no way diminished as an ethical obligation by our decision to honor the competing ethical obligation to protect the innocent from harm.

The distinction between prima facie and actual duty requires that we discern our ethical responsibilities carefully and sensitively but with

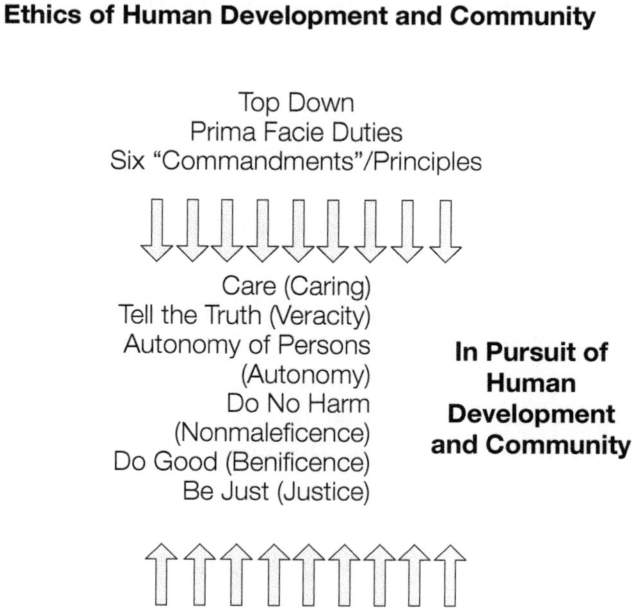

Ethics of Human Development and Community

Top Down
Prima Facie Duties
Six "Commandments"/Principles

⇓⇓⇓⇓⇓⇓⇓⇓

Care (Caring)
Tell the Truth (Veracity)
Autonomy of Persons
(Autonomy)
Do No Harm
(Nonmaleficence)
Do Good (Benificence)
Be Just (Justice)

In Pursuit of Human Development and Community

⇑⇑⇑⇑⇑⇑⇑⇑

FIGURE 2-4. Decision-making framework

common sense (the virtue of prudence). We must simultaneously understand that our professional ethical duties obligate (or don't obligate) in particular contexts. In Piagetian terms, we must be able to decenter—simultaneously to recognize the moral force of both (1) *top down prima facie duties* in the form of ethical principles and (2) *bottom up actual duties* in everyday concrete situations in their particularity and historical context. Principles and their attendant prima facie duties, therefore, constitute a general ethical framework that obligates us to make *this* rather than *that* choice. The distinction between prima facie and actual duty is useful in helping address the controversy over the need for and feasibility of a universal approach to ethics. One of the assignments in an Ethics for Human Development Professionals course entails requiring students to develop good reasons for and against universal ethics. They are presented with many of the arguments for and against universal ethics covered in the paragraphs that follow.

Among the factors in contemporary society that suggest that universal ethical perspectives should be developed are the following: (1) The planet has been described as "spaceship earth" on which we are all passengers, suggesting that what any of us do has implications for all the rest of us. (2) The development of computer and information technology suggests that we all live in the "global village." (3) Catastrophic events, such as the massive nuclear accident at Chernobyl, may have measurable negative effects throughout the world. (4) Threats to the environment, such as global warming and acid rain, result from actions and policies that transcend local or national boundaries. (5) Wars, such as World War I and World War II, have been waged by many nations and have had major destructive consequences throughout the world. (6) Weapons of mass destruction will not respect national boundaries in the harm and death they inflict on people. (7) Terrorists often come from more than one country, and the chaos they intend to produce transcends local or national boundaries. (8) We live in an interdependent world. Witness especially the inexorable move toward the globalization of most businesses and the way economic crises affect the whole world. (9) Virtually every profession is practiced in most countries of the world: Witness the existence of many international professional associations.

While there are numerous factors in contemporary society that suggest that universal ethical perspectives shouldn't be developed, the following are the most important: (1) Anthropology has demonstrated that the world is culturally pluralistic and that different cultures often seem to have vastly different lifestyles and understandings of ethics. (2) Differing cultural and religious perspectives must be understood and respected, and we must learn to be tolerant and respect, even encourage, diversity. (3) Among the most important human rights are freedom of religion and freedom of cultural expression. (4) Universal ethical codes may be impractical because they would seem to be difficult to enforce. Students are, in effect, asked to project the EHDC onto the global stage and consider how their particular professions might or might not be helped to deal with the global challenges using the theory.

Much of what we have written thus far can be understood as a specification and elaboration of the principle of *respect for the autonomy of persons*—the duty to treat all human beings as persons not things and to respect them as ends in themselves not as means to our own ends. Beyond autonomy, codes of professional ethics are typically imbued with the principles of *beneficence* (do good) and *nonmaleficence* (do no harm). In its most basic form, the principle of *justice* entails the notion of distributive justice as equality of treatment (treat like cases alike and different cases differently in doing good and avoiding harm).

Incorporating Ethics in Human and Community Development

By definition, the concept of professional ethics is broad and potentially vague. Although we suggest that certain examples of ethical behavior are widely understood, more direct examples of how to incorporate ethics individually and collectively may be needed. For example, this chapter includes two specific sections to guide readers interested in generatively cultivating ethics and care during instruction and research as well as reflective practice in the classroom and community. Specific course assignments, as well as insights in Tables 2-1 and 2-2 and Figures 2-3 and 2-4, can be directly applied to both classroom and workshop settings. Furthermore, the "Getting Started!" table provides additional direction to help readers interested in translating professional ethics from academics and theory into practice. Many of these strategies are appropriate for students, faculty, and community residents with whom you may be involved.

Chapter 2: Getting Started!
The Ethical Foundations of Human and Organizational Development Programs:
The Ethics of Human Development and Community Across the Curriculum

Action Item 1: Update your reading list.
Assign Dewey's *The Public and Its Problems* (1927/1954) as required reading. In addition to introducing individuals to a seminal Deweyan text, it will also provide the broad context from which discussions on ethical issues can emerge. Incorporate books or book excerpts from Mayeroff's *On Caring* (1971), Freire's *Pedagogy of the Oppressed* (1970), and Addams's *Democracy and Social Ethics* (1902) to prepare them to grapple with ethical issues. Be sure to identify central concepts and themes for students to uncover. Including readings by scholars on diverse experiences is also essential to broaden views about ethics. Be prepared to possibly provide free copies of key book excerpts to community members who cannot easily locate or afford to purchase them.

Action Item 2: Enhance course syllabus format.
Revise the course syllabus to increase the number of group activities that foster discussion. Consider reducing the number of lectures to encourage a more dialogic learning environment.

Action Item 3: Introduce new concepts.
Introduce and define concepts such as the social construction of reality, dramatic instance, democracy, reflexivity, and community. Be sure to provide several examples of each concept and discuss how and why these concepts are important for the study of ethics. Help individuals broaden their ethical compasses empathetically beyond traditional "either/or" and "right/wrong" dichotomous ways of thinking.

Action Item 4: Incorporate cooperative problem solving.
Case studies and group discussions based on real-world problems will help students apply course concepts and readings. For example, the 2004 *Harvard Business Review* case study "Oil and Wasser" by Byron Reimus could be used in a variety of classes to study cultural differences, ethnocentrism, stereotypes, international issues, and ethical business decisions.

Action Item 5: Incorporate experiential learning.
Incorporate service learning at local food banks, elder care centers, schools, and homeless shelters based on course and/or project themes. For example, requiring students in your classes or students on your project teams to volunteer at an assisted living facility will provide valuable insight as you focus on issues such as ageism, vulnerable populations, and economic inequality.

Action Item 6: Learn about Participatory Action Research (PAR).
The following types of articles will provide essential information and guidance for persons interested in expanding their research tool kit: Kidd, S. A., & Kral, M. J. (2005).

(*continued*)

Chapter 2: Getting Started! *(continued)*

Practicing participatory action research. *Journal of Counseling Psychology, 52*(2), 187–95; Cahill, C. (2007). Repositioning ethical commitments: Participatory action research as a relational praxis of social change. *ACME: An International E-Journal for Critical Geographies, 6*(3), 360–73; and, Fine, M. (2009). Postcards from Metro America: Reflections on Youth Participatory Action Research for Urban Justice. *The Urban Review, 41*, 1–6. For new readers of this subject, scholarship by Michelle Fine provides an excellent instructional model to follow. Be prepared to possibly provide free copies of key readings to community members who cannot easily locate or afford to purchase them.

Action Item 7: Create culturally sensitive spaces.
An essential part of the process for discussing ethical issues in class, mentoring sessions, or research projects requires intentionally cultivating safe spaces where individuals feel comfortable discussing potentially sensitive, often controversial issues in non-judgmental ways, particularly if one's university or school does not have such a reputation. Teachers who are not trained to create such spaces should consider taking classes or workshops on cultural sensitivity and combating discrimination sponsored by local colleges or organizations such as the NAACP.

Action Item 8: Be self-reflexive.
Purposely engage in self-reflection and encourage students and community members to do so. Read books such as Schön's *The Reflective Practitioner* (1983) and Bellah's *Habits of the Heart* (1985) for insight. Include a semester-long journal assignment for individuals and yourself to reflect upon experiences inside and outside the classroom as a way to begin to engage in the generative-reflective process. Consider concepts such as power, virtue, ethics, social justice, and human respect, as well as new knowledge that emerges during the journaling process. Help those persons involved understand and acknowledge that self-reflection is a process that can be personally challenging and beneficial.

Action Item 9: Honestly and directly assess issues of power.
Discuss varying forms of power, why they exist, where, how they are maintained, and the groups that tend to benefit or be hurt by different forms of power. As an instructor or group leader, be willing to cede some of your power. For example, enabling students to lead class discussions is one approach to empower them and share power. Placing community members in key, influential positions during a research project also helps foster shared power.

Action Item 10: Consider the study of ethics as a process rather than an outcome.
Anticipate certain outcomes as individuals grapple with this topic (for example, changes in students' remarks during discussions and written comments on assignments). However, do not consider the course or module unsuccessful if such outcomes are not immediately apparent. Individuals may not fully understand and appreciate this topic until months or years after exposure. The process of engaging the topic of ethics is as important as outcomes.

Conclusion

Based on what we have written about the EHDC, we argue that each HOD course promotes human development and community as a central concern. We are educating, motivating, and attempting to transform our students to become reflective-generative practitioners who, in enacting their varied professional roles, will care, tell the truth, respect the autonomy of persons, do no harm, do good, and be just in pursuit of human development and community. We are worthy of our inheritance of the legacy of Nicholas Hobbs: The EHDC operates across the HOD curriculum and is a candidate for adoption in the social and behavioral sciences and the professions more generally.

References

Addams, J. (1902). *Democracy and social ethics*. New York: Macmillan.
Bellah, R. N., Madsen, R., Sullivan, W. M., Swidler, A., & Tipton, S. M. (1985). *Habits of the heart: Individualism and commitment in American life*. New York: Harper & Row.
Bok, S. (1978). *Lying: Moral choice in public and private life*. New York: Pantheon.
Boydston, J. A. (ed.). (1985/2008). *The later works of John Dewey, Volume 7, 1925–1952: 1932, Ethics*. Carbondale, IL: Southern Illinois University Press.
Browning, D. S. (1973). *Generative man: Psychoanalytic perspectives*. Philadelphia: Westminster Press.
Browning, D. S. (1991). *A fundamental practical theology*. Minneapolis: Fortress Press.
Craig, J. H., & Craig, M. (1973). *Synergic power: Beyond domination and submissiveness*. Berkeley, CA: Proactive Press.
Dewey, J. (1960). *Theory of the moral life*. New York: Irvington Publishers, Inc.
Dokecki, P. R. (1996). *The tragicomic professional: Basic considerations for ethical reflective-generative practice*. Pittsburgh, PA: Duquesne University Press.
Dunst, C. J., Trivette, C. M., & Deal, A. G. (1988). *Enabling and empowering families*. Cambridge, Mass: Brookline Books.
Erikson, E. H. (1967). *Insight and responsibility*. New York: Norton.
Fischer, F. (1980). *Politics, values, and public policy: The problem of methodology*. Boulder: Westview Press.
Frankena, W. K. (1963/1973). *Ethics*. Englewood Cliffs, NJ: Prentice-Hall.
Freire, P. (1970). *Pedagogy of the oppressed*. New York: Herder & Herder.
Fromm, E. (1955). *The sane society*. New York: Rinehart.

Gergen, K. J. (1978). Toward generative theory. *Journal of Personality and Social Psychology, 36*, 1344–60.

Green, J. M. (1999). *Deep democracy: Community, diversity, and transformation.* Lanham, MD: Rowman & Littlefield.

Hobbs, N., Dokecki, P. R., Hoover-Dempsey, K. V., Moroney, R. M., Shayne, M. W., & Weeks, K. H. (1984). *Strengthening families.* San Francisco: Jossey-Bass.

Lebacqz, K. (1985). *Professional ethics: Power and paradox.* Nashville, TN: Abingdon Press.

MacIntyre, A. (1981). *After virtue.* Notre Dame, IN: University of Notre Dame Press.

Marrow, A. (1969). *The practical theorist: The life and work of Kurt Lewin.* New York: Basics.

Mayeroff, M. (1971). *On caring.* New York: Harper and Row.

Moroney, R. M. (1986). *Shared responsibility: families and social policy.* New York: Aldine.

Moroney, R., Dokecki, P. R., Gates, J., Haynes, K. N., Newbrough, J. R., & Nottingham, J. (1998). *Caring and competent caregivers.* Athens, GA: University of Georgia Press.

Nussbaum, M. (2011). *Creating capabilities: The human development approach.* Cambridge: Belknap.

Polkinghorne, D. E. (1988). *Narrative knowing and the human sciences.* Albany: State University of New York Press.

Schmidt, P. R., & Finkbeiner, C. (Eds.) (2006). *ABC's of cultural understanding and communication: National and International Adaptations.* Charlotte, NC: Information Age Publishing.

Schön, D. (1983). *The reflective practitioner.* New York: Basic Books.

Schön, D. (1987). *Educating the reflective practitioner.* San Francisco: Jossey-Bass.

Part II: Implications and Responses: *Academics in Action!*

According to American educator, philosopher, and psychologist Williams James, "Act as if what you do makes a difference. It does."[1] This charge is the impetus behind the four chapters in Part II. Each piece describes systematic attempts to respond to social ills in society; each also recognizes the difficult task of combating community problems, the need for both academic and applied research, as well as the importance of community partnering during the process. Concerns about homelessness, youth development, public health inequities, and community development in general often seem untenable. Yet according to the writers in these chapters, it is imperative that the academy actively and intentionally participate in scholarly inquiry, classroom instruction, and social engagement to combat such social problems for the common good. Such involvement reflects its reasonable service. The efforts described are not presented as cure-alls but rather possible approaches to community-based action-oriented work to address specific social concerns. The chapters highlight the importance of context when developing prevention and intervention initiatives and research agendas that aim to alleviate complex social problems. Each chapter also illustrates some of the strengths associated with studying and responding to social issues using an interdisciplinary approach, and examines how other scholars, practitioners, and students can proactively move their work from the classroom to the community.

The four chapters in this section enable readers to consider some of the real-world local, regional, and/or national implications of community engagement that are theoretically presented in Part I as well as prepare readers for additional insights on programmatic processes and structures that undergird such research in Part III. Moreover, they reflect contemporary

---

1. *The Correspondence of William James: April 1908–August 1910* (1908/2004, Vol. 12, p. 135, Charlottesville: University of Virginia Press). Correspondence with Helen Keller.

examples of Deweyism in their ability to empirically and directly consider problems, tensions, nuances, and implications of the models detailed in the initial section of this volume. Equally important, each chapter illustrates how these principles can be applied to specific issues that continue to plague our complex, multicultural global society in a way not previously considered by Dewey. Each chapter also illustrates the importance of empirical and practical results to augment theory to construct useful knowledge tied to ideas and social experiences (Dewey, 1927/1954, 1938).

Chapter 3, "Using Research to Guide Efforts to Prevent and End Homelessness," documents the role of research in efforts to alleviate homeless in the United States. According to the chapter authors, preventing and ending homelessness for families require both intellectual and practical action at local, regional, national, and international levels. The authors introduce several existing studies to better understand and counter this chronic social problem, including systemic correlates to homelessness such as historic inequality and poverty, solutions that have had some degree of success, cutting-edge prevention and intervention strategies, and some of the experiences of homeless persons as they seek shelter. By candidly discussing the benefits and challenges of university involvement in work around homelessness, this chapter provides insight for readers through an example of active dialogue and work between academia and public spheres (Dewey, 1927/1954). Next, how do students, academicians, and practitioners work together to develop and implement effective youth prevention programs for healthy youth development? This query is the focus of Chapter 4, "Ecological Research Promoting Positive Youth Development." The authors posit that research, scholarship, and teaching in the arena of prevention and youth development can be significantly improved by informing the conventional scientific approach with ecological systems theory and partnering with community groups. Specific research and resulting best practices for three projects—Strong African American Families Program (SAAF) to counter HIV/AIDS among African Americans, the Alignment Enhanced Services (AES) initiative that promotes the well-being and success of Nashville public school students, as well as the South African Field School project to foster high school retention rates—clearly illustrate the beneficence of combining evidenced-based research with community-centered preventions and solutions.

Health care inequities and diminishing quality of life among increasing numbers of U.S. citizens provide the premise for Chapter 5, "Putting Boyer's Four Types of Scholarship into Practice: A Community Research and Action Perspective on Public Health." The authors challenge disciplinary divisions as well as methodological and analytical schisms that undermine common goals of investigating social determinants of health and developing effective public health interventions. They further contend that scholarship would benefit from interdisciplinary, holistic studies of the social context of health that inform remedies and strategies. Applying a key feature of Dewey's treatise, communities matter in understanding health challenges (Dewey, 1927/1954, 1938). The chapter illustrates how a social justice lens and Boyers's scholarly framework, coupled with the systematic inquiry evident in HOD's Ph.D. program,[2] can translate into cooperative problem solving and experiential learning that are crucial for comprehensive remedies to health-related problems.

Lastly, some of the contemporary challenges and possible benefits associated with university-community partnerships are documented in Chapter 6, "Conducting Research on Comprehensive Community Development Initiatives: Balancing Methodological Rigor and Community Responsiveness." This chapter examines specific approaches and processes to minimize the research-practice gap that is so common in academia. Community-based participatory research and action research are presented as models to cultivate meaningful relationships and successful applied work between the "researcher" and the "researched." This chapter offers a case study of a partnership linked to a Promise Neighborhoods (PN) planning project to provide suggestions, strategies, and lessons to minimize group tensions, increase inter-group collaboration, identify and cultivate diverse forms of expertise, overcome institutional barriers, and work together to accomplish significant goals for community improvement.

2. The Ph.D. degree in Community Research and Action (CRA) prepares action-oriented researchers for academic or policy-related careers. The program has a social justice orientation and areas of emphasis include community psychology/development, organizational change, health policy, prevention, and social policy. CRA is unique in its combination of community psychology, sociology, and social psychology, with an emphasis on empirically grounded practice, rigorous applied research, and human and community development.

The four chapters in Part II reflect twenty-first century Deweyism by providing direct evidence that projects to promote the common good can still occur, yet they must be nuanced to reflect the current political, cultural, economic, and social mosaic of our time. In addition to empirical analyses, the authors introduce novel concepts and methodologies as well as present strategies and policy suggestions. Furthermore, the chapters show that evidence-based work can be thoughtfully used to champion a myriad of social concerns, particularly when coupled with an interdisciplinary lens. The chapters ultimately provide evidence that intellectual interests, professional development, and community engagement are not necessarily mutually exclusive goals for faculty, practitioners, community members, and students alike.

References

Dewey, J. (1927/1954). *The public and its problems.* Chicago: The Swallow Press.
Dewey, J. (1938). *Education and experience.* New York: Touchstone, Simon & Schuster.

3 Using Research to Guide Efforts to Prevent and End Homelessness

MARYBETH SHINN, LINDSAY S. MAYBERRY,
ANDREW L. GREER, BENJAMIN W. FISHER,
JESSICA GIBBONS-BENTON, AND
VERA S. CHATMAN

We only think when we are confronted with problems.

—John Dewey, 1933

People who are homeless are not social inadequates. They are people without homes.

—Sheila McKechnie[1]

Homelessness is a pressing national problem afflicting 578,000 Americans on a given night (U.S. Department of Housing and Urban Development, 2014, Annual Homeless Assessment Report to Congress, hereafter AHAR, 2014). Far larger numbers of people will experience homelessness in their lifetimes. Although progress was interrupted by the recent recession (AHAR, 2014; Sard, 2009), rates of homelessness have decreased since 2007, with larger decreases for single individuals than for families (AHAR, 2014).

Preventing and ending homelessness requires theory and action at multiple levels, from local housing and service programs to national and even international policy. Researchers are neither policy makers nor service providers (although individuals may play more than one of these roles), but they can work collaboratively with others to make policies and programs more effective. In this chapter, we describe briefly our understanding of the structural causes of homelessness and explain how our research is contributing to efforts to prevent and end it. Our student-faculty

---

1. Dame Sheila Marshall McKechnie (May 3, 1948–January 2, 2004) was a Scottish trade unionist, housing campaigner, consumer activist, and executive director of an organization called Shelter. The quote from 2004 was retrieved from Scotsman.com.

group in the department of HOD is engaged in a national multi-site study (the Family Options study) and its spinoffs, and also works with local government agencies in New York City; Alameda County, California; and Nashville, Tennessee to improve the efficacy of efforts to prevent and combat homelessness. In particular, our recent research addresses the following issues:

> What works to *end* homelessness for families?
> How can housing services best address the unique needs and experiences of families who become homeless?
> What works to *prevent* homelessness, and how can prevention services be directed to people most likely to become homeless without them?

In addition to research that addresses these questions, we work with the local homeless service system in Nashville, Tennessee. Most of the projects in this multi-site endeavor were developed in collaboration with government agencies and thus directly inform the policy process. We will also describe how working in an interdisciplinary department in a research university often facilitates and occasionally hinders these efforts.

Structural Origins of Homelessness

We have argued elsewhere (for example, Shinn, 2007a; Shinn, 2010; Shinn & Gillespie, 1994) that homelessness originates as a result of income inequality that puts even inexpensive market-rate housing beyond the reach of many poor households. For example, data from the American Community Survey show that 18 percent of all American households paid over half of their income for housing in 2010 (Joint Center for Housing Studies of Harvard University, 2012, p. 27) and an overlapping 18.3 percent were doubled up (living with relatives or friends) in 2011 (Johnson, 2011). Both doubled-up households and those with high cost burdens are at risk of homelessness (indeed some definitions of homelessness include doubling up because of lack of resources). Further, social exclusion leads some groups in society (for example, racial minorities, people who are poor or experience mental illness) to be systematically disadvantaged in terms of employment and income, wealth, housing, and incarceration, each of which increases risk for homelessness and accounts for its uneven distribution across social groups (Shinn, 2010). The same patterns are evident in all industrialized societies, but inequality is particularly egregious in the United States, where taxation and social expenditure do less to alleviate it than in other developed countries. Thus, it is not surprising that telephone surveys to assess lifetime prevalence of homelessness find higher levels of homelessness in the United States than in other industrialized countries in Europe or in Japan (Shinn, 2007a, 2010). Although rates of homelessness are best understood in structural terms, individual characteristics and luck also influence which members of high-risk groups manage to maintain housing stability or succumb to homelessness.

Our research group recognizes that reductions in income inequality and efforts to combat racism and other forms of social exclusion require political leadership beyond the reach of most academics. Academics can and—in our view—should bear witness, but we should also roll up our sleeves and work with policy makers to improve the effectiveness and efficiency of programs to prevent and end homelessness in the existing socio-political environment. Hopper (2003) describes such work as "waltzing with a monster"—researchers don't typically get to call the tune, but if they are willing to come to the dance, they can have some influence on the steps (see also Shinn, 2007b). This chapter reflects some of our group's efforts.

What Works to End Homelessness for Families?

The gold standard for understanding what works to prevent or end homelessness is an experiment in which people from some defined group are randomized to receive particular interventions and followed over time to assess how they fare. Experiments typically build on earlier studies that show that interventions are associated with positive outcomes. Our research team is currently collaborating with Abt Associates in the Family Options experiment to evaluate the relative effectiveness of three housing and service interventions for 2,307 families recruited from shelters in twelve sites across the country.

One intervention is ongoing housing subsidies, typically provided by Housing Choice Vouchers that reduce a family's rent to 30 percent of its income. The central rationale for housing subsidies is that families become homeless because they cannot afford market-rate housing. Although subsidies have been shown to prevent homelessness (Wood, Turnham, & Mills, 2008) and to end it in quasi-experiments (Cragg & O'Flaherty, 1999; Shinn et al., 1998; Wong, Culhane, & Kuhn, 1997), they are an expensive intervention, and limited Congressional appropriations mean that relatively few of the households that are eligible, by reason of income, receive them. Thus, a second intervention under trial is a short-term and often "shallow" subsidy (that is, one that requires households to pay more toward rent than they would with a Housing Choice Voucher), funded by the Homelessness Prevention and Rapid Re-housing Program (HPRP) as part of the American Recovery and Reinvestment Act (the stimulus program). The rationale for this intervention, called community-based rapid re-housing, is that most families who experience homelessness do so briefly, suggesting that a short-term subsidy may be sufficient to help families get back on their feet. HPRP subsidies lasted from three to eighteen months and could decline over time. In addition to housing stipends, rapid re-housing may be accompanied by services focused on housing and self-sufficiency. The third intervention, unlike the first two, provides case management and multi-faceted social services in program-based transitional housing for a period of up to two years. The rationale for transitional housing is that many homeless families have problems that interfere with their ability to secure housing and that services to improve job skills, repair credit, or deal with trauma, mental health or substance problems will position families to succeed in the private rental market on their own.

The experiment compares all three interventions to one another and to usual care, in which families work with shelter staff to secure whatever resources may be available in their communities. The Family Options study examines five outcomes: residential stability, economic self-sufficiency, family preservation, and adult and child well-being. Results of 18-month follow-up assessments will be available in late 2015 and 36-month follow-ups are being fielded. Because the core Family Options study was funded by a contract from the Department of Housing and Urban Development (HUD), federal policy makers are following its progress closely. HUD is the primary federal funder of shelters and housing programs for homeless and low income Americans and wants maximum impact from its expenditure of funds. Therefore, we designed the study to address questions that HUD wanted to answer and consulted with them about key choices (for example, which interventions to include). After the study ends, HUD will make the data available as a public-use file that other researchers can continue to mine for insights.

How Can Housing Services Best Address the Unique Needs and Experiences of Families Who Become Homeless?

In addition to HUD funding, our group has also secured supplemental funds from the National Institute of Child Health and Human Development (NICHD) to take a more comprehensive look at child outcomes, including direct interviews and assessments of children. NICHD also funded qualitative interviews with a non-random subsample of 80 families from the larger study to examine families' experiences with the interventions. The qualitative interviews enabled us to address several questions: (1) How do different living situations commonly experienced by families who become homeless affect family processes? (2) How do families experience the housing service system, including housing assistance interventions, and what strategies do they use to obtain housing services? (3) How do different housing services affect families' access to their support networks? (4) How do families make housing decisions—specifically, how do they choose whether or not to accept a particular type of housing assistance offered them through the intervention? What are the key factors in their decisions about where to move and when? (e) How do parents become separated from a child or a partner? In the following sections, we highlight our findings germane to each of these questions, and offer suggestions as to how policy may integrate such research into practice.

(1) **How do different living situations commonly experienced by families who become homeless affect family processes? (Mayberry, Shinn, Benton, & Wise, 2014)** Even though we interviewed families an average of only six months after they received an offer for housing assistance, most families had already experienced several living situations, including the shelter at which they were recruited, during that short interval. We asked parents to discuss their experiences with parenting in each living situation and to compare that living situation to the others. We analyzed their experiences with maintaining family routines and rituals in shelter, in transitional housing programs, in temporary living

situations with friends or family members (i.e., doubled up), and in their own place (with or without housing assistance subsidies). We found that family routines in independent living situations were organized around pursuing goals (for example, finding resources, obtaining education, working, or looking for employment), public transportation availability, family activities, and children's waking and sleeping cycles. In contrast, family routines in service-intensive housing programs—shelter and transitional housing—were organized around imposed schedules for meals and curfews, *demonstrations* of seeking resources or employment (activities that demonstrate to staff that families were seeking resources and employment, whether or not families felt such activities were helpful), and attending mandatory meetings and services. A participant offered an example of such a routine:

> We wake up, get the girls ready. I had to have my room clean every day. We had things that we had to do like the computer thing you had to sign up for a job or something. You had to have an activity and you had to do like community service for the court. And that's like stuff around the [shelter] facility, not even leaving. [Note: all quotations preserve respondents' wording.]

Those interviewed indicated that rules and surveillance by program staff and other residents presented major impediments to family routines and rituals in shelters and transitional housing programs. Parents described how rules that specified acceptable and unacceptable discipline made it difficult to maintain consistency with children. In addition, they reported that these rules allowed program staff to surveil their parenting, interrupt them when they were disciplining their children, and correct their parenting in front of their children. Parents reported having to work to reestablish authority and regain children's respect after shelter or transitional housing stays:

> If I tell [my children] something and they didn't feel like doing it, they would boldly tell me in the shelter "I don't want to do it" because then you have all these people watching you telling you, "You can't discipline your child because you're in the shelter." So once you get out of the shelter, you have to go through a whole new ballgame to get your kids reprogrammed.

Parents indicated that they employed strategies to maintain consistency with their children during shelter stays and blocked out criticism of their parenting by staff and other program residents by focusing on their positive relationship with their children.

While prior research has been conducted on the effects of shelter stays on family processes, our study was one of the first to examine experiences across numerous shelters, project-based transitional housing programs, and other living situations in several sites. As a result, our findings indicate that problematic applications of program rules are common although not universal. Our findings and others (Cosgrove & Flynn, 2005; Hausman & Hammen, 1993; Lindsey, 1998) emphasize the challenges inherent in parenting without a private residence and accentuate the need for programs to train staff to model supportive parenting, to strive to enhance parenting self-efficacy (Schulz, 2009), and to work collaboratively with parents to make a plan for consistent parenting in the context of the program environment and rules. In addition, our findings suggest that parenting interruptions by program staff should not be allowed, as parents are unlikely to receive the correction as constructive and children may be confused.

(2) How do families experience the housing service system, including housing assistance interventions, and what strategies do they use to obtain housing services? (Mayberry, in press) Service use is one of the pathways through which families obtain stable housing and re-achieve stability, but the challenges to successful service use are rarely examined. Analyses revealed that confusion or uncertainty about requirements for services were a consistent problem. Participants reported trouble contacting service providers to ask questions or get clarification about requirements or services. They also described not knowing which service provider was associated with which service (for example, not knowing whether "the lady" they talked to was affiliated with the shelter or the subsidy program), making it difficult to know whom to contact about specific programs or resources:

> It's really hard for me to get accurate information as far as assistance . . . There's situations where someone would tell me, "Oh, this place or that place will help you with assistance." And I get all my stuff together and

go there and they're like, "Oh, well we don't do that anymore." Or "The program is shut down. We don't have funding for it anymore." And it's like, "Oh wow, I kind of did all this work for nothing."

Participants also recounted how their applications would initially get accepted and subsequently be denied or rescinded, often without a clear sense of who was responsible. In response to these challenges, participants often activated official resources (for example, police, lawyers) and/or filed complaints with agencies when service providers were not helping them reach their goals. They also developed and leveraged relationship with service providers to learn about resources.

Participants reported that checking their spot on waiting lists was critical to staying on the list. Calling or visiting weekly was necessary to ensure eventual placement or receipt of resources.

The uncertainty and confusion associated with service use across all sites and several programs within each indicate that these problems are not solely attributable to the service user. During times of extreme stress and first exposure to various types of services, each with different paperwork and eligibility requirements, families need clearer communication from service providers. Providers should check to ensure families understand processes by helping them plan next steps or asking them to explain the requirements back to the provider. Key characteristics of positive service experiences also emerged from interviews. These included communication across service programs and with participants, clear and consistent requirements, and the opportunity to choose or tailor services to meet family needs. When participants encountered shelter programs or other services with these characteristics, they reported feeling empowered to meet requirements, obtain needed services, and make progress toward their goals.

(3) How do different housing services affect families' access to their support networks? (Mayberry, 2012) We asked parents in different living situations to identify people who fostered or stymied parental support (supportive and non-supportive social network members). Mixed-methods were used to describe support networks and compare network characteristics across living situations. Results showed that participants in service-intensive living situations had more support for parenting than those in independent or doubled-up living situations.

Although participants in service-intensive housing programs did not have more network members, they had more access to them. Participants who lived in shelters located closer to friends with whom they had had relationships prior to entering the shelter reported more support for parenting than did participants in independent living and doubled-up situations.

These findings suggest that families may lose access to their support systems as they relocate to obtain independent housing. Participants felt that the shelter environment provided access to other parents in similar situations, formal childcare services and informal assistance with childcare from other shelter residents, and parenting classes/activities for children. Participants in independent living situations sometimes felt a loss of access to these resources upon leaving the shelter:

> That was one of the things I liked at [shelter] is having like, you know, everybody there was in the same situation and being able to socialize with people with similar situations and not having to be like embarrassed or anything like that because everybody was in the same boat. And then they also had the kids around the same age, and you could discuss things . . . I definitely don't have as much of a social connection with people now because I'm all the way out here [in my own place]. And most [of those] people don't have transportation a lot of times.

Based on these results, we recommend that housing programs allow participants to continue to participate in services that are provided by shelters and transitional housing, or help them identify and access new resources as they transition to independent living situations.

(4) How do families make housing decisions? What are the key factors in their decisions about where to move and when? (Fisher, Mayberry, Shinn, & Khadduri, 2014) Homelessness intervention services are designed to present attractive options for families. However, families often choose not to use available housing programs (Edin, DeLuca, & Owens, 2012; Jacob & Ludwig, 2012). Families may decline to pursue offers or leave programs before they are required to do so. To understand these phenomena, we asked the 80 families to tell us about the places they lived after leaving shelters, the housing programs they used, as well as how they made housing decisions, and we compared patterns with tracking data from the larger study.

Participants' responses revealed a number of reasons they might not use housing interventions offered to them. For example, participants cited the desire for stability, although they were not always able to attain it; families wanted to find living situations that were relatively permanent and affordable and that allowed the entire family to be together. Participants also emphasized the importance of living near existing resources such as friends, family, transportation, jobs, and children's schools that helped to make their daily family life feasible. For instance, one mother turned down her assigned offer for transitional housing because it was located too far from her mother and grandmother, who provided childcare support that allowed her to work full-time. Another refused to move because her mother was ill and she wanted her children to spend time with her before she passed away. Additionally, many families avoided living in neighborhoods that they perceived as unsafe or otherwise undesirable for children. Ineligibility for programs sometimes constrained families' options. Families reported that the restricted options from which to choose often led to compromises in an effort to find places that were "good enough," rather than optimal:

> I wasn't being too picky at the time because the shelter I was in was a short-term shelter, and they were getting ready to kick us out. So I could not afford, really, to be picky. So I seen one unit, I didn't like it at all. It was on a third floor, it was really small, and can you imagine six people in a small apartment? So then I saw this one and I said "Well, this is decent." And it had a washer and dryer, first floor, which I felt I wouldn't bother anyone with the kids and everything, and I just said, "I'll just take this."

As a result, several had already moved from their first post-shelter residence within the first six months, and others hoped to relocate as new opportunities arose, potentially leading to continued high rates of residential mobility.

Families also reported some concerns specific to each intervention. Transitional housing was the offer most frequently turned down by families. Participants cited reasons such as poor facilities, bad locations, and a one-bag restriction on what they were allowed to bring. Some families left transitional housing before they had to because they felt the environment was bad for their children:

[There's a] lot of arguing. All the cigarette smoking going on. It's always some kind of drama going on up in here. And I'm not—you know, I left the shelter because . . . there was some drama there, and I didn't want my daughter to be in that situation. So that's another reason. And I'm really considering just, like just getting out of this program, period, and just doing it on my own. Cause it's not helping me.

Families reported that the temporary nature of community-based rapid re-housing generated a significant amount of anxiety for them. The recertification process seemed enigmatic, and many indicated that they did not fully understand how long and at what level funding would last:

Well, she said [the funding would last] up to a year, so it's kind of in the air, I guess. Every three months they let me know, and it depends on the funding, which is nerve-wracking for me.

Several participants expressed concern that the income ceilings for community-based rapid re-housing made it difficult for them to save enough money to sustain their independent housing after the subsidy ended. Long-term housing subsidies were the most sought-after option:

[We're] very grateful [for the subsidy] because we've been paying fair market and I've never had Section 8 or anything or any kind of HUD assistance. So for me to actually have a nice house for our children without having to be completely worried about rent, rent, rent for this month because my husband is trying to go back to school full-time and so am I . . . that way we know we're supported and we don't have to worry about losing the house because we are trying to go to school and work and we're safe, we're okay and we'll get things back on track.

Although some families encountered landlords who would not accept vouchers as payment, all of these families did eventually find accepting landlords. These findings may inform policies to make housing interventions more appealing to homeless families.

(5) How do families become separated from a child or a partner? Families frequently are separated because of homelessness. Past research has focused most attention on separations of children from parents. Park, Metraux, Brodbar, & Culhane (2004) found that 16 percent of children in families experiencing homelessness in New York City had been placed in foster care five years after their families entered shelter. Cowal, Shinn,

Weitzman, Stojanovic, & Labay (2002) included informal placements with relatives as well as formal foster care, and found that 44 percent of homeless mothers in the same city were separated from one or more children by five years after shelter entry. New York City allows all family members to stay together in shelters, but not all communities are equipped to do so. Thus, our research examined parents' separation from partners as well as children (Shinn, Gibbons-Benton, & Brown, in press).

Across the twelve sites in the larger Family Options study, 23 percent of the 2,307 families in shelter were two-parent families, and an additional 10 percent had a partner living elsewhere. Survey data for 80 families who participated in qualitative interviews were similar (25 percent and 10 percent), but the interviews revealed additional separations, many of which had ended in reunification. Such reunifications frequently depended on securing housing that would accommodate the entire family.

Twelve respondents had been separated from a partner, half because of rules in shelters or housing programs that excluded men, unmarried partners, or people with criminal convictions, sometimes putting mothers in the difficult position of turning down a housing option to keep her family intact, or separating from a partner to accept a housing subsidy. The extent to which the homeless service system forces partner separations is an important concern.

Forty-three of the 80 families had experienced 57 instances of child separation. The most common reason (15 families) had to do with economic hardship that left parents unable to provide for children's basic needs:

> I was pregnant, and we were living in motels. I found myself getting broke. We were eating fast foods I got paid from my job and I called their dad, and I said, "[Ex-Partner], I love my boys, I know you love them too, but I need help right now." We met and he took the boys . . . I didn't have a refrigerator or nothing like that, so I don't want my boys to—it was beginning to be too much.

Housing programs are less likely to separate parents from children than from partners. However, not all shelters accept older boys, and some families separated so that children would not be exposed to shelter conditions. In all, nine separations had to do with some aspect of shelter. Six families were separated when the parent was arrested, and five when the parent was unable to parent to her own or her family's standards. Child

Protective Services was involved in only four cases (including one of the arrests).

Congregate settings such as shelter and transitional housing often have a difficult time balancing the different needs associated with different family structures (for example, two-parent versus single-parent, older children versus younger children). In our interviews, some respondents complained of forced separation from partners, while another respondent (quoted previously) worried about the safety of her daughter in a program that also housed adult men. More independent forms of housing for families experiencing homelessness, such as apartment style shelters or transitional housing with independent units scattered throughout a community, would lead to less conflict among the needs of families with different structures. Social policies that support families, such as the family allowances, universal health care, and childcare policies prevalent in Europe (Shinn, 2010), would make it possible for more families to stay together in the face of economic hardship and homelessness.

What Works to Prevent Homelessness, and How Can Prevention Services Be Directed to People Most Likely to Become Homeless in the Absence of Services?

The Family Options study attempts to discover cost-effective ways of ending homelessness and promoting positive outcomes for families who are recruited from homeless shelters. However, researchers and policy makers also want to know how to prevent homelessness from happening in the first place. Broad-based social policies to reduce income inequality and make housing affordable would go a long way toward eliminating homelessness. In the current policy environment, policy makers often hope to reduce homelessness by offering services and supports to those at risk. Local administrators charged with dealing with homelessness are particularly eager to prevent it, and efforts to do so transcend partisan boundaries. For example, the U.S. Conference of Mayors (2008) reported that in 2007 all but one of twenty-five cities surveyed had programs to prevent homelessness among families facing eviction. However, evidence that these or other prevention efforts reduce homelessness remains sparse.

Efforts to prevent homelessness must be both effective (reduce rates of homelessness among people at high risk) and efficient (target people who are most likely to become homeless in the absence of services) (Burt, Pearson, & Montgomery, 2007). Efficiency may be the more difficult problem because many people are at risk but most avoid using shelters or sleeping in public places. Identifying those who are likely to become homeless in the absence of help is challenging. A long literature in decision-making suggests that "actuarial" predictions based on statistical models are more accurate than professional or "clinical" judgments in predicting individual outcomes across diverse domains including medicine, mental health, personality, and education (Ægisdóttir et al., 2006; Dawes, Faust, & Meehl, 1989; Grove, Zald, Lebow, Snitz, & Nelson, 2000). Thus, through partnerships with local government programs in New York City and Alameda County, California, our group has developed and evaluated statistical targeting models to predict which households end up in shelter and which avoid it, despite poverty and other risk factors. In Alameda County, we are also evaluating the effectiveness of prevention services. In the following sections, we highlight two promising approaches to prevention, and the specific ways our group's research seeks to inform practice.

HomeBase, New York City. HomeBase, run by New York City, is the largest community-based homelessness prevention program in the United States. It offers individually tailored services that can include cash grants, job training, assistance with childcare, and help accessing benefits such as tax credits (Hess, 2006). These services are desirable and the program has many applicants. A quasi-experimental evaluation suggested that such services were effective (Messeri, O'Flaherty, & Goodman, 2011). However, very few families in the control group became homeless—even in the absence of services. Thus, improvements in prevention may depend more on accurate targeting than on making services more effective. To improve the city's targeting, we followed 11,105 families who applied for HomeBase between 2004 and 2008 using city records to determine whether they entered shelter within three years after application. We used survival analysis to show that the hazard of entering shelter was highest shortly after application for services (remaining elevated for about a year and a half) as well as to model factors that put families at highest risk of shelter entry. As expected, an easily implemented statistical model using fifteen risk factors was more accurate than workers' judgments in predicting who would enter shelter, and services appeared to make the most difference for families at highest risk. If the city had served the same proportion of applicants during the study period but selected them using the empirical model, it would have increased correct targeting of families entering shelter by 26 percent and reduced misses by almost two-thirds. Alternatively, with the same funds, the city could provide more extensive services to fewer families, but still reach more of those who would enter shelter without help (Shinn, Greer, Bainbridge, Kwon, & Zuiderveen, 2013).

New York's Department of Homeless Services then requested that we develop a parallel model for individual applicants for services (Greer, 2014), and it has adopted both of our empirical models to identify which applicants to serve. Workers are permitted to override the model decision in up to 5 percent of cases, with written explanations and approval from the Department of Homeless Services. The possibility of overrides is important to get workers to buy into the empirical system. In addition, later analysis of these explanations may identify new trends in risk factors. Administrators in Alameda County, California asked for a similar model based on their data (Greer, 2014). They also asked for help with examining the effectiveness of their homelessness prevention program, as described in the next section. Across all three models for different populations and locations, prior episodes of homelessness were the strongest predictor of new episodes. Other important predictors included aspects of housing, income, and public assistance, which we consider to be individual manifestations of structural causes of homelessness. For families, youth, pregnancy, and presence of young children—factors that increase needs for housing and reduce the ability to work—also mattered. Interestingly, factors suggesting individual vulnerability, such as mental illness, substance abuse, and domestic violence that are prominent in the literature, played little role in any of the models.

Homelessness Prevention and Rapid Re-Housing Program Evaluation, Alameda County. The American Recovery and Reinvestment Act offered communities $1.5 billion from 2010 to fall 2012 to prevent homelessness and/or rapidly re-house people who experienced it through the Homelessness Prevention and Rapid Re-Housing Program (HPRP) (Witte, 2012). The goal was to quickly allocate these funds and few communities made much effort to evaluate their programs. As federal stimulus funds ended and communities had to decide whether to invest their own funds in homelessness prevention, administrators wanted to know whether programs succeeded in keeping people housed. In the process of setting up the Family Options study, members of our team became acquainted with administrators in Alameda County, California. Thus, when administrators wanted to evaluate their prevention program, we were asked to complete the task. This evaluation used a regression-discontinuity design to compare the treatment group that received services through HPRP funds to a comparison group of people who did not because their risk was deemed too low or so high that services would not help. The core idea of the design is that applicants on either side of the cutoff in assessed risk are almost alike, so their outcomes can be compared to determine the effectiveness of the program. Results suggest that the program made little difference for those at low risk who are unlikely to become homeless, but that it may have been helpful for those at high risk. The sample size was insufficient to answer the question definitively (Greer, 2014).

How Can Local Homeless Services Be Improved?

Our team does not presently conduct research in Nashville, but we have participated in local street counts and "vulnerability" surveys to identify individuals on the street with medical vulnerabilities to whom the Homeless Commission has given priority for housing. One member of our group serves on the governance group for the local Continuum of Care—a HUD-mandated group that sets priorities for the HUD funding for local services. Two efforts to engage Nashville providers in research were met with enthusiasm in some quarters and more resistance in others and have not come to fruition, but we remain open to more local endeavors. Engaging local practitioners is an important challenge confronting academic-based researchers who desire to create practical outlets for their research findings, as is addressed in other chapters of the present volume.

Developing a Policy-Oriented Academic Agenda

The creation of academic departments framed by an overarching commitment to social justice offers an exciting hub in which scholars and practitioners from a wide range of sectors and disciplines may connect to conduct progressive research on social problems. Such research creates opportunities to link academic scholars to policymakers in meaningful ways. How-

Chapter 3: Getting Started!
Using Research to Guide Efforts to Prevent and End Homelessness

Action Item 1: Take advantage of the freedom universities provide to study pressing social questions.
Faculty and students have enormous freedom to select areas in which they will work. Pick one that inspires your passions.

Action Item 2: Collaborate with cross-disciplinary partners, both within and beyond your institution.
Social issues are not the provenance of one discipline, and it is not only academic colleagues but also administrators and the people affected who have worthy ideas. Reach out to diverse stakeholders to jumpstart collaborations.

Action Item 3: Embrace applied research.
Applied research is sometimes snubbed by the academy because of perceptions of limited rigor. However, when developed intentionally, it can be as conceptually and methodologically challenging as other research approaches.

Action Item 4: Address questions that policy makers want answered.
It is not enough for studies to simply be "policy-relevant" for researchers to expect that policymakers will be interested. When taking on a research agenda with potential policy implications, academics must consider what kinds of information are useful in the policy arena. Some policy makers may not appreciate academic research but just as often have questions they are eager for researchers to answer. Creating intentional connections between the overlapping goals of researchers and policy makers should be a core part of research development and execution.

Action Item 5: Be ready to use a variety of methods.
Once members of the research team agree upon the core research questions, they should next consider a range of appropriate methods, which may include quantitative, qualitative, multi-level, and participatory approaches. When research teams are situated within a university setting, they may seek out experts in particular methods for advice on their development and execution. These methods should aim to capture the impact of social settings and policies, and avoid attributing negative outcomes to decontextualized individual behaviors.

Action Item 6: Take advantage of opportunities.
In the academy, it is important that research is programmatic—that is, multiple studies should build on one another to get a deeper understanding of a problem. In the applied world, researchers must jump on opportunities when they present themselves, but they can still endeavor to build a coherent body of expertise.

(continued)

Chapter 3: Getting Started! (continued)

Action Item 7: Create opportunities.
Although researchers must remain flexible to opportunities that arise throughout their research, they must also actively create opportunities. This is most likely to occur when engagement with policy makers and administrators is sustained intentionally over time, even in the absence of specific projects.

Action Item 8: Translate findings for diverse audiences.
Work published in academic journals will have little influence unless the researcher takes the initiative to translate it for diverse audiences. Potential outlets may include practitioner conferences and informal discussions, webinars, and newsletters.

ever, the questions of importance for policymakers often differ from those that guide scholarly work. As a result, this chapter identifies a number of steps that academics should take in framing their research agendas to meet the diverse but interconnected goals of the two groups. The "Getting Started!" table presents eight distinct action steps that are critical to the development of a policy-oriented academic agenda.

Conclusion: Support and Hindrance of Such Efforts in a Research University

In sum, the research agenda as we have described in this chapter is well situated in an interdisciplinary department committed to social justice and action. Faculty have the freedom to select projects and work with collaborators, both within and outside the university; graduate students are in a position to influence national policy while still in training. Perhaps the biggest support that the university provides is financial. Research is a core part of the university's mission; therefore, faculty with full-time salaries and graduate students with assistantships can choose additional work they think is important without worrying about whether a particular project has outside funding. The interdisciplinary environment means that we do not have to justify projects in disciplinary terms (for example, to explain to skeptical colleagues why our work is "psychology" or "sociology") or to publish in particular outlets.

The work summarized in this chapter poses an array of conceptual and methodological challenges, similar to those found in more basic research.

Through our research experience, we have found that the best solutions to such challenges include the input of diverse, invested stakeholders, not simply that of university colleagues. For example, in the Family Options study, it was key to reconcile the demands of random assignment with the fact that the fifty-one transitional housing programs, eighteen subsidy programs, and twenty-eight rapid re-housing programs participating in the study had scores of requirements families must meet (ranging from behavior, such as sobriety or participation in mandatory programs, to income and employment status, to demographics, such as family size and composition). We did not want to send families to programs we knew would turn them down, but how could we do so without damaging the integrity of the experiment? The solution was to screen families for program requirements for all programs with openings and randomize them only among interventions when they passed the screening for at least one program with an opening representing that intervention at that site. (Note: randomization was at the intervention level, rather than program level.) To preserve the integrity of the experiment, all analyses compare pairs of interventions and include only families who were eligible for both intervention arms and assigned to one.

Additionally, given the diverse range of expertise found within our group, the projects involve a variety of methods. In an earlier study to evaluate how many people are missed by street counts in New York, we used a plant-capture methodology, in which we sent volunteers ("plants") to bed down on the streets on the night of the count to determine whether they were in fact enumerated (Hopper, Shinn, Laska, Meisner, & Wanderling, 2008). To construct models to identify households for preventions services, we used survival analysis (a statistical technique originally developed in medical settings) to model the fact that people can enter shelter after delays of various lengths of time. We used "receiver-operating characteristics" (ROC curves developed by psychologists) to graph hit rates (successful targeting of people who enter shelter) against false alarm rates (incorrect targeting of people who do not enter shelter) to help administrators choose the appropriate proportion of families to serve (Shinn, et al., 2013). Further, work with administrative records often requires multiple imputation of missing data. In addition, qualitative methods are important tools to make sure that participants' experiences are taken into account, and that the right questions are posed in future work with larger samples.

The interventions themselves, as in the Pathways Housing First program that we helped evaluate, sometimes emerge from participatory research methods (Tsemberis, Moran, Shinn, Asmussen, & Shern, 2003). Thus, students interested in applied problems can receive excellent and varied methodological training for which research universities can provide support.

Despite the evidence of departmental and institutional support, it is also important to note the ways in which research universities may also hinder work. Perhaps the biggest barrier, which also manifests as the biggest facilitator, stems from the competing demands of full-time employment. With classes to take or teach and administrative work to perform, clearing the time to respond nimbly to policy maker's deadlines or to work with collaborators who are solely focused on particular issues and tasks can be difficult. Language in collaborators' contracts or mission statements can also pose impediments to collaboration. For instance, Vanderbilt University initially declined to accept a subcontract for the Family Options study because the language in the standard contract from HUD required that the agency accept the final report, and the University interpreted this as a restriction on publication. Freedom to publish findings is integral to work in the academy, so HUD staff had to clarify their meaning. Accordingly, they re-wrote the contract to state that researchers would not be required to *"modify or eliminate independent opinions, judgments, conclusions, or views"* but might be asked to label such views as our own. Successful research collaborations require flexibility and conversation between multiple, invested stakeholders, processes that may take time and delay the research process.

No work environment is perfect, but few are as supportive of efforts both to accumulate knowledge about a major social problem, such as homelessness, and its broader context and also to work with policy makers as the academy. We feel privileged to be able both to contribute to national policy studies of approaches to ending homelessness and to promote the efficiency and effectiveness of local efforts to prevent it. We can apply our research findings to practices and policies, while we simultaneously advocate for the kinds of structural changes required to render this research topic obsolete (Dewey, 1933).

References

Ægisdóttir, S., White, M. J., Spengler, P. M., Maugherman, A. S., Anderson, L. A., Cook, R. S., . . . Rush, J. D. (2006). The meta-analysis of clinical judgment project: Fifty-six years of accumulated research on clinical versus statistical prediction. *The Counseling Psychologist, 34*(3), 341–82. doi: 10.1177/0011000005285875

Burt, M. R., Pearson, C. L., & Montgomery, A. E. (2007). *Homelessness: Prevention, strategies and effectiveness.* New York: Nova Science Publishers, Inc.

Cosgrove, L., & Flynn, C. (2005). Marginalized mothers: Parenting without a home. *Analyses of Social Issues and Public Policy, 5*(1), 127–43. doi: 10.1111/j.1530-2415.2005.00059.x

Cowal, K., Shinn, M., Weitzman, B. C., Stojanovic, D., & Labay, L. (2002). Mother-child separations among homeless and housed families receiving public assistance in New York City. *American Journal of Community Psychology, 30*(5), 711–30. doi: 10.1023/A:1016325332527

Cragg, M., & O'Flaherty, B. (1999). Do homeless shelter conditions determine shelter population? The case of Dinkins Deluge. *Journal of Urban Economics, 46*(3), 377–414. doi: 10.1006/juec.1998.2128

Dawes, R. M., Faust, D., & Meehl, P. E. (1989). Clinical versus actuarial judgment. *Science, 243*(4899), 1668–74.

Dewey, J. (1933). *How we think: A restatement of the relation of reflective thinking to the educative process.* Boston: Heath.

Edin, K., DeLuca, S., & Owens, A. (2012). Constrained compliance: Solving the puzzle of MTO's lease-up rates and why mobility matters. *Cityscape: A Journal of Policy Development and Research, 14*(2), 181–94.

FEANTSA. (2005). *European typology of homelessness and housing exclusion.* Brussels, Belgium: Author.

Fisher, B. W., Mayberry, L. S., Shinn, M., & Khadduri, J. (2014). Leaving homelessness behind: Housing decisions among families exiting shelter. *Housing Policy Debate, 24*(2), 364–86. doi: 10.1080/10511482.2013.852603

Greer, A. L. (2014). *Preventing homelessness in Alameda County, CA and New York City, NY: Investigating effectiveness and efficiency.* Doctor of Philosophy, Vanderbilt University, Nashville, TN.

Grove, W. M., Zald, D. H., Lebow, B. S., Snitz, B. E., & Nelson, C. (2000). Clinical versus mechanical prediction: A meta-analysis. *Psychological Assessment, 12*(1), 19–30. doi: 10.1037/1040-3590.12.1.19

Hausman, B., & Hammen, C. (1993). Parenting in homeless families: The double crisis. *American Journal of Orthopsychiatry, 63*(3), 358–69. doi: 10.1037/h0079448

Hess, R. (2006). HomeBase homelessness prevention services. Retrieved from http://www.innovations.harvard.edu/awards.html?id=52611.

Hopper, K. (2003). *Reckoning with homelessness.* Ithaca, N.Y.: Cornell University Press.

Hopper, K., Shinn, M., Laska, E., Meisner, M., & Wanderling, J. (2008). Estimating numbers of unsheltered homeless people through plant-capture and postcount survey methods. *American Journal of Public Health, 98*(8), 1438–42. doi: 10.2105/ajph.2005

Jacob, B. A., & Ludwig, J. (2012). The effects of housing assistance on labor supply: Evidence from a voucher lottery. *The American Economic Review, 102*(1), 272–304. doi: 10.1257/aer.102.1.272

Johnson, D. (2011). Households doubling up. Retrieved August 16, 2012, from http://blogs.census.gov/2011/09/13/households-doubling-up/.

Joint Center for Housing Studies of Harvard University. (2012). *The state of the nation's housing.* Cambridge, MA: Harvard University.

Lindsey, E. W. (1998). The impact of homelessness and shelter life on family relationship. *Family Relations, 47*(3), 243–52. doi: 10.2307/584973

Mayberry, L. S. (2012). *Family processes in the context of housing instability and intensive service use: Implications for parenting and caregiver well-being.* Doctor of Philosophy, Vanderbilt University, Nashville, TN.

Mayberry, L. S., Shinn, M., Benton, J. G., & Wise, J. (2014). Families experiencing housing instability: The effects of housing programs on family routines and rituals. *American Journal of Orthopsychiatry, 84*(1), 95–109. doi: 10.1037/h0098946

Messeri, P., O'Flaherty, D., & Goodman, S. (2011). Can homelessness be prevented? Evidence from New York City's HomeBase program. Retrieved from http://jagiellonia.econ.columbia.edu/~bo2/research/homebase.pdf.

Park, J. M., Metraux, S., Brodbar, G., & Culhane, D. P. (2004). Child welfare involvement among children in homeless families. *Child Welfare, 83*(5), 423–36.

Schulz, B. (2009). Commentary: A provider perspective on supporting parents who are homeless. *American Journal of Orthopsychiatry, 79*(3), 301–4. doi: 10.1037/a0017238

Shinn, M. (2007a). International homelessness: Policy, socio-cultural, and individual perspectives. *Journal of Social Issues, 63*(3), 657–77. doi: 10.1111/j.1540-4560.2007.00529.x

Shinn, M. (2007b). Waltzing with a monster: Bringing research to bear on public policy. *Journal of Social Issues, 63*(1), 215–31. doi: 10.1111/j.1540-4560.2007.00505.x

Shinn, M. (2010). Homelessness, poverty, and social exclusion in the United States and Europe. *European Journal of Homelessness, 4*, 19–44.

Shinn, M., & Gillespie, C. (1994). The roles of housing and poverty in the origins of homelessness. *American Behavioral Scientist, 37*(4), 505–21. doi: 10.1177/000276429403700404

Shinn, M., Greer, A. L., Bainbridge, J., Kwon, J., & Zuiderveen, S. (2013). Efficient targeting of homelessness prevention services for families. *American Journal of Public Health, 103*(S2), S324–S330. doi: 10.2105/ ajph.2013.301468

Shinn, M., Weitzman, B., Stojanovic, D., Knickman, J., Jimenez, L., Duchon, L., . . . Krantz, D. (1998). Predictors of homelessness among families in New York City: From shelter request to housing stability. *American Journal of Public Health, 88*(11), 1651–57. doi: 10.2105/ AJPH.88.11.1651

Strauss, A., & Corbin, J. (1990). *Basics of qualitative research.* Newbury, CA: Sage.

Tsemberis, S., Moran, L., Shinn, M., Asmussen, S. M., & Shern, D. L. (2003). Consumer preference programs for individuals who are homeless and have psychiatric disabilities: A drop-in center and a supported housing program. *American Journal of Community Psychology, 32*(3–4), 305–17. doi: 10.1023/B:AJCP.0000004750.66957.bf

The United States Conference of Mayors. (2008). *Hunger and homelessness survey: A status report on hunger and homelessness in America's cities: A 25-city survey.* Washington, DC: Author.

U.S. Department of Housing and Urban Development. (2010). *The 2009 Annual Homeless Assessment Report to Congress.* Washington, DC Author.

Witte, P. (2012). The State of Homelessness in America. Washington, DC: National Alliance to End Homelessness.

Wong, Y. L. I., Culhane, D. P., & Kuhn, R. (1997). Predictors of exit and reentry among family shelter users in New York City. *Social Service Review, 71*(3), 441–62.

Wood, M., Turnham, J., & Mills, G. (2008). Housing affordability and family well-being: Results from the Housing Voucher Evaluation. *Housing Policy Debate, 19*(8), 367–412. doi: 10.1080/10511482.2008.9521639.

4 Ecological Research Promoting Positive Youth Development

CAROL T. NIXON, BERNADETTE DOYKOS,
VELMA McBRIDE MURRY, MAURY NATION,
NINA C. MARTIN, ALLEY PICKREN, AND
JOSEPH GARDELLA

> All education which develops power to share effectively in social life is moral. It forms a character which not only does the particular deed socially necessary but one which is interested in that continuous readjustment which is essential to growth. Interest in learning from all the contacts of life is the essential moral interest.
>
> —John Dewey, 1916

> Until the great mass of the people shall be filled with the sense of responsibility for each other's welfare, social justice can never be attained.
>
> —Helen Keller

Research in the fields of prevention and youth development has tended to focus on the mechanisms through which youth intra- and/or interpersonal processes affect individual youth outcomes. The predominant prevention research paradigm recommended by the Institute of Medicine is predicated on identifying problems or disorders and their antecedents (Mrazek & Haggerty, 1994). Interventions targeting these problems typically are tested progressively, moving from randomized controlled trials to large-scale studies in real-world community settings. This traditional approach has contributed to an accumulation of research identifying risk and protective factors associated with substance use, adolescent pregnancy, violence, delinquency, school dropout, and other negative youth behaviors (Balfanz, Herzog, & MacIver, 2007). Consequently, intervention programs and practices informed by this body of research are designed to minimize youth exposure to risk factors (for example, negative peer influences) and strengthen protective factors (self-management and awareness, social awareness, decision-making, and relationship skills) (Catalano, Hawkins, Berglund, Pollard, & Arthur, 2002).

While the traditional prevention science paradigm has helped expand the knowledge base about risk and protective factors, it has multiple limitations. Primarily, it fails to capture individual behavior in relation to social interactions and the environment (Eisner, 1992). In reality, the lives of youth are inherently complex. Youth navigate multiple environments and demands on a daily basis, and, as a result, their developmental outcomes and behavior vary considerably across time and contexts. Ignoring the variation in youth experiences across home, school, and neighborhood environments has several key consequences for research and practice. First, explanations of youth development tend to be overly reductionist—focused on single, isolated problems—and primarily linear and causal (Catalano, Hawkins, Berglund, Pollard, & Arthur, 2002; Price & Behrens, 2003). Moreover, focusing solely on preventing negative outcomes has resulted in a relative neglect of research promoting positive development for all youth, as well-being is not defined simply by the absence of negative outcomes (Flay, 2002; Lerner, 2002). Further, ignoring context restricts a theory-driven understanding about why, when, and under what circumstances youth outcomes vary (Granger, 2011) and, in turn, limits the effectiveness of prevention efforts and contributes to the gap between research and practice (Catalano et al., 2002; Stokols, 1996).

In this chapter, we assert that research, scholarship, and teaching in the fields of prevention and youth development can be greatly enhanced by extending the traditional scientific paradigm by integrating ecological systems theory and collaboratively engaging community members and organizations. We begin by describing the departmental context within which we work as well as three recent research projects conducted by our faculty and students. We then discuss how the department's mission and our action-oriented, ecological systems theoretical orientation permeate multiple aspects of the research process, including the conceptualization of projects, articulation of research questions, intervention design, research methods, project oversight and management, and use of findings. Finally, we describe three projects to illustrate a balanced approach to generating knowledge simultaneously and effecting social change in applied, community settings. By so doing, we highlight an approach to research that is one of democratic participation, harkening back to the principles of Dewey (1916).

Departmental Mission and Context

The research, scholarship, and teaching conducted within the Department of HOD in Peabody College at Vanderbilt University are deeply rooted in the core mission of the department:

> The Department of HOD is committed to promoting individual, relational, and collective well-being by enhancing the development of individuals, organizations, communities, and societies. We strive to achieve these aims by creating and disseminating knowledge about how people, groups, and systems influence one another.

The department's mission also integrates three essential principles. *Simultaneity* asserts that human, organizational, and community development, as well as teaching, research, and action, should progress at the same time. *Complementarity* implies that knowledge and skills across development and domains must be integrated. Finally, *Contextualism* supports understanding of behavior and outcomes as influenced by multiple environments and social influences. The values and principles of our mission provide the scaffolding for our work and have far reaching implications for research, practice, and teaching. HOD's mission and essential principles highlight the importance of context and the interactions among systems and promotes *the use of knowledge* about personal, organizational, and community development and interdependent systems for *social action*. Research findings are used to advocate for and empower disadvantaged youth and their families, as well as to promote youth and community development for social justice. Although tensions between the scientific paradigm and community action are inevitable, over the past decade, several researchers have highlighted the need to integrate research and action to promote more effective practice (Wandersman, 2003).

Overview of Research Projects

The three projects described in this section vary in terms of primary aims, setting, research design, and methods. Yet each employed an ecological systems framework to explore and document the complexity of intrapersonal, interpersonal, and setting-level influences on youth outcomes. Moreover, each ecological space ultimately informed a series of research-based actions to respond to social challenges.

Strong African American Families Program

As many as 1 in 30 African American women and 1 in 16 African American males will be diagnosed with HIV at some point in their lifetime (Centers for Disease Control and Prevention, 2006). Prevention programs designed to deter HIV-related behaviors, such as substance use and high-risk sexual behavior, are implemented primarily through schools. However, these programs are typically scarce in the rural South where there is often inadequate resources and incentives for prevention programming (Murry & Brody, 2004). Further, the effectiveness of interventions to deter substance use and high-risk sexual behavior specifically among rural African American adolescents has been largely unknown. Moreover, research has revealed that rural African American families are more reliant on other family members when challenges arise (Murry, Heflinger, Suiter, & Brody, 2011). Thus scholars have suggested that the family is a primary protective agent for most African American youth, growing up in either urban and rural environments, rather than social institutions such as schools.

In response, Brody and Murry developed and implemented the Strong African American Families (SAAF) Program (Brody, Murry, Gerrard, et al., 2004). SAAF is a family-centered intervention designed to address youth risk behaviors associated with the epidemic rates of HIV/AIDS among African Americans (Brody et al., 2004). It was developed to extend evidence-based family-centered prevention and draws on more than a decade of work with rural African American youth and their families (Brody et al., 2004; 2005; Murry & Brody, 1999; 2002). The program targets first-born, early adolescents and their families. Early adolescence is an important developmental period for youth as they transition to middle school and is thus an optimal time to implement prevention initiatives. The seven-week SAAF intervention includes separate programming for youth and their parents as well as joint family activities. Curriculum content for intervention sessions is presented via videotapes depicting family interactions that illustrate targeted intervention concepts. SAAF is designed to support involved, vigilant parenting practices to foster positive youth outcomes. The intervention also aims to improve youth intrapersonal skills to promote future-oriented goals, self-regulation, effective coping, resistance efficacy, and negative images of risk-taking peers. It also supports racial socialization to promote effective strategies for overcoming the realities of discrimination and strengthening racial identity and pride (Stevenson, 1997).

In a randomized controlled trial with 667 rural African American young adolescents, researchers (Brody et al., 2004) found positive outcomes for all targeted parenting and youth intrapersonal processes. Families who participated in SAAF experienced increases in regulated-communicative parenting practices that were associated with more proximal outcomes, such as risk-related attitudes, future orientation, self-regulation, and resistance efficacy and with HIV-related risk behaviors, including early onset of substance use and sexual initiation. Follow-up analyses have documented sustained effects in deterring risky sexual practices and escalation of alcohol and substance use 65 months post-SAAF exposure (Brody, Chen, Kogan, Murry, & Brown, 2010). Further analyses have demonstrated mediating and moderating effects. Changes in parenting practices among SAAF participants mediated the onset and escalation of risky sexual behavior in youth (Murry et al., 2011). Program attendance also moderated change in regulated-communicative parenting. High attendance was associated with greater changes in parenting practices, which in turn fostered greater change in youth intrapersonal skills. Murry and colleagues (2011) examined the extent to which the program differed for families who were confronted with challenges. They defined high-risk families as those reporting elevated parental depression, low religiosity, economic hardship, youth nonconventional behavior, and a high ratio of children to adults in homes. Results revealed that high-risk families benefited more from SAAF program participation more than those raising children under less challenging circumstances. High-risk families reported greater changes on the use of monitoring and consistent inductive discipline, adaptive racial socialization, communication about sex, and clear expectations about high-risk behavior than low-risk families.

Alignment Enhanced Services School Climate Improvement Project

The Alignment Enhanced Services (AES) project emerged from the work of a community-based coalition formed to support public education in Nashville, Tennessee. Formed with combined funding from the chamber of commerce, school system, and philanthropic funders, Alignment Nashville, a small non-profit organization, was formed to facilitate school improvement initiatives promoting the well-being and success of students. Its staff organized committees focused on specific issues (for example, behavioral health) and the needs of elementary, middle, and high school students. The committees consisted of stakeholders from schools, central office, community-based organizations, city agencies, and postsecondary institutions.

The Middle School Committee wished to decrease disruptive, aggressive, and violent behaviors among middle school students. Rather than implement an evidence-based program, the committee opted to develop its own intervention based loosely on student assistance programs (SAP). Rather than focus on individual student barriers to learning (for example, substance use, mental health, and truancy) as most SAP programs do, the AES project aimed to decrease violence by systemically improving school climate. The committee invited HOD researchers to partner with them to help fund, refine, and evaluate the AES intervention as part of the Nashville Urban Partnership Academic Center of Excellence (NUPACE), funded by the Centers for Disease Control and Prevention (CDC). The HOD team helped revise the intervention model to better reflect evidence-based practices. Components of Positive Behavioral Intervention and Supports (PBIS) and the Olweus Bullying Prevention Program (OBPP) were incorporated into the AES intervention model. For example, the project conceptualized student supports ranging across a three-tiered system, similar to that promoted by PBIS, to suggest that universal, secondary, and tertiary supports are needed to support skill development and to address individual barriers to learning. However, the AES model also differed from the two models. Although the OBPP focuses on bullying behaviors and PBIS on barriers to learning, the AES model was conceptualized to promote positive youth development and capacity building within schools.

The AES model reflected the idea of synergy through cooperation. A full-time AES Coordinator in each intervention school was responsible for aligning school administrative and organizational processes, prevention programs and support services, and community and parent engagement. Coordinators' work was predicated on developing positive relationships and networks within and external to the school based on the school's needs. Action plans were collaboratively developed with school leadership and community partners to leverage existing resources through coordination and scaffolding rather than simply adding new programs. For example, Coordinators frequently found that students with the greatest needs often were not receiving services from community organizations serving the school. Furthermore, some students, with less risk were receiving services from multiple providers. Regular community partnership meetings were established to identify gaps and duplication of services.

The research team, consisting largely of HOD faculty and students, implemented a quasi-experimental research design to evaluate the effectiveness of the AES model. A total of twelve middle schools (grades 5–8), identified as having relatively high rates of disciplinary incidents, were included in the evaluation. The AES model was implemented in four schools; the OBPP was introduced in four schools; and practice as usual was observed in another four schools. Numerous educational and social emotional outcomes were measured using administrative and student survey data. Outcomes of interest included disciplinary as well as student perceptions of school climate, including bullying and victimization, peer and student-teacher relationships, and school engagement.

The evaluation has suggested several positive outcomes for students and schools (for example, Nation et al., 2010). Coordinators were able to increase personnel's capacity to create positive learning environments through in-service professional development and classroom coaching. They were also able to increase programmatic and community-based services to address student needs. All AES schools implemented PBIS to promote stronger behavioral norms and diversified referral mechanisms for community-based services and supports. As a result, discipline referrals and out-of-school suspensions decreased. Student reports of peer and student-teacher relationships also predicted bullying perpetration, attendance, classroom engagement, and math and reading achievement. Nation, Voight, and Nixon (2011) showed that student-teacher relationships impacted student outcomes and narrowed outcome gaps between minority and white students and between students enrolled in special education or English Language Learner (ELL) programs and those who were not. The project also elevated conversation about the importance of school climate on student and school outcomes at the district-level. New district-led plans include strategies to promote prosocial learning environments, social emotional learning, and positive student-adult relationships. Indicators of progress also include the measurement of school climate from multiple perspectives (for example, student, teacher, and parent).

South African Field School Project: Understanding Factors Contributing to High School Dropout

During the summer of 2012, sixteen graduate students from Vanderbilt participated in a six-week field school in South Africa. Six of the students participated in collaborative research with a school-based nonprofit agency to explore high school dropout rates in the township of "Gardenia Valley" (a pseudonym), near Cape Town. In addition to describing the complexity of pull and push factors and contexts that influence dropout rates, project goals included developing local prevention capacity, including the development of a survey to assess these factors annually. The historically *coloured* township (South African term referring to individuals of mixed-race) was constructed in the 1970s as a result of government-sanctioned segregation practices that relocated non-white residents from the nation's city centers to distant and densely populated townships, in effect isolating them from educational and employment opportunities (Galvaan, 2012). Scholars have argued that relative to white and black communities, coloured communities are in a state of despair because they did not receive the same privileges as whites under apartheid and have less political representation and access to affirmative action programs in the post-apartheid era (Bray et al., 2010). High school dropout rates are an immense problem throughout South Africa. At Gardenia Valley High School, dropout rates have been consistently about 70 percent, higher than the 55 percent average rate for Cape Town (Flisher et al., 2010). Youth of color are more likely to drop out than their white peers (Department of Basic Education, 2011). Over 80 percent of white youth aged 21–25 years old complete high school compared to 35 percent of black and 40 percent of coloured youth (Ministerial Committee, 2007).

The HOD research team conducted an exploratory, qualitative study on factors impacting school dropout. They engaged community stakeholders using semi-structured interviews, focus groups, and observations of community meetings. The team met with members of the school and broader community, including students, after-school sports coaches, representatives from local nongovernmental organizations (NGOs), school board trustees, school administrators, and the local police. Research design and protocols were informed by preliminary conversations with school and NGO administrators and feedback solicited during community meetings. Staff revealed that the oft-cited causes of dropout in the township—including gang involvement and teenage pregnancy—were considered symptoms of complex, compounding risk factors students experience across multiple environments, including homes, schools, and communities. Given the specific interest of community partners to move beyond symptom-driven explanations for student dropout, the interview protocol included questions to explore the impacts of family, school, and community experiences on students' school engagement.

The HOD team engaged with local adults familiar with the school, students, and afterschool program to assist in recruiting students for interviews and focus groups. They conducted twenty-nine interviews with students, ranging from grades 8 to 11 and varying in perceived risk of school dropout; seven interviews included a community mapping activity, during which students were asked to draw a map to identify locations where they spent time, felt safe or unsafe, bored or excited, and respected or disrespected. Teachers and administrators were interviewed and focus groups were held with after-school staff and NGO representatives. Researchers constructed a broader understanding of the students' experiences by speaking to multiple stakeholders from diverse youth-serving settings. The research team also examined the impact of out-of-school experiences on students' school engagement and the role of educational policies.

The research team developed a conceptual model depicting push and pull factors for students across their multiple environments that contributed to their decisions to dropout or remain in school. Results also suggest that the legacy of apartheid greatly influences students' life experiences and opportunities. The deleterious effects of this macro-level force, in addition to contemporary manifestations of racial inequity, further exacerbate the quality of life of students, their families, and communities (Feagin, 2006). This model was used further to develop a quantitative survey so that NGO staff can annually assess students' experiences as they relate to school completion and dropout. Moreover, the survey includes questions that highlight the cumulative role of multi-layer influences (for example, family expectations and fear of violence in the community) on students' decisions to remain in or leave high school prior to completion.

Research in Action: Actualizing our Mission to Promote Youth Development

Although these HOD projects differ in methodologies and target populations, collectively they illustrate several common characteristics in scholarship central to promoting civically engaged and socially just research. We now highlight the dynamic nature of research and action in promoting youth development by drawing on literature and experiences from the SAAF, AES, and Gardenia Valley projects. We assert that two features are foundational to conducting balanced, integrated, and meaningful research: applying ecological theory and using a collaborative community model of research to ultimately narrow the research to practice gap.

Utilizing Ecological Theory in Research

Prevention programs and practices must be founded on etiological and intervention theory and grounded in sound empirical evidence (Chen, 1990). Nation et al. (2003) noted several theory-driven practices in prevention programming that promote intervention effectiveness. Researchers also have called for the integration of multiple theories across disciplines to further youth development and prevention. According to Tebes (2005), the reliance on contextualism in research implies that multiple theories are needed to advance knowledge. The three HOD studies suggest that simultaneously including related theories provides the scaffolding for integrating the department's mission and principles into research, scholarship, and teaching. Researchers have highlighted the importance of social processes within settings as the basis for youth development and learning (Tseng & Seidman, 2007). Similarly, ecological systems theory

(Bronfenbrenner, 1979; Friedman & Allen, 2011) posits that youth behavior and development are influenced by youth interactions within and across contexts (ecology) and systems (for example, intrapersonal, interpersonal, family, community, cultural). These influences are dynamic, reciprocal, and transactional (Darling, 2007). Thus, youth behavior cannot be understood apart from an environment that can impede or enhance it (Conyne & Cook, 2004). Multiple theories can be integrated into a framework to address intrapersonal, interpersonal, organizational, environmental, and/or cultural processes (Flay, 2002; Stokols et al., 1996; Tebes, 2005). Ecological systems theory can be used to provide an overarching framework to integrate multiple theories within and across these levels to promote positive youth development (Best et al., 2003; Stokols, Allen, & Bellingham, 1996).

We have highlighted the ways in which the three HOD projects integrate and ecological approach to design prevention programs and research protocols. Based on their longitudinal research with rural African Americans, Murry and colleagues incorporated multiple theories in designing SAAF. In addition to Bronfenbrenner (1979), the model integrates individual and family theories within an ecological framework, including Cicchetti's (1997) conceptions of the ecology of development, Zimbardo's (1999) time perspective theory, Bandura's (1997) and Barkley's (1997) theories about the development of self-regulatory mechanisms, and, finally, Gibbons and Gerrard's (1997) prototype/willingness model of adolescent health risk behavior. The AES model was founded on an ecological model, cognitive theory, which suggests that an aggressive predisposition in social information processing may contribute to bullying behavior (Crick & Dodge, 1994), and theories that suggest low self-esteem may contribute to bullying behavior (Roberts & Morotti, 2000). The AES model further acknowledges that bullying is affected by peer behaviors and reactions, norms, and school characteristics such as adult supervision and peer or student-teacher conflict (Kasen, Berenson, Cohen, & Johnson, 2004).

Failure to recognize the power of contexts and the influences of teacher, family, and community processes on student behavior has limited the effectiveness of traditional school-based bullying prevention programs (Hong & Espelage, 2012). During the project, a powerful example emerged. In a review of office referral data, an AES Coordinator identified roughly a dozen students as "high flyers," those who were responsible for roughly 80 percent of the school's disciplinary referrals. However, rather than to simplistically target the negative behavior of these students, the AES Coordinator dug deeper and discovered that the majority of referrals came from one teacher. Subsequent classroom observations made clear that the teacher struggled with classroom management, which resulted in over-referring "disruptive" students to the office. Thus, attention to context promotes intervention that shifts away from marginalizing youth by exclusively labeling or diagnosing their risk or deviant behavior and provides a richer set of responses to promote wellness for all youth in the classroom and school community.

Similarly, the Gardenia Valley project exemplifies how ecological systems theory influenced research on school dropout rates in the township. Community partners and the research team chose to go beyond commonly cited individual and social causes of school dropout to understand better the root causes of the problem as well as more proximal antecedents to students' decision-making about school completion or dropout. To this end, HOD researchers met with a wide range of stakeholders to gain a broad and comprehensive understanding of how culture, history, social policy, and environment interacted with youth, family, and social factors in ultimately assessing youth educational outcomes.

The Need for Collaborative Community Research

Over the past two decades, policy makers and researchers have lamented the research to practice gap (Granger, 2011; Stokols, 1996). Interventions shown to be efficacious under controlled conditions have rarely been scaled in real-world practice settings, and when they have, they often have failed to demonstrate effectiveness. In part, the gap has been perpetuated by the limitations of the traditional prevention research paradigm outlined previously. To narrow this gap, researchers, primarily from the fields of community psychology and public health, have suggested blended research-practice models to increase the use of evidence-based programs and practice in community settings (Best et al., 2003; Davidson, 2011; Wandersman, Flaspohler, Lesesne, Puddy, & Phillips, 2012). Price and Behrens (2003) argued for equal focus on building knowledge and improving practice that is grounded in the context of applied settings.

However, the philosophical underpinnings for most community-centric models are different from and often in sharp contrast to those on which the traditional research paradigm is grounded (Nation et al., 2011; Spencer, 2006; Tebes, 2005). This difference in philosophical orientations has implications for the conceptualization and practice of research. Tensions can arise related to stakeholder engagement, articulation of the research questions, and choice of research design and methods. Thus these tensions often present challenges to closing the research-to-practice gap (Spoth & Greenberg, 2005). Nonetheless, a balance between the traditional prevention research paradigm and community-based research is achievable, as reflected in the HOD projects highlighted in this chapter. While all of the projects take place in community settings, SAAF and AES employed rigorous experimental and quasi-experimental research designs, respectively, typically characteristic of the traditional research paradigm.

Moreover, all three projects engaged community stakeholders in an intentional process to inform intervention practices, promote youth outcomes, and enhance study findings. Engagement of community members in the research process is an essential practice in research for most HOD researchers. Various terms have been used to describe this process, including community-based participatory research (Israel et al., 2005; Wallerstein & Duran, 2010), community-engaged research (Nation et al., 2011), and participatory or community-based action research (Kidd & Kral, 2005). Each of the studies benefited from the ongoing input of multiple stakeholders throughout the research process. Creating such opportunities for stakeholder involvement results in rich opportunities to advance both research methods and questions that may enhance the overall importance and implications of work targeting a broader understanding of youth processes. Participatory research may be driven by philosophical and/or practical reasons. From a theoretical perspective, contextualism implies the need to integrate multiple perspectives, because "the truth" is grounded in contexts or systems (Tebes, 2005). Participatory research can facilitate the implementation of an intervention and enhance its relevance, effectiveness, and sustainability (Israel et al., 2005; Spoth & Greenberg, 2005). Involving youth, families, and community members more readily illuminates contextual factors so that interventions can be adapted and tailored to unique needs of youth and their families.

Engaging multiple stakeholders in research, however, can be challenging. Stakeholders' roles and levels of engagement in the process can vary tremendously. Many factors influence the balance of power, decision-making authority, resources, and use of results among research and community partners (Baker, Homan, Schonhoff, & Kreuter, 1999). The strengths and challenges of community-engaged research are evident across the HOD projects. Often, the impetus of a project has implications for roles, power, and levels of engagement among the collaborating partners. While each of the projects presented in this chapter grew from community needs, their development ranged from direct requests from community partners for research assistance to project initiatives that arose to address unmet youth and/or family needs. In the AES project, Vanderbilt researchers were invited to join an existing community coalition after practitioners and administrators had initially conceptualized the "solution." Even though the balance of power rested with the community, and particularly the facilitating organization, HOD researchers were able to negotiate changes to the AES model to reflect more strongly evidence-based practices (Nation, Bess, Voight, Perkins, & Juarez, 2011). Even then, the multiplicity of community partners with differing program delivery models posed challenges to implementing the Coordinators' scope of services throughout the project. Tensions arose related to the Coordinators' job descriptions and chain of command. Regular meetings and considerable negotiation with school and community stakeholders were required to address these challenges.

For the Gardenia Valley project, although the community invited the research team to participate in addressing specific concerns related to school dropout, the community relied on the research team to lead the development of the evaluation design and protocols. Thus, although the community partners remained engaged in the process, their role was one of providing feedback and facilitating communication with stakeholders rather than dictating knowledge generation. Finally, the SAAF project illustrates a researcher-initiated project driven by community needs. In contrast to the AES project, the research team had more control over intervention design and implementation as well as evaluation methods. Yet their engagement of families and community members in the design and implementation was strategic and yielded significant contributions. For instance, including community members as project liaisons and gathering feedback through focus groups helped garner community trust and influenced intervention design. As a result, transportation, childcare, and meals were added to the SAAF program activities to increase program attendance. Feedback from participants also contributed to the inclusion of racial socialization and racial identity in the SAAF causative model.

Benefits of Community-Engaged Research

Despite the challenges of participatory research practices, a number of benefits often result. First, the "fit" between the needs of youth, families, school, or communities and the intervention approach may be improved with increased community engagement. Community engagement enables researchers to "learn from communities" to develop tailored, indigenous programs adapted to the capacity and values of community organizations (Miller & Shinn, 2005). In the Gardenia Valley project, existing research focused predominantly on students' individual risk and behavior. However, the research team explored factors affecting school dropout with the assumption that it is heavily influenced by deleterious episodes in history and national policy. Similarly, Murry and colleagues used focus groups in testing and revising the cultural appropriateness of conceptual models, prevention topics, program content, research protocols, and measures (Brody et al., 1994; Murry & Brody, 2004). Based on this input, racial socialization and racial identity were included in the program model and session topics. Participants' feedback led directly to the creation of co-developed content, celebrating the diversity of African American families and Black Pride. Finally, in the AES project, school climate improvement strategies differed considerably across schools. Each approach reflected the philosophies and leadership styles of principals, student and school needs, local service providers, and the community within which the school was embedded. As a result, responses were tailored to align with school improvement plans, which created more buy-in across personnel.

Second, stakeholder involvement enables access to research participants. In the AES project, the mechanism for community engagement and access to schools was predetermined. However, once AES Coordinators were embedded in schools, it was essential that they build trusting relationships with administrators, teachers, and other personnel as well as community providers to promote effectively school climate change through services coordination and intervention (Nation et al., 2010). In the SAAF project, community residents with positive reputations and extensive social contacts were hired as liaisons. They worked with project staff to enroll families, track attendance and contact information, and communicate with families between sessions to resolve barriers to their participation. The high retention rate of 90 percent of SAAF participants is likely attributable to enhanced trust, buy-in, and efforts of the liaison network (Murry & Brody, 2004). Similarly, the Gardenia Valley project utilized community meetings and key stakeholders to obtain feedback as well as participant recruitment. In short, the increased access to and participation of youth, families, schools, and community organizations enhances the external validity of our research findings and facilitates exploration of what works for whom and under what circumstances. Increased engagement with community partners may engender trust and buy in, increase willingness to share information, and foster support during implementation. This process may help to span the research-practice gap in important ways.

Third, community collaboration can increase implementation of effective community-based programs and practices (Davidson, 2011; Wandersman et al., 2012). Murry and colleagues were able to leverage the cumulative evidence base on family-centered prevention, particularly the Strengthening Families Program (Molgaard, Kumpfer, & Fleming, 1996), in designing SAAF. In the AES project, although the Middle School Committee was not willing to replace the AES model with a pre-packaged evidence-based program, the research team was able to negotiate stronger emphasis on evidence-based practices. They also strengthened the theoretical orientations framing the intervention. Consequently, while also addressing student risk, the AES model placed greater emphasis on positive youth development as well as the importance of the school environment. This orientation provided relatively more intervention strategies (for example, student-adult relationships, school engagement, civic engagement, and parent involvement) as levers of change.

Finally, researcher-practitioner collaboration can facilitate capacity building within families, organizations, and communities. When researchers shift their focus to include families, schools, practitioners, organizations, and communities in addition to youth, capacity building becomes a crucial factor illuminated by ecological systems theory. Research guided by the traditional prevention research paradigm has often failed to take into account contextual fit and the influences of macro- and mesosystems in the design and implementation of youth prevention efforts, thereby perpetuating the gap between research and practice (Miller & Shinn, 2005; Spoth & Greenberg, 2005).

For example, family-based youth prevention programs need to address capacity building in families. Studies have consistently shown that powerful factors that protect rural African American youth from high-risk behaviors originate in the family environment, particularly in parents' care-giving practices (Brody et al., 2010; Murry & Brody, 1999). Many rural African Americans direct their parenting processes toward enhancing their children's resilience, enabling them to withstand the challenges associated with *growing up Black in America* (Peters & Massey, 1983). Thus SAAF targets parenting processes that have implications for adolescents' positive development. These practices can be categorized as both universal (that is, strategies that are considered important for all groups) and racially specific (strategies that are especially important for African American families). SAAF empowered families to serve an instrumental role to deter early sexual debut and alcohol use (Murry et al., 2011). In addition, SAAF intervention-induced changes in parenting behaviors facilitated an increase in self-pride among youth, as evidenced by positive racial pride and self-esteem.

Similarly, organizational capacity needs to be developed to support implementation of evidence-based youth programs and practices (Miller & Shinn, 2005; Spoth & Greenberg, 2005). According to Fixsen and colleagues, "implementation is synonymous with coordinated change at system, organization, program, and practice levels" (Fixsen, Naoom, Blase, Friedman, & Wallace, 2005, p. vi). Organizations implementing prevention programs must build in mechanisms for ongoing training, coaching, and performance feedback. Organizational policy and norms need to be aligned and consistent with prevention messaging. In the Gardenia Valley project, the HOD team provided training and technical assistance to community partners' staff to support their understanding of qualitative research and program improvement, administration of the survey, data analysis, and intervention. In the AES project, the research and coordinators held regular weekly meetings and the research team provided on-site technical assistance related to data collection, analysis, use, and evidence-based intervention. The Coordinators developed an understanding about the empirical evidence supporting the AES model, were able to monitor the fidelity of intervention implementation, and strengthened their skills in collecting and utilizing data in decision-making. Further, the researchers were exposed to the realities and demands of daily school life. This contextual knowledge enabled more successful navigation of implementation challenges as they arose.

Promoting Positive Youth Development

In this chapter, we propose that research, scholarship, and teaching in the field of prevention and youth development should incorporate an ecological systems model, working collaboratively with community partners to ensure that prevention efforts best meet the needs of the communities in which they are delivered. We present three sample research programs, conducted by research teams of students and faculty within the department of HOD, which illustrate the ecological systems approach to generating knowledge and effecting social change in applied community settings. In the "Getting Started!" table, we present specific suggestions that cut across the sample projects and provide various printed and online resources that support those suggestions. By so doing, we hope to provide readers with a foundation for developing similar research programs within their own department, programs that are decidedly Deweyan in their focus on democratic participation.

Conclusion

For the past decade, prevention and youth development researchers have called for integrated research-practitioner models of research to promote the use of evidence-based programs and practices in community settings. We have argued that ecological systems theory and community engagement are essential for narrowing the research-to-practice gap and advancing youth development. In particular, theoretical pluralism is needed to further our understanding of how culture, norms, and the capacity within contexts—families, schools, organizations, and communities—

Chapter 4: Getting Started!
Ecological Research Promoting Positive Youth Development

Action Item 1: *Use additional readings to broaden the definition of "prevention science."*
Students should be encouraged to go beyond the traditional definition of prevention science as a reductionistic concept that focuses on avoiding negative outcomes to one that honors the complexity of youths' lives and includes a focus on positive youth development within the context of ecological systems theory. Nation et al.'s (2003) article, "What works in prevention: Principles of effective prevention programs" (*American Psychologist, 58*[6/7], 449–56), can serve as a foundational reading, as can Dahlberg & Krug's (2002) "Violence—a global public health problem" (in Krug et al. [eds.], *World Report on Violence and Health*, Geneva, Switzerland: World Health Organization [pp. 1–56]). Other readings by such authors as Nation, Murry, Olweus, and Pittman (see reference list in this chapter) can serve as additional sources of information.

Action Item 2: *Bring attention to CDC efforts in promoting the social-ecological model of prevention.*
An additional source of information for both students and researchers is the website of the Center for Disease Control (CDC), specifically the Division of Violence Prevention. This site outlines the public health approach to violence prevention, delineating the major steps within and provides additional information about prevention efforts in such fields as youth violence, global violence, and child maltreatment (http://www.cdc.gov/violenceprevention/overview/publichealthapproach.html).

Action Item 3: *Promote qualitative data usage.*
First-hand information from research partners is critical to understanding the complexity of their worlds and the social processes that inform their lives. Focus groups allow for cost-effective methods of gaining valuable information from research participants before a prevention effort begins to ensure its relevance and effectiveness. Through the use of such groups, researchers can gain information about opinions, beliefs, and attitudes about the problem under study and can build excitement and "buy in" from participants. Focus groups can also be employed at later stages of prevention, to provide ongoing feedback and to process results upon conclusion. Numerous guidelines for how to gather and analyze focus group data exists (refer to http://assessment.aas.duke.edu/documents/How_to_Conduct_a_Focus_Group.pdf).

Action Item 4: *Identify and involve community stakeholders in all stages of prevention.*
Community stakeholders can provide critical information about the needs and viewpoints of the community in which prevention efforts are conducted. Numerous guidelines for identifying and involving stakeholders exist. For example, the Building a Blueprint for Change online manual, sponsored by the Corporation for National and

Chapter 4: Getting Started!

Community Service (CNCS), can be incorporated as part of a course about ecological research efforts and/or as part of training for researchers (refer to http://blueprintfor changeonline.net/pages/other/about.php).

Action Item 5: Consider mediators and moderators in the design stage.
Mediators point to mechanisms of change and identify possible vehicles or pathways through which an intervention may have its effect. Consideration and identification of important potential mediators for a proposed intervention during the design stage allow research teams not only to conceptualize the pathways through which an intervention may be effective but also to include measures of such mediators before the research project begins. Moderators can point to important differences among groups, serving to distinguish those groups for whom an intervention may be most or least effective. Like mediators, potential moderators should be considered and included in the design stage of an intervention, thereby increasing the chance that efforts are appropriately tailored to the groups they may most benefit and allowing for the analysis of such moderators at the conclusion of the prevention effort. Researchers and others involved in prevention efforts should have a working understanding of the concept of mediators and moderators in general, such that important variables can be considered and included in the design phase of the research program. Articles that present the conceptual ideas associated with mediators and moderators in a clear and coherent way and provide relevant examples of these ideas in action should be part of the training program for researchers, faculty, and students alike. Magill's (2011) "Moderators and mediators in social work practice: Toward a more ecologically valid evidence base for practice" (*Journal of Social Work, 11*[4], 387–401) is a particularly useful example of such a source. For a more statistical treatment, consult "Testing moderator and mediator effects in counseling psychology research," by Frazier, Tix, and Barron (2004) (*Journal of Counseling Psychology, 51*(1), 115–34).

---

influence youth behavior and development. Use of theoretical knowledge in civic participation, practice, and community-engaged research maximizes opportunities for meaningful social change by supporting effective collaboration (Price & Behrens, 2003). This foundation should facilitate investigation of effective practices or active ingredients that are common across effective programs and thus inform what works for whom and under what circumstances.

Collaborative community-based approaches to research enhance intervention design, implementation, and research. Although many researchers claim a philosophical orientation that supports stakeholder engagement, in practice, the research process often fails to reflect meaningful stakeholder involvement. Although several specific models of community engagement have been proposed (Bryk, Gomez, & Grunow, 2010), effective practices for engagement may vary depending on research goals, community needs, power sharing, data use, and other factors (Nation et al., 2011). Nonetheless, researchers should be intentional and strategic in engaging stakeholders throughout the research process and be prepared to address the challenges of collaboration (Wallerstein & Duran, 2010). In addition to the challenge of defining roles and balancing power, researchers need to address the tensions that will arise related to implementation fidelity when implementing evidence-based programs in applied settings. Meaningfully engaging community stakeholders likely will lead to opportunities to tailor programs to the specific needs within contexts. Better "fit" between programs and contexts should lead to better outcomes. Researchers must be prepared to include evaluation strategies that explore flexibility in implementation practices to advance translation science. Despite these challenges as well the implications of continued economic, political, and social inequities, community-engaged research, informed by ecological systems theory, will enable more relevant action and thus promote meaningful youth, organizational, and community development.

By extending the traditional research paradigm in these ways, this modern, more progressive approach to research can be said to rest on the foundations of Dewey (1916), espoused long ago. The projects described in this chapter are examples of participatory democracy at its finest, where the research team is defined to include researchers, students, and members of the community alike and where the task of this team is one of working collaboratively to elucidate problems and generate solutions. It is an approach that is neither "top down" nor "bottom up" but rather transactional and reciprocal—an approach that involves "dialogic communication" dependent upon active participation by all.

References

Baker, E. A., Homan, S., Schonhoff, R., & Kreuter, M. (1999). Principles of practice for academic/practice/community research partnerships. *American Journal of Preventive Medicine, 16*(3 Suppl), 86–93.

Balfanz, R., Herzog, L., & MacIver, D. (2007). Preventing student disengagement and keeping students on the graduation track in high-poverty middle-grades schools: Early identification and effective interventions, *Educational Psychologist, 42*(4), 223–36.

Bandura, A. (1997). *Self-efficacy: The exercise of control.* New York: Freeman.

Barkley, R. A. (1997). Behavioral inhibition, sustained attention, and executive functions: Constructing a unifying theory of ADHD. *Psychological Bulletin, 121*, 65–94.

Brody, G. H., Chen, Y. F., Kogan, S. M., Murry, V. M., & Brown, A. C. (2010). Long-term effects of the Strong African American Families program on youths' alcohol use. *Journal of Consulting and Clinical Psychology, 78*(2), 281–85.

Brody, G. H., Murry, V. M., Gerrard, M., Gibbons, F. X., Molgaard, V., McNair, L., . . . Neubaum-Carlan, E. (2004). The Strong African American Families Program: Translating research into prevention programming. *Child Development, 75*(3), 900–17.

Brody, G. H., Murry, V. M., McNair, L., Chen, Y., Gibbons, F. X., Gerrard, M., & Wills, T. A. (2005). Linking changes in parenting to parent-child relationship quality and youth self-control: The Strong African American Families Program. *Journal of Research on Adolescence, 15*(1), 47–69.

Bronfenbrenner, U. (1979). *The ecology of human development: Experiments by nature and design.* Cambridge, MA: Harvard University Press.

Bryk A. S., Gomez L. M., Grunow A. (2010), Getting ideas into action: Building networked improvement communities in education, Carnegie Foundation for the Advancement of Teaching, Stanford, CA, essay, retrieved from http://www.carnegiefoundation.org/ spotlight/webinar-bryk-gomez-building-etworkedimprovement-communities.

Catalano, R. F., Hawkins, J. D., Berglund, M. L., Pollard, J. A., & Arthur, M. W. (2002). Prevention science and positive youth development: Competitive or cooperative frameworks? *Journal of Adolescent Health, 31*, 230–39.

Centers for Disease Control and Prevention (2006). Racial/ethnic disparities in diagnoses of HIV/AIDS—33 states, 2001–2004. *MMWR: Morbidity & Mortality Weekly Report, 55*(5), 121–25.

Chen, H. (1990). *Theory-driven evaluation.* Newbury Park, CA: Sage.

Cicchetti, D., & Toth, S. L. (1997). Transactional ecological systems in developmental psychopathology. In S. S. Luthar, J. Burack, D. Cicchetti & J. Weisz (Eds.), *Developmental psychopathology: Perspectives on adjustment, risk, and disorder* (pp. 317–49). New York: Cambridge University Press.

Conyne, R. K., & Cook, E. P. (2004). Understanding persons within environments: An introduction to ecological counseling. *Ecological counseling: An innovative approach to conceptualizing person-environment interaction.* Alexandria, VA: American Counseling Association.

Crick, N. R., & Dodge, K. A. (1994). A review and reformulation of social information-processing mechanisms in children's social Adjustment. *Psychological Bulletin, 115,* 74–101.

Darling, N. (2007). Ecological systems theory: The person in the center of the circles. *Research in Human Development,* 4(3–4), 203–17.

Davidson, W. S. (Ed.). (2011). *American Journal of Community Psychology,* 48(1–2).

Department of Basic Education. (2011). Report on dropout and student retention strategy. Retrieved from http://www.education.gov.za/LinkClick .aspx?fileticket= jcSsY0rHcME%3D&tabid=422&mid=1261

Dewey, J. (1916). *Democracy and education.* New York: The Free Press, Simon & Schuster.

Eisner, E. W. (1992). Are all causal claims positivistic? A reply to Francis Schrag. *Educational Researcher,* 21(5), 8–9.

Feagin, J. R. (2006). *Systemic racism: A theory of oppression.* New York: Routledge.

Fixsen, D. L., Naoom, S.F., Blase, K. A., Friedman, R. M., & Wallace, F. (2005). *Implementation Research: A Synthesis of the Literature.* (FMHI Publication #231). Tampa: University of South Florida, Louis de la Parte Florida Mental Health Institute. Available online at http://cfs.cbcs.usf.edu/_docs/ publications/NIRN_Monograph_Full.pdf.

Flay, B. R. (2002). Positive youth development requires comprehensive health promotion programs. *American Journal of Health Behavior,* 26(6), 407–24.

Flisher, Alan J., & Chalton, Derek O. (1995). High school dropouts in a working-class South African community: Selected characteristics and risk-taking behavior. *Journal of Adolescence,* 18, 105–21.

Friedman, B., & Allen, K. N. (2011). System theory. In J. R. Brandell (Ed.), *Theory & practice in clinical social work* (pp. 3–20). Washington, DC: Sage Publications.

Galvaan, R. (2012). Occupational choice: The significance of socioeconomic and political factors. In G. E. Whiteford & C. Hocking (Eds.), *Occupational science: Society, inclusion, participation* (pp. 152–62). Somerset, NJ: Wiley-Blackwell.

Gibbons, F. X., & Gerrard, M. (1997). Health images and their effects on health behavior. In B. P. Buunk & F. X. Gibbons (Eds.), *Health, coping, and wellbeing: Perspectives from social comparison theory* (pp. 63–94). Mahwah, NJ: Erlbaum.

Granger, R. C. (2011). The big why: a learning agenda for the scale-up movement. *Pathways,* Winter 2011, 28–32.

Hong, J. S., & Espelage, D. L. (2012). A review of research on bullying and peer victimization in school: An ecological system analysis. *Aggression and Violent Behavior,* 17, 311–22.

Kasen, S., Berenson, K., Cohen, P., & Johnson, J. G. (2004). The effects of school climate on changes in aggressive and other behaviors related to bullying. In D. L. Espelage & S. M. Swearer (Eds.), *Bullying in American schools: A social-ecological perspective on prevention and intervention* (pp. 187–210). Mahwah, NJ: Lawrence Erlbaum.

Kidd, S. A., & Kral, M. J. (2005). Practicing participatory action research. *Journal of Counseling Psychology, 52*(2), 187–95.

Lee, C. D. (2010). Soaring above the clouds, Delving the ocean's depths: Understanding the ecologies of human learning and the challenge for education science. *Educational Researcher, 39*(9), 643–55.

Lerner, R. M. (2002). *Concepts and theories of human development* (3rd ed.). Mahwah, NJ: Lawrence Erlbaum Associates Publishers.

Miller, R. L., & Shinn, M. (2005). Learning from communities: Overcoming difficulties in dissemination of presentation and promotion efforts. *American Journal of Community Psychology, 35*(3/4), 169–83.

Ministerial Committee on Student Retention in the South African Schooling System (2007). *Progress report to the minister of education.* Retrieved from www.info.gov.za/view/DownloadFileAction?id=79404

Molgaard, V. K., Kumpfer, K., & Fleming, E. (1996). *The Strengthening Families Program: For parents and youth 10–14—Revised.* Ames: Iowa State University Extension Service.

Mrazek, P. J., & Haggerty, R. J. (Eds.) (1994). *Reducing risks for mental disorders. Frontiers for preventive intervention research.* Washington, DC: National Academy Press.

Murry, V. M., Berkel, C., Chen, F., Brody, G. H., Gibbons, F. X., & Gerrard, M. (2011). Intervention induced changes on parenting practices, youth self-pride and sexual norms to reduce HIV-related behaviors among rural African American youths. *Journal of Youth and Adolescence, 40*(9), 1147–63.

Murry, V. M., & Brody, G. H. (1999). Self-regulation and self-worth of Black children reared in economically stressed, rural, single mother–headed families: The contribution of risk and protective factors. *Journal of Family Issues, 20*(4), 458–84.

Murry, V. M., & Brody, G. H. (2002). Racial socialization processes in single-mother families: Linking maternal racial identity, parenting, and racial socialization in rural, single-mother families with child self-worth and self-regulation. In H. P. McAdoo (Ed.), *Black children: Social, educational, and parental environments* (2nd ed., pp. 97–115). Thousand Oaks, CA: Sage.

Murry, V. M., & Brody, G. H. (2004). Partnering with community stakeholders: Engaging rural African American families in basic research and the Strong African American Families preventive intervention program. *Journal of Marital and Family Therapy, 30*(3), 271–83.

Murry, V. M., Heflinger, C. A., Suiter, S. V., & Brody, G. H. (2011). Examining perceptions about mental health care and help-seeking among rural African American families of adolescents. *Journal of Youth and Adolescence, 40*(9), 1118–31.

Nation, M., Bess, K., Voight, A., Perkins, D. D., & Juarez, P. (2011). Levels of community engagement in youth violence prevention: The role of power in sustaining successful university-community partnerships. *American Journal of Community Psychology, 48,* 89–96.

Nation, M., Collins, L., Nixon, C., Bess, K., Rogers, S., Williams, S., Juarez, P. A. (2010). Community-based participatory approach to youth development and school climate change: The Alignment Enhanced Services project. *Progress in Community Health Partnerships, 4*(3), 197–205.

Nation, M., Crusto, C., Wandersman, A., Kumpker, K., Seybolt, D., Morissey-Kane, E., & Davino, K. (2003). What works in prevention: Principles of effective prevention programs. *American Psychologist, 58*(6/7), 449–56.

Nation, M., Voight, A., & Nixon, C. T. (June 2011). School climate and academic achievement: Unpacking the relations between school context and the academic achievement of at-risk students. Paper presented at the Society for Community Research and Action Biennial Conference, Chicago, Illinois.

Olweus, D. (2004). The Olweus Bullying Prevention Programme: Design and implementation issues and a new national initiative in Norway. In P. K. Smith, D. Pepler, & K. Rigby (Eds.), *Bullying in schools: How successful can interventions be?* (pp. 13–36). Cambridge, UK: Cambridge University Press.

Peters, M. F., & Massey, G. (1983). Mundane extreme environmental stress in family stress theories: The case of black families in white America. In H. I. McCubbin & M. B. Sussman (Eds.), *Social Stress and the Family* (pp. 157–70). Binghamton, NY: Haworth.

Price, R. H., & Behrens, T. (2003). Working Pasteur's quadrant: Harnessing science and action for community change. *American Journal of Community Psychology, 31*(3/4), 219–23.

Roberts, W. B., & Morotti, A. A. (2000). The bully as victim: Understanding bully behaviors to increase the effectiveness of interventions in the bully-victim dyad. *Professional School Counseling, 4,* 148–55.

Spencer, M. B. (2006). Phenomenology and ecological systems theory: Development of diverse groups. In W. Damon & R. M. Lerner (Eds.), *Handbook of child psychology* (6th ed., Vol. 1, pp. 829–93). New York: Wiley.

Spoth, R. L., & Greenberg, M. T. (2005). Toward a comprehensive strategy for effective practitioner-scientist partnerships and larger-scale community health and well-being. *American Journal of Community Psychology, 35*(3/4), 107–26.

Stevenson, H. C. (1997). Managing anger: Protective, proactive, or adaptive racial socialization identity profiles and African American manhood development. In R. J Watts & R. J. Jagers (Eds.), *Manhood development in urban African-American communities* (pp. 35–61). New York: Haworth Press.

Stokols, D., (1996). Translating social ecological theory into guidelines for community health promotion. *American Journal of Health Promotion, 4*(10), 282–98.

Stokols, D., Allen, J., & Bellingham, R. L. (1996). The social ecology of health promotion: Implications for research and practice. *American Journal of Health Promotion, 10*, 247–51.

Tebes, J. K. (2005). Community science, philosophy of science, and the practice of research. *American Journal of Community Psychology, 35*(4/5), 213–30.

Tseng, V., & Seidman, E. (2007). A systems framework for understanding social settings. *American Journal of Community Psychology, 39*, 217–28.

Wallerstein, N., & Duran, B. (2010). Community-based participatory research contributions to intervention research: The intersection of science and practice to improve health equity. *American Journal of Public Health, 100*(S1), S40–S46.

Wandersman, A., Flaspohler, P., Lesesne, C. A., Puddy, R., & Phillips, E. (Eds.). (2012). Advances in bridging research and practice using the interactive system framework for dissemination and implementation (Special issue). *American Journal of Community Psychology, 50*(3–4).

Wandersman, A., & Florin, P. (2003). Community interventions and effective prevention. *American Psychologist, 58*(6–7), 441–48.

Zimbardo, P. G., & Boyd, J. N. (1999). Time perspective: A valid, reliable individual-differences metric. *Journal of Personality and Social Psychology, 77*, 1271–88.

5 Putting Boyer's Four Types of Scholarship into Practice

A Community Research and Action Perspective on Public Health

LAUREN BRINKLEY-RUBINSTEIN,
VERA S. CHATMAN, LAUREL LUNN,
ABBEY MANN, AND CRAIG ANNE HEFLINGER

> Things gain meaning by being used in a shared experience or joint action.
>
> —John Dewey, 1916

> What we now have is a more restricted view of scholarship, one that limits it to a hierarchy of functions. Basic research has come to be viewed as the first and most essential form of scholarly activity, with other functions flowing from it. Scholars are academics who conduct research, publish, and then perhaps convey their knowledge to students or apply what they have learned . . . If the nation's higher learning institutions are to meet today's urgent academic and social mandates, their missions must be carefully redefined and the meaning of scholarship creatively reconsidered.
>
> —Ernest Boyer, 1991

There is an increasing awareness that health is influenced by a variety of factors that were not traditionally considered impactful. This evolution in thinking has resulted in the need for public health interventions to become increasingly interdisciplinary and relevant to the unique characteristics of communities that are affected by various health issues. Consideration of the social determinants of health as primary contributors to health status has also become increasingly common. However, although current research may sometimes employ holistic approaches to public health interventions, there remain disciplinary and sector divisions that diminish the relevance and application of research and intervention endeavors. We assert that scholarship will benefit from multidisciplinarity, holistic considerations of the social context of health that inform subsequent remedies and strategies. John Dewey (1927/1954) relayed the need to make education more holistic and to include communities at risk as key partners. In this chapter, we build on this central theoretical tenet, acknowledging that communities matter when attempting to understand health disparities, and use Boyer's four types of scholarship as a lens through which to attain inclusive understanding of health. After briefly reviewing the traditional approaches to public health intervention, we present two case studies that used the Community Research and Action (CRA) approach to conduct research relevant to health disparities.

Traditional Approaches to Public Health and Persistent Divides

While the discipline of public health has evolved over the years, it has also increasingly become siloed. The public health field was originally created as a response to community health risks in the early nineteenth century such as lack of sanitary water and subsequent disease risk. Initially, those who were trained in public health were individuals with medical backgrounds (Rosenstock, Helsing, & Rimer, 2011). In response to increasing urbanization and resulting public health threats, such as tuberculosis, the American Public Health Association was formed in the 1860s. Soon after, the first schools of public health were organized and reports that outlined the system of public health education were released (Flexner, 1910; Welsh & Rose, 1915). These first examples of public health scholarship focused primarily on the control of infectious diseases. Still applicable today, public health was originally defined as "the science and art of preventing disease, prolonging life and promoting health through the organized efforts and informed choices of society, organizations, public and private, communities and individuals" (Winslow, 1920, p. 21). However, the role of public health has transformed over the course of the past century. While still focusing on the same issues identified earlier, public health has become a fairly interdisciplinary field incorporating perspectives from epidemiology, biostatistics, nursing, community development, sociology, and other scholarly arenas (Joint Task Group on Public Health Human Resources, 2005).

Although efforts have been made to make the public health discipline more interdisciplinary, divides persist. For instance, funding streams are distinctly disciplinary; interdisciplinary spaces in which scholars, community members, and practitioners can share ideas are relatively rare. Interventions in public health often: lack cross-sectorial collaboration; do not involve the public or interested community members in the design, administration and analysis phase of the research process; and, do not produce products that have application in the communities under study. Finally, there is often a divide between the research that is conducted and the subjects taught in classrooms. Rarely are students a part of the research process. Therefore, this chapter presents a definition and framework, undergirded by Boyer's four types of scholarship (1991), in an attempt to reconcile disciplinary divides, incorporate communities as key stakeholders, and translate research findings into teaching scholarship. It is our hope that this framework, called the Community Research and Action (CRA) approach to health, can serve as a guide for academics, practitioners, advocates, and interested community members to engage in extant community-based health prevention, intervention, and research.

The Community Research and Action Approach

The Community Research and Action (CRA) approach views health through a social justice lens with the overarching ideal that every human, regardless of social or economic characteristics, should be able to experience good health in the broadest sense, including physical, economic, and social dimensions.[1] It is influenced by numerous disciplines, from traditional public health to progressive paradigms found in community-based action research. Furthermore, it places explicit attention on multiple levels of analysis and intervention, especially at the community level. The CRA framework is undergirded by Boyer's four types of scholarship—discovery, integration, application, and teaching—and emphasizes the

---

1. Department of Human and Organizational Development. (n.d.). Mission Statement. Retrieved May 20, 2015 from http://peabody.vanderbilt.edu/departments/hod/graduate-programs/mission_statement.php.

interconnectedness among these functions to encourage strategies for researchers and practitioners that:

> *Investigate* the causes and consequences of health- and mental health–related issues that affect individuals and communities. Researchers using this approach must explore the social and institutional determinants of health and acknowledge the roles of historical circumstances, as well as the "structure versus agency" discourse in the determination of health status. Researchers must recognize that health status changes over time and is influenced by a complex network of processes and social structures. For instance, researchers must take into account the social and environmental context in which people live and its effect on health (for example, neighborhood characteristics). Researchers should rely on multidisciplinary theoretical foundations and mixed-methodological approaches (for example, using interviews and surveys in combination), including those that consider partnership with the targets of social interventions as active participants in the production of knowledge. In many cases, such participation does not represent a threat to validity or objectivity but rather an opportunity to draw from diverse perspectives and skills to produce knowledge and evidence of use to multiple audiences. Drawing on the expertise of community members is an essential component to authentic understanding of the issues under study. This may take the form of collaborating with community members as co-researchers or creating community advisory boards that provide input throughout the research project.
>
> *Engage* interdisciplinary and inter-sector collaborators and partners. Frameworks employed by the CRA approach to health should be informed by multiple disciplines, such as public health, community health, nursing, sociology, anthropology, geography, policy, psychology, psychiatry, medicine, and the social sciences more broadly. Using multiple frameworks can add dimensionality to research because scholars can understand the complexity of issues related to health by using different lenses. For instance, when considering a particular health problem, researchers using the CRA approach seek to understand the individual health behaviors that may be undermining health; service systems that may be

affecting health status; the effect of the social and contextual community in which people reside that may result in barriers to healthcare access; and the health *and* social policies in place in the region, state, and nation that may be impacting individual health and decision-making behaviors. Equally as important is developing partnerships with those practicing in different disciplines. Research can often be siloed and housed in one academic department. The CRA approach values the skills, perspective, and input of those from various departments, disciplines, and areas of expertise. Research endeavors, then, should include a team of scholars tackling issues from diverse angles.

Apply to community-oriented issues. This can take the form of population-based intervention strategies or local, state, and national policy change. Researchers must consider wide ranges of interventions beyond traditional medical care and place a special emphasis on preventing illness (or the risk of illness) and working with individuals and communities to act on their own behalves through capacity building. Those who are affected by health issues are often included through consultation with community members, needs and assets assessments conducted in concert with community members, or action-oriented approaches that include community members at each phase of the research process. This application of research to address community-oriented issues must include the input of community members and, subsequently, incorporate the issues that the community finds important into the research aims. This may require researchers to modify pre-existing research plans to accommodate important community-driven, relevant issues.

Bridge the gap between scholars' and students' understandings of individual and community health issues. A range of courses associated with the CRA approach address issues directly related to health, methods, methodology, and epistemology of health and mental health research while also noting communities and numerous social and cultural factors that affect health. Through engaging with students at the undergraduate, master's, and doctoral levels, faculty and students gain mutually from the advancement in understanding and knowledge related to factors affecting health and interventions addressing these issues. In the classroom, students and instructors work together to generate new ideas that often serve as the inspirational fuel needed to perform the functions of investigation, engagement, and application. Building teams of students and faculty at different levels (undergraduate, graduate, non-tenure and tenure track) to collaborate on research projects, writing and other aspects of scholarship (for example, creating and giving presentations), and teaching can help bridge the gap between individuals at differing points in their career and can also help catalyze the interests of young researchers and scholars.

Relating the Four Types of Scholarship to the CRA Approach to Health

According to Ernest Boyer (1991), "Every scholar must . . . demonstrate the capacity to do original research, study a serious intellectual problem and present to colleagues the same results" (p. 15). The challenge then becomes how do we as scholars translate our findings to others (both peers and students) and to communities that are affected? Boyer suggests four types of interrelated scholarship that can provide a map to follow to make research more inclusive, applied, and relatable to students, those new to the field, community members, or those completely unfamiliar with the discipline of public health. The four types include discovery, integration, application, and teaching. Each type of scholarship is described in the sections that follow and related to the CRA approach to health.

The Scholarship of Discovery

Boyer (1991) defines the scholarship of discovery as "transforming knowledge through original research and advancement of knowledge, scholarship that makes up intellectual fields and disciplines" (p. 18). This stage of research is traditionally the first, during which researchers investigate phenomena, searching for new ideas, information, and ways of seeing the world. This step includes gathering information related to the problem a researcher is trying to solve or better understand such as community characteristics; identifying existing community initiatives or existing research that has investigated this problem; locating infrastructure available to support the work (for example, possible community partners and funders); and utilizing varied research methods to gain a more complete understanding of the issue under investigation.

The Scholarship of Integration

Among the unique qualities of the CRA approach to health is its interdisciplinary nature. The approach necessitates inclusion of faculty and students from a number of different disciplines and integrates scholarship, methods, and theory from a wide range of sources. Researchers utilizing the CRA approach also engage with collaborators from different organizational settings, including hospitals, health departments, and human service organizations. Perspectives on health come in different forms and, therefore, can be measured using different methodologies. Researchers using this approach are also expected to cite research across disciplines and to use theory and evidence from a diverse array of sources. In so doing, they are exemplifying what Boyer (1991) refers to as "integration." Instead of understanding health disparities through a single lens, individuals utilizing the CRA approach rely on multiple frameworks with the goal of viewing problems from diverse standpoints, developing solutions that are new and innovative as well as involving stakeholders from a variety of different standpoints and with a variety of skills and expertise levels.

Students and faculty utilizing the CRA approach must also be engaged in ongoing discussions regarding the nature of interdisciplinary scholarship—often engaging in discourse related to why it is important, challenges and/or benefits of cross-discipline partnerships, and how to communicate the work (for example, journal publication or report creation) in a way that is mutually beneficial to all partners involved. For instance, scholars engaging in interdisciplinary work informed by Boyer (1991) must reconcile the benefits of diverse partnerships with the realization that they are also expected to conduct work and publish in journals relevant to the work that is valued by their home department or institution. Therefore, careful consideration must be given to planning work that may be outside the realm of traditional scholarship so that those involved can have the maximum benefit. In addition, students must frequently take courses in various disciplines, such as women and gender studies, integrating feminist theory into the understanding of the ways in which race, class, and gender intersect and affect health outcomes. Those utilizing the CRA approach to health should also engage in cross-sector partnerships when considering interventions or research collaborations. This may include working with public health entities as well as non-profit social agencies that might not have an explicit health mission but understand the impact of social issues on overall individual and collective wellness. In sum, the CRA stresses the importance of interdisciplinary work and, as such, can impact the way health research is conceptualized and conducted within and across disciplines and sectors of expertise.

The Scholarship of Application

Generating knowledge and putting it in context are worthwhile, but ultimately, scholarship requires the application of this knowledge to problems in a rigorous and responsible way. Boyer (1991) explains that such application must go beyond vague conceptualizations of "service" to connect our knowledge to life. Furthermore, application itself can be a knowledge-generating activity in which those involved learn more about concepts related to the problem as well as practical issues or logistical considerations of implementing successful interventions. Application includes a number of important sub-concepts that should be given careful attention, such as which ecological level to target to address a problem most effectively (i.e., individual, community, or institutional).

The CRA approach is strongly committed to its application in community settings, primarily those that demonstrate at least one measure of disadvantage. In fact, the program's name was chosen specifically to highlight the importance of research *and* action, based on the knowledge generated from the landscape of existing research, or methods in which the research itself acts as an intervention (for example, community capacity building via action research approaches, community empowerment via acting as research collaborators). Community-engaged research is especially conducive to the application of the CRA approach because of the integral inclusion of the target community itself throughout the research process. This approach allows for a more intimate knowledge and understanding of context, processes, and nuances that are typically rare for academics whose project design and result interpretation are disconnected from the population of interest. Of course, Boyer (1991) and those utilizing the CRA approach would argue that it is because of insights that are available to the researcher through community involvement that community-based research may, in some cases, prove to be more rigorous, accurate, useful, and responsible than other approaches.

In its highest form, Boyer (1991) implies, "application" might manifest such that social problems themselves define the research agenda. Indeed, this is common for those who research health, who identify research questions based on the health problems that are salient at the time. Though this is rarer, in a truly community-based project, community members themselves would define the research agenda instead of "outside" researchers. Identification of appropriate topics to study could occur by convening a community forum in which researchers ask community members what issues are most important to them. Additionally, researchers should be open to modifying their own pre-existing research aims and also be willing to alter the research plan throughout the duration of a study. This research fluidity is important because the community's research agenda and prioritization of issues may change or evolve over time.

The Scholarship of Teaching

The last type of scholarship is related to teaching. Research endeavors often fall short and do not fully recognize the importance of multidirectional knowledge transfer in the classroom and in the field. The CRA approach recognizes this possible limitation and is grounded in the idea that mastery of knowledge and facilitating learning to include integral opportunities that encourage students to immerse themselves in it allow students to learn *and* add to their existing knowledge. Boyer (1991) states that "teaching, at its best, means not only transmitting knowledge, but transforming and extending it as well" (p. 34). Therefore, those utilizing the CRA approach must constantly ask themselves, "How can knowledge best be learned by others?" and subsequently construct educational strategies that produce desired learning. Creative strategies must be utilized to fully transfer knowledge to students in such a way that encourages them to extend their current understandings of complex, multi-layered issues. Possible strategies in line with the CRA approach might include service learning initiatives and graduate student, undergraduate student, and faculty research initiatives in which students are full participants in the research process. Inclusion of student collaborators can take place at any stage of research but works best if they can participate at all stages as stakeholders.

Service learning is defined as the incorporation of community service within an educational system (Eyler & Giles, 1999). Examples include collaborations with community-based organizations and institutions and academic departments or individual classes in which some joint project is created and completed in concert. Specific activities might include students conducting research; the creation of needs assessments, policy guides, or resource materials; or the actual provision of services (for example, volunteering to meet a common goal of both the classroom and the organization). Students utilizing the CRA approach to health have engaged in collaborations with a local children's hospital to create a web portal that provides information on the importance of health literacy for parents and children; other students have conducted health impact assessments for the local health department to evaluate how local policies affect the health of community members. The idea behind this type of practice is one of exposure and reflection where students from diverse backgrounds experience the practical reality of community organizations and immerse themselves in relevant research to complete a shared goal. Students are also encouraged to engage in iterative reflection of the processes so that knowledge transfer can occur and they can better understand how to further existing efforts.

Case Study Examples That Embody the CRA Approach to Health

But what exactly does the CRA approach to health "look like" in real life? Two case studies of research that were undertaken and planned using the CRA approach illustrate this methodology in action. Both cases are related to the social determinants of health and their impact on health disparities among minority populations.

An Exploration of the Health Impact of Incarceration on HIV-Positive African American Men

Given the intersections of health disparities and incarceration, a research project was developed to understand some of the health impacts incarceration has on HIV-positive African American men.

SCHOLARSHIP OF DISCOVERY

During the initial research stage, while the researchers were conceptualizing the scholarship of discovery phase, it was decided that a mixed-method approach that included ethnographic methods, administration of a quantitative survey, and a series of focus groups would be used to uncover important nuances in the participants' lives that might remain undetected by conventional research approaches. During this phase, those principles embodied by the scholarship of discovery were deployed. The researchers consulted with both the local health department and an AIDS Service Organization (ASO) to develop a research plan that included the priorities of all partners. This included adding a new component to the existing survey that investigated the impact of health literacy on HIV outcomes. Although this was not originally a primary aim for the researchers, the investigation of health literacy led to a deeper understanding of how incarceration acts as a barrier to development of health literacy.

Although the primary goal of the scholarship of discovery is to add to the existing body of knowledge, this study also endeavored to make this stage as collaborative as possible by encouraging participation with organizational entities. This collaborative effort embodied the CRA approach and could be easily replicated in other studies. One strategy could involve approaching governmental or community-based representatives and presenting them with a mutually beneficial research plan. Although we added an element to the survey, a mutually beneficial partnership could also include a "service trade" wherein the researcher and institution could each provide one another with a product or service such as grant writing or help with recruitment.

SCHOLARSHIP OF INTEGRATION AND APPLICATION

Researchers engaged in the scholarship of integration and application by first collaborating with community members who had a history of incarceration and who were HIV-positive, and continued collaboration with the local ASO and health department. Multiple faculty and staff members across a number of disciplines both inside and outside academia offered input about the research design. Researchers frequently consulted with community stakeholders and cross-sector partners and incorporated their feedback throughout the study period. The quantitative survey was developed in collaboration with four HIV-positive African Americans who had recently experienced incarceration; they also aided in survey administration, conducting focus groups and interpreting results. Findings were shared with participants and they were asked to suggest possible policy changes and future programs.

SCHOLARSHIP OF TEACHING

The final stage of scholarship, teaching, reflected the inclusion of undergraduate students in each stage of the research project (from design to writing manuscripts and policy reports). Additionally, details of the study were presented to several undergraduate courses each semester during various phases of the project and participants of the study guest lectured and discussed the importance of research collaboration with community members. After many of the presentations, undergraduates approached researchers and asked to participate in the study. Their inclusion led to new pathways of discovery as well as the creation of new ideas related to application and integration of the results.

Therefore, the *discovery* of knowledge was founded on partnerships between researchers and local agencies and relied upon community-level knowledge of participants; *integration* was attained via cross-sector collaboration that included input from scholars from multiple disciplines; *application* of findings included creating an ongoing, sustained partnership between the researchers and local agencies by writing grants and developing projects based on the findings; and, finally, study results were used in *teaching* endeavors where participants shared their experiences, students worked on the project during each stage, and findings were presented at various stages of the research process. Using the CRA approach allowed researchers to uncover findings that might have otherwise been unavailable to them by including participants and community members as stakeholders during each phase. The approach also presented an opportunity to further the field of knowledge via collaborations and partnerships with undergraduate students. Additionally, community involvement led to an ongoing relationship in which a number of projects (funded by various co-written grants) are still continuing.

Investigating the Impact of the Social Determinants of Refugee Health

As a grant-funded non-profit organization, the Center for Refugees and Immigrants of Tennessee (CRIT) houses operations and programming that are financed by time-limited resources. The Community Development Director at the center noted to a doctoral student who had volunteered with the organization that many of the services they provide to refugees are somewhat "obvious" and therefore easy to justify to funders (for example, English language classes, assistance finding employment, assistance with citizenship applications), but that the health needs of such communities are "hidden." Without data about health status and unmet need for health care, services end up focusing on other needs, defined largely by the central priorities of grant applications that are more easily demonstrable. This conversation spurred a fruitful partnership between the organization and the university.

SCHOLARSHIP OF DISCOVERY

The student and CRIT director co-wrote a mini-grant to fund data collection on refugee health status in Nashville, which was funded by the Community Engaged Research Core, a collaboration between the Meharry Medical College and Vanderbilt University Medical Center. The research team consists of members from both Vanderbilt and CRIT, and both organizations have contributed to project design and the early stages of data collection. The study aims to collect information about the health status, service need, life stressors, and a number of contextual and social factors for the two largest groups of refugees in Nashville. These data will create knowledge (*discovery*) about resettled refugee health that will advance current literature. The study also reflects collaboration between the researcher and a community-based organization. Both the researcher and the organizational leadership recognized a mutual need for data on refugee health. This led to collaborative grant writing that resulted in funding to enable the project to begin.

SCHOLARSHIP OF APPLICATION AND INTEGRATION

The primary purpose of the study is its *application* to a real community need. Data can justify funding for organizations and inform the design of service provisions. It is already apparent that the data must be *integrated* with other knowledge to be of greatest potential. The academic disciplines that relate to the study span public health, social epidemiology, and community psychology. The community knowledge about behaviors, beliefs, and social structures that affect these groups will be invaluable in situating the results of the study in context. The project enabled the creation of data, with the help of interdisciplinary and inter-sector (academic, practitioner, community member) contributors. The team will have a strong chance at making substantive meaning from the data that will inform its application. Furthermore, health is a component of well-being that affects and is affected by many other factors in life, such that some topics that one may not automatically associate with health (for example, housing, social networks) are indeed embedded in a complex system of relationships that involve health. Without the existing work to integrate knowledge from diverse disciplines, sectors, and people, the depth of our understanding of health would be diminished.

One of the major lessons for the researchers has been the realization that accessing refugee communities in Nashville would be nearly impossible without direct personal connections. CRIT, as an organization founded by Somali refugees and still serving a large number of Somali clients, has strong community ties. Because prospective participants trust CRIT, and CRIT trusts the research team, Somalis are far more willing to contribute to the study than they would be if contacted by a stranger from the university who was disconnected from their community. In addition, many respondents are motivated not by the monetary compensation offered by the study but by the possibility that the knowledge generated will be of use to their community.

In this project, it was essential to establish institutional trust between the researcher and organization. This trust was key to gaining access to a "hidden" population and typified the CRA approach to health via both community integration and application that is relevant to the social context that mirrors the lived experience of participants. Because of the initial and continual institutional involvement, the data have a very real

138 IMPLICATIONS AND RESPONSES

application that will inform service delivery to Somali refugees who seek care via CRIT. Other researchers might also consider collaborating with organizations to develop alternate products such as reports, training manuals, or brochures such that organizations can use research data to directly impact their service delivery processes.

SCHOLARSHIP OF TEACHING

A service learning component could easily be included in this type of study. For example, after data collection and analysis, students could work with CRIT to aid in implementation of change. This could take the form of follow-up projects to continue investigating health disparities among refugees, grant writing to fund future interventions or projects, or development of programmatic changes or additions based on the survey results. Researchers and practitioners could also engage in a service-learning project with students to sustain ongoing community relationships. And by doing so, all parties involved would be participating in the creation of usable knowledge that may be implementable for the common good (Dewey, 1927/1954, 1938). This project exemplified the CRA approach while keeping focus on both the importance of community participation and the social context in which the study occurred. Via discovery, new knowledge was added about refugee health that was subsequently integrated into the community via a community-based organization as an institutional research partner. Application was the primary study goal and the results will help inform policy and practice. Finally, service learning has the potential to maintain partnerships and make the discovery of new knowledge iterative rather than static.

Putting Boyer's Typology into Action

The CRA approach is undergirded by a multidisciplinary approach to health. Informed by Boyer's four types of scholarship–discovery, integration, application, and teaching–interconnectedness is emphasized when pondering and exploring complex health problems and possible solutions. The "Getting Started!" table provides a number of actionable steps to integrate Boyer's four types of scholarship into a new or existing program or research agenda.

Chapter 5: Getting Started!
Putting Boyer's Four Types of Scholarship into Practice: A Community Research and Action Perspective on Public Health

Action Item 1: *Bring fieldwork into the classroom.*
There is often a divide between research and teaching. Consider making ongoing research projects a key component to courses. Bringing the instructor's research into the classroom may catalyze the interests of young researchers and scholars. Examples might include examining survey tools or interview protocols via workshops, taking students to field sites, or asking community partners to present results during class.

Action Item 2: *Include community members as key partners throughout the research process.*
Value the expertise that community members bring to the table and include them, where appropriate and possible, throughout the research process. Their involvement can take many shapes but might include aiding in the design of the research plan, working on and editing surveys, interviewing participants, engaging in data analysis or member-checking, writing publications, participating in conference presentations, and disseminating results.

Action Item 3: *Embrace interdisciplinarity.*
Avoid getting trapped in disciplinary silos. Consider the contributions to your field of study from various disciplines. Consult scholars and community members who have diverse backgrounds to gain insight into the problems you hope to solve. Public health practitioners have much to learn from the theoretical and empirical work of (to name a few): sociologists, psychologists, philosophers, and practice-based interventionists.

Action Item 4: *Don't neglect the "action" component of Community, Research and Action.*
Equally value each components of the CRA approach. To maximize the benefits of the four types of Boyer's scholarship, each type must be considered. Engage in action that makes tangible your research findings. This might include presenting your work to community partners, working with community-based organizations to widely distribute your findings to community members, writing an editorial in a local newspaper, or contacting local governmental officials to share your results to advocate for policy change.

Action Item 5: *Involve students in research endeavors.*
In addition to bringing fieldwork into the classroom, also involve students in research endeavors. Possible strategies might include service learning initiatives and research in which students are full participants in the process. Inclusion of student collaborators can take place at any stage of research but often works best if they can participate as stakeholders at all stages.

Conclusion

Although practitioners and researchers alike have incorporated more holistic approaches in their investigation and intervention efforts around health, inclusive discovery across disciplines and sectors, applied to practical problems and then presented in the classroom in a way that furthers our collective understanding, is lacking. However, we posit that using the CRA approach to health, undergirded by Boyer's (1991) framework and a modern embodiment of Deweyism (1927/1954, 1938), provides an opportunity to engage in meaningful public health research that illuminates community and individual issues that would often otherwise be unavailable or "hidden" to individuals in the ivory tower.

References

Boyer, E. L. (1991). *Scholarship reconsidered: Priorities of the professoriate.* New York: The Carnegie Foundation for the Advancement of Teaching.

Department of Human and Organizational Development. (n.d.). Mission statement. Retrieved May 20, 2015 from http://peabody.vanderbilt.edu/departments/hod/graduate-programs/mission_statement.php.

Dewey, J. (1916). *Democracy and education.* New York: Simon & Schuster.

Dewey, J. (1927/1954). *The public and its problems.* Chicago: The Swallow Press.

Dewey, J. (1938). *Education and experience.* New York: Touchstone, Simon & Schuster.

Eyler, J., & Giles Jr., D. E. (1999). *Where's the learning in service-learning?* San Francisco, CA: Jossey-Bass Higher and Adult Education Series.

Fazel, M., Wheeler, J., & Danesh, J. (2005). Prevalence of serious mental disorder in 7000 refugees resettled in western countries: A systematic review. *Lancet, 365,* 1309–14.

Flexner, A. (1910). *Medical education in the United States and Canada: A report to the Carnegie Foundation for the Advancement of Teaching.* New York: Carnegie Foundation for the Advancement of Teaching.

Frenk, J., & Chen, L. (2010). Health professionals for a new century: Transforming education to strengthen health systems in an interdependent world. *Lancet, 376,* 1923–58.

Kennedy, C., & Baker, T. Changing demographics of public health graduates: Potential implications for public health work force. *Public Health Reports, 120,* 355–57.

Rosenstock, L., Helsing, K., & Rimer, B. K. (2011). Public health education in the United States: Then and now. *Public Health Reviews, 33* (1), 39–65.

St. Lawrence, J. S., Snodgrass, C. E., Robertson, A., & Baird-Thomas, C. (2008). Minimizing the risk of pregnancy, sexually transmitted diseases and HIV among incarcerated adolescent girls: Identifying potential points of intervention. *Criminal Justice Behavior, 35*(12), 1500–14.

Welsh, W. H., & Rose, W. (1915). *Institute of hygiene: A report to the general education board of Rockefeller Foundation.* New York: The Rockefeller Foundation.

Wilkinson, R. G., & Marmot, M. G. (2003). *Social determinants of health: The solid facts.* Geneva: World Health Organization.

Winslow, C. (1920). The untitled fields of public health. *Science, 51*(1306), 23–33.

6 Conducting Research on Comprehensive Community Development Initiatives

Balancing Methodological Rigor and Community Responsiveness

KIMBERLY D. BESS, BERNADETTE DOYKOS,
JOANNA D. GELLER, KRISTA L. CRAVEN,
AND MAURY NATION

> The path of least resistance and least trouble is a mental rut already made. It requires troublesome work to undertake the alternation of old beliefs.
>
> —John Dewey[1]

> Tolerance, inter-cultural dialogue and respect for diversity are more essential than ever in a world where peoples are becoming more and more closely interconnected.
>
> —Kofi Annan[2]

Over the last twenty years, a number of scholars have examined the complexities of university-community partnerships. The majority of such work has resulted from collaborative approaches to prevention and intervention and disproportionately exists in the public health field (Israel, Schultz, Parker, & Becker, 1998). The impact of such efforts has coincided with the emergence of academic programs, including Community Research and Action (CRA) and Community Development and Action (CDA) in the HOD department, which consider applied coursework and

---

1. Dewey, John (author) and J. A. Boydston (ed.). 1986. *The Later works, 1925–1953: Volume 8, 1933*, Carbondale, IL: Southern Illinois University Press, p. 136.

2. From "Tolerance, Inter-Cultural Dialogue, Respect for Diversity More Essential Than Ever," a press release by Secretary-General Kofi Annan for the International Day for the Elimination of Racial Discrimination, March 21, 2004. Retrieved from http://www.un.org/News/Press/docs/2004/sgsm9195.doc.htm.

research essential to advanced degrees. The foundation of such work is undergirded by Dewey's scholarship that emphasized the engagement of experts, community members, and other members of society in collaborative endeavors (Dewey, 1916; Oakes and Rogers, 2006). Community of inquiry approaches recognize that knowledge is always nested in a particular social context. As such, different types of expertise representative of diverse interested parties (for example, community members, researchers, academics, and community organization representatives) must be included (Lipman, 2003). Such efforts also aid in bridging the research-practice gap. Additionally, through more recently developed methods, such as community-based participatory research (CBPR) and action research, these partnerships challenge traditional power hierarchies between the "researcher" and the "researched."

In recent years, expectations of third-party funders, including federal granters and foundations, have prioritized the integration of results-driven evaluation, increasing the technical reporting requirements for award recipients. In many ways, these opportunities create a natural space for collaboration between university researchers and community partners. However, as we will illustrate in this chapter, academic demands frequently conflict with community needs, creating tensions that threaten to limit the authenticity and potential success of these types of collaboration. This chapter offers a case study of a partnership that emerged as a result of a Promise Neighborhoods (PN) Planning grant from the U.S. Department of Education to a Nashville-based human service organization, the Martha O'Bryan Center. We examine challenges in relation to three key tensions: defining expertise, institutional barriers, and expectations of scientific rigor. In addition, we explore approaches to overcome those challenges and lessons for academics in creating rewarding partnerships that satisfy the needs and expectations of all invested parties.

An Overview of Participatory Action Research

Research about university-community collaboration has examined community-based Participatory Action Research (PAR) projects that seek to engage community members as critical contributors throughout the research process (Israel et al., 1998; Minkler, Blackwell, Thomson, &

Tamir, 2003). For example, Israel and her colleagues (1998) argue that recent prioritization of randomized control trials as the "gold standard" for outcomes research obscures the social and environmental variables that directly impact individual level outcomes. In contrast, community-based research allows for the direct consideration of "social, structural, and physical inequalities" (Israel et al., 1998, p. 173) through the integration of community expertise, from conceptualization to execution and analysis of research. Although there is immense potential in this type of work, both academics and community partners must be intentional in developing systems and practices that ensure equal participation to achieve the best results (Lentz et al., 2001). Participatory action-oriented research involves identifying issues that are relevant to a particular group or community through a process of engaged dialogue. This process results in the creation and implementation of a plan of action to address issues to improve community conditions (Craig, 2009). Participatory methods entail power sharing and co-learning through the equitable participation of partners (Israel et al. 2008). This requires intentionality in expanding the traditional "expert" role and recognizing and addressing institutional barriers and expectations of scientific rigor.

Expanding the "Expert" Role

The belief that community members have a right to research the conditions that shape their lived experiences is a central tenet of participatory, action-oriented research. This complements Appadurai's (2006) call to democratize academic research endeavors:

> [Everybody has the] right to research [because] research, in this sense, is not only the production of original ideas and new knowledge (as it is normally defined in academia and other knowledge-based institutions). It is also something simpler and deeper. It is the capacity to systematically increase the horizons of one's current knowledge, in relation to some task, goal or aspiration. (p. 176)

Scholars who embrace this principle recognize that community members possess critical expertise about their social and structural context that is essential in understanding the complex nature of the social issues that lie at the center of analysis but oftentimes beyond the confines of traditional methods (Fine, 2009; Rodriguez & Brown, 2009).

Through strategic partnerships, traditional notions of "expertise" have the potential to be expanded when local knowledge—both of community residents and community practitioners—is combined with the technical skills of university-trained researchers to address localized problems or concerns (Wilson, 1997). For projects that center on a place-based community development initiative, the recognition and inclusion of community voice from the outset allows for a broader understanding of individual and collective experiences in the context of intense poverty, limited resources, and various institutional barriers. The lived experiences of individuals affect how and why community members engage with programs and use resources that are intended to support their broader well-being (Geller, Doykos, Craven, Bess, & Nation, 2014). The most effective community development initiatives provide more than basic programming and interventions but rather build social capital in the target community that solicits resident engagement and lays the foundation for sustainable change (Wilson, 1997). Recognizing the expertise and knowledge of community residents throughout the research process also promotes social justice, as traditionally underrepresented populations are identified as experts. However, it is important to note, "analysis without action does not produce tangible change" (Watts, Williams, & Jagers. 2003, p. 186). Thus, an essential element of working toward social justice is an approach that addresses the issues that are of collective interest and concern to a community.

Yet researchers often overlook institutionalized power that can impact these collaborations and how roles are established throughout the research process (Bess, Prilleltensky, Perkins, & Collins, 2009; Cahill, 2007). Thus "community involvement," as defined by a researcher, may exclude particular subpopulations, especially those with the most limited voice. Continuing difficulties to authentic community engagement are often the byproduct of power structures rooted in a history of racism, xenophobia, classism, sexism, and other institutions of privilege (Bonilla-Silva, 2006; Fine, 2009). As a result, power inequalities must be explicitly addressed during the entire research process; alternately, they may potentially influence both the processes (for example, sample selection and selected methods) and, ultimately, the findings.

Institutional Obstacles

The ways universities are structured can present challenges for community-based researchers. Participatory approaches to research often require a substantial investment of time in the initiation, facilitation, and dissemination phases of the research process, which can challenge one's ability to dedicate the necessary time to other academic activities required by universities (Kidd & Kral, 2005). For instance, the tenure and promotion process typically requires faculty to produce a substantial number of publications and allot considerable time to teaching and other university-based activities. Graduate students face similar constraints, including dissertation fieldwork, scholarly writing and publishing, teaching courses, and completing coursework and research training. While these activities are crucial to becoming a successful academic, this system can create a space that discourages scholars from dedicating their time to engaging in emergent, community-driven research projects (Hall, 1992; Kidd & Kral, 2005; Rodriguez & Brown, 2009). Moreover, the significant amount of time spent building connections and working in partnership with communities and local organizations is often not considered a crucial component of faculty hiring processes or tenure applications (Hall, 1992; Kidd & Kral, 2005). These time constraints are further complicated by the academic calendar, which often does not align with the schedules of community organizations and other key stakeholders and can impede collaboration between university researchers and community members.

Moreover, academics following principles of community-based participatory research may face university challenges with respect to research "quality." Traditionally, academic research has been disproportionately framed by a positivist approach that seeks to identify causal relationships (Hesse-Biber, Leavy, & Yaiser, 2004). Quantifiable outcomes are typically desired, and there may be little opportunity for critical inquiry about how specific contexts may impact analyses. Additionally, institutional processes, such as approval from the Institutional Review Board (IRB), can reify role division between researchers and non-researchers. The IRB restricts who can participate as a researcher within a university-sanctioned research project. Finally, because the IRB is based primarily on a medical model of research, it may not lend itself to studies in the social sciences, particularly those that deviate from traditional experimental or researcher-initiated studies. As a result, scholars are often encouraged to shape their research to mirror narrow definitions of "rigor" (Cahill, 2007). This may pose a problem for those attempting to employ participatory methods. For example, to gain approval, IRB proposals must pre-state both the research questions of interest and the methods to be employed *a priori*, limiting the possibilities for community engagement in such processes. This transforms participants into passive contributors in a research project where their key concerns may not be considered or elucidated (Cahill, 2007). Considering that one cannot initiate a research project that includes human participants without IRB approval, the institutional norms of research embraced by some IRBs can make the process of designing and facilitating a participatory community-based research project difficult.

Expanding the Notions of Rigor

Traditionally, academic research is bound by expectations of rigor, defined in large part by the methods used and notions of validity and reliability. Scholars who advocate for the use of participatory methods suggest that, within the context of community research, notions of scientific rigor need to expand beyond traditional definitions that hold up randomized control trials as the gold standard. Instead, they argue, fully engaging traditionally underrepresented populations throughout an iterative research process results in enhanced validity (Cahill, 2007). It must be noted that these two approaches to research are not strictly dichotomous. However, more often than not, participatory methods preclude randomization and challenge traditional notions of rigor. To guide this practice, Bradbury and Reason (2006) raise six framing questions: (1) Is the action research explicit in developing a praxis of relational participation? (2) Is it guided by reflexive concern for pragmatic outcomes? (3) Does it ensure conceptual and theoretical integrity? (4) Does it include extended ways of knowing? (5) Can it be considered significant? and (6) Does it lead toward a new and enduring infrastructure? Several studies that have pushed traditional boundaries and included community members as essential partners have demonstrated the merit of participatory methods across multiple disciplines, including education (Duncan-Andrade & Morrell, 2008), public health (Minkler & Wallerstein, 2008), and geography (Al-Kodmany, 2002). Yet a stated intention to include multiple partners to enhance validity and rigor is insufficient in guaranteeing it in practice. Academic partners must be intentional as they approach collaboration to reflexively consider how to ensure rigor throughout the research endeavor (Bradbury & Reason, 2006).

The Nashville Promise Neighborhood: A Case Study of Collaboration

The following case study examines three key tensions related to expanding definitions of expertise, institutional barriers, and expectations of rigor within the context of a collaborative partnership between researchers from Vanderbilt University (VU) and representatives from the Nashville Promise Neighborhood (NPN). For over 65 years, the Martha O'Bryan Center (MOBC) has served the James A. Cayce Homes (Cayce Homes), providing a broad range of programs and services to children and families. Cayce Homes is Nashville, Tennessee's largest public housing complex, serving nearly 3,000 people. According to the U.S. Census (2010), the neighborhood that MOBC serves exhibits some of the most alarming statistics in the city: 87 percent of children live in poverty and the median household income is $10,412—over $47,000 lower than the citywide median income. Beyond Cayce Homes, the impacts of extreme poverty are evident across other institutions in the surrounding community. For example, in 2011, over half of the students scored at a basic or below basic level on the reading and math portions of the state test (Tennessee Department of Education, 2012).

With a clearly stated need, a well-defined plan for assessing current community needs and resources, and the stated support of a number of local partners, MOBC was awarded a grant from the U.S. Department of Education (DoE) to spearhead the Nashville Promise Neighborhood (NPN) in December 2011. MOBC received a planning grant, $500,000 over a 12-month period, for the development of the precise blueprint of how the NPN would respond to specific needs of the targeted geographic area. Like other PN initiatives around the country, the hope of the NPN is to bring together diverse stakeholders around the common goal of creating a cradle-to-career system of resources and supports that foster the healthy development of children and families.

In the months following the award announcement, MOBC approached a diverse set of potential partners, including local schools, nonprofits, community groups, and researchers from VU. Prior to the planning grant award, a small VU research team led by a faculty member from the Human and Organizational Development department (HOD) had collaborated with MOBC on several projects, including a program evaluation, professional development delivery, and grant consultation. The new award offered the opportunity to expand the involvement of faculty and students in HOD and across other departments. The primary role of the VU team was to provide assistance with the technical requirements of the grant, including the development and execution of a community needs assessment (CNA). In partnership with NPN, the research team conducted an extensive literature review, assisted in collecting local data from existing sources, and developed and conducted a door-to-door community survey. The goal of the partnership was to develop a comprehensive assessment of the community's assets and challenges that could inform the development of a data-driven intervention plan as well as identify the most relevant and potentially successful approaches to comprehensive community change.

According to Arthur and Blitz (2000), there are two important reasons researchers and practitioners conduct CNAs before implementing interventions. First, interventions must be adapted to local context. For example, the programs that constitute the Harlem Children's Zone may not work in communities with a unique set of needs and resources. Thus, conducting a needs assessment helps identify unmet service needs and local assets within a particular community. Second, research demonstrates that community-level interventions are more likely to succeed when residents have been involved in their development (Chaskin, 2001). CNAs endeavor to gather information on community assets and challenges that can be used to create interventions, initiatives, and opportunities that are responsive to community needs, as defined by residents. In relation to expanding expertise through a CNA, some scholars argue that surveys with questions designed by researchers run the risk of asserting professional perceptions and definitions of need on the community, while others argue that entirely qualitative techniques are too nebulous and do not enable generalizability (Billings & Cowley, 1995). The following sections describe specific tensions that arose through joint efforts to design, plan, and implement a CNA to inform the development of the PN implementation grant. We examine how the methods employed in the development and the execution of the CNA served to engage community partners at various points in the process.

Expanding Expertise: Conducting the NPN Community Needs Assessment

From the outset, the MOBC staff members responsible for the NPN set the research agenda. This arrangement is in line with CBPR or PAR endeavors, in which university researchers cultivate a community-driven process and create conditions for expanding expertise. We acknowledge that the technical and content-specific expertise that we brought as trained researchers was important to the successful execution of a research partnership. However, we posit that the success of the project ultimately depended on leveraging our skill set with community input and participation throughout the CNA process. The complexities and demands of the context created particular challenges to the collaboration. The CBPR value of recognizing community members' expertise requires collaborators to identify stakeholder groups in the community that can make unique contributions to the research and to determine how these community members will participate in the research process. As with many collaborative initiatives, the question—*Who is the community?*—was not entirely clear. For this project, three key collaborators emerged: MOBC staff who managed NPN, members of NPN partner organizations, and community residents.

CBPR principles encourage community participation in all aspects of the research; however, it became clear early on that a number of variables, including differences in level of interest, availability, and capacities, would influence each group's participation. In the case of MOBC, staff members, charged with completing the CNA for NPN, had high levels of interest, availability, and professional expertise. Therefore, it was natural for them to take the lead role in its development and implementation. Additionally, they had the organizational support, especially in the form of time, to commit to collaborate. In contrast, participation among members of NPN partner organizations and community residents was also critical, but they played a more restricted role, as will become evident.

COMMUNITY PARTICIPATION IN THE CNA RESEARCH PROCESS

Our VU research team worked closely with NPN staff to develop a three-part research strategy for gathering local-level data related to the education, family, and community support indicators outlined in the PNP grant. First, we culled information about the neighborhood from a diverse set of resources, analyzing publically available datasets and conducting a comprehensive literature review. This strategy was used to collect data related to a number of the education indicators. For example, for the indicator "Children demonstrate achievement of grade-level proficiency in major subjects including math and reading," data from grade-level reports of Adequate Yearly Progress (AYP) were gathered for all NPN targeted schools (six elementary, two middle, and one high school). Several partner organizations were crucial during this phase of the CNA process, providing access to datasets as well as information about existing programs, services, and resources for community members.

Second, the research team, with the support of NPN staff, conducted a series of focus groups (n = 9) with key stakeholders, including students, school administrators, nonprofit program staff, and parents to identify specific community needs and interests that would help NPN staff tailor their CNA to the local context. The research team and NPN staff worked together to analyze focus group data and identify major themes. Findings were triangulated from existing literature, secondary datasets, and focus groups to inform the thematic priorities of the CNA. The focus groups highlighted some important gaps that were not initially evident in our preliminary analyses. For example, residents of Cayce Homes cited a number of institutional barriers that limited their participation in a number of local activities. One primary issue was a lack of trust, which many parents identified as a critical precursor to engaging in community activities (for a more detailed summary of this finding, please see Geller, et al., 2014). As an essential part of the CNA strategy, the focus groups captured the expertise and knowledge of community residents and professional staff from NPN partner organizations. However, the role individuals from these groups played was largely that of research participant because we were unable to include them in the analysis process because of emerging barriers such as the grant deadline, academic pressures, and lack of resources to reconvene the groups.

The final phase of our CNA strategy was the development and execution of a door-to-door community survey of NPN residents to gather local-level data unavailable from existing sources and to explore more systematically the focus group results. We collaboratively developed the survey for the CNA collaboratively with the NPN staff. Once a preliminary draft was finalized, it was piloted with community residents to assess cultural and linguistic reliability. We identified a number of questions that concerned respondents and solicited their feedback about how to change the wording or question format. This phase was a critical step in finalizing the community survey. Had we not engaged in a piloting process, data quality would have suffered.

Billings and Cowley (1995) note the tendency to only gather opinions in a CNA from residents who are most able and willing to participate; thus, it was crucial to consider how to promote maximum community representation in the sampling processes for the survey. To capture a statistically representative sample from the target geographic area and high priority zones, we developed an extensive data-sampling framework. We worked with representatives from the NPN and MOBC to identify the most strategic approach. Collectively, our primary concern was to capture the voices of the most disenfranchised residents, specifically those who lived in the high priority zone around Cayce Homes and the adjoining CWA Plaza Apartments. The sampling frame included an oversampling of 120 households in the highest-risk census tracts in the geographic zone. In doing this, we prioritized responses from the most marginalized subpopulations in the cluster—those for whom the proposed program of services had the greatest potential impact. This approach to sampling proved to be successful. Over a three-week period, we collected a total of 485 surveys, with over 40 percent (n = 200) from priority neighborhoods. Underrepresentation would have posed a serious problem had the process not included the input and participation of MOBC staff, community residents, and NPN partner organizations as well as the technical training of the VU research team.

MULTIPLE PATHS FOR EXPANDING PARTICIPATION AND EXPERTISE

As researchers, we aimed to involve community participation at each step of the research process. In practice, this was not always feasible or necessarily desirable for our partners. Yet having this goal did establish a value for expanding expertise through various opportunities for participation.

As noted earlier, we worked closely with NPN staff members to leverage expertise—including our own—in ways that acknowledged, but did not overburden, stakeholders. At various times, different stakeholder groups brought different types of expertise to the project. Thus, the stakeholders involved at any particular stage depended upon the specific nature and requirements of the task. For example, given the technical requirements for data analysis and other pragmatic concerns, members of the VU research team mainly took on this task. However, we relied on community residents and practitioners to help interpret analysis results. This collaborative process combined various types of expertise, which helped convert initial findings into locally relevant and applicable information. However, tension emerged between our desire to enact the value of participation and expand the notion of expertise and pragmatic concerns around resources and timelines that were externally imposed.

Our team was aware of the ongoing need to be sensitive to how considerations about "expertise" both facilitated and deterred the inclusion of all invested stakeholders. We believe that with the NPN staff members leading the CNA, our team's role as research experts only enhanced the process and did not diminish or undermine NPN staff participation in the research. It resulted in a process that drew on and potentiated the expertise of multiple stakeholders. However, beyond our relationship with NPN staff, one could argue that our practice was more limited and resembled traditional research despite attempts to integrate multiple stakeholders. Community residents and members of NPN partner organizations often played consultation roles and participated in very limited ways in the development and execution of the research. The focus groups and survey were traditional approaches to capture community voice, knowledge, and expertise but largely consigned these stakeholders to a more passive role in the research process. Although this reality diminished the ways in which the "community" participated in the research process, it served the goals of NPN staff and NPN partners and resulted in a successful CNA process overall.

Overcoming Institutional Barriers: Working in an Academic System

A central aspect of the CNA was the development and execution of the community survey. Several institutional obstacles were encountered during its completion. One key tension was adhering to IRB requirements while honoring the CBPR value of a community-driven, organic process. The role of IRB in the academy "is to make sure that all the necessary steps are taken to safeguard the privacy, confidentiality, rights, and privileges of those individuals who participate in and share information for the study" (Bronte-Tinkew, Allen, & Joyner, 2008, p. 1). Despite a good working relationship with the VU IRB, a number of procedural issues arose that had important consequences for the project timeline and potential opportunities for engagement of the community partners.

The first challenge involved how to "officially" include persons outside the university in the research process. The VU IRB requires all data collectors to complete a basic credential from the Collaborative Institutional Training Initiative (CITI). To begin training, individuals were required to have a VU electronic login. However, because the university research system is set up to include only university employees, it was necessary to work with administrators to create a temporary solution. The training process itself posed another challenge. The online CITI training module consists of a series of thematic subjects and reading of technical material and requires access to a computer and the Internet. These two requirements limited the potential pool of data collectors. Ultimately, we solicited data collectors from a number of sources, including VU graduate students in HOD and AmeriCorps volunteers from the MOBC. However, local residents were largely excluded from the data collector role, given the technical requirements and time commitment for training, effectively limiting opportunities for the full participation of community members in this phase of the research process. To meet this challenge of inclusion, we created a second role—survey volunteers—that allowed for more participation of residents and other NPN stakeholders without directly involving them in the data collection process. Volunteers accompanied data collectors into the field and often served as the "first knock," providing information about NPN and introducing the purpose of the survey. Multiple roles created an interesting paradox. Although the inclusion of volunteers offered increased opportunities for resident involvement, there was still a hierarchy among research teams. Data collectors were the only team members who could "officially" collect data, while volunteers were relegated to more administrative tasks, such as tracking paperwork. The volunteer and data collector worked as a team to create connections with the residents we sought to survey.

Another unanticipated obstacle was the lag time between when data collectors completed CITI training and when the credential was processed through the VU IRB system. An individual was ineligible to serve on a research team until both steps were complete, and in some cases was forced into volunteer roles until his or her paperwork was approved. Given the abbreviated timeline with which we were working to complete the community survey, this delay resulted in a loss of workforce during the first phase of data collection. Despite these frustrations, we were able to develop relationships within the VU IRB, which helped navigate obstacles as they arose and expedite the administrative process as our enumerators completed the training module. We also experienced a more fundamental tension in CBPR between balancing community needs and goals and those of academia. Conflicting timelines with community partners was the biggest challenge, given their narrow window of time to collect data to fulfill the requirements of the planning grant. As a result, members of the VU team faced the challenge of committing the time necessary to engage in CNA activities while fulfilling other aspects of their university roles, such as teaching and publishing. This led to long periods of time in which members of the VU team felt stretched in their ability to meet university responsibilities. The academic calendar also conflicted with the timeline that our community partner created. For example, the community survey was originally scheduled by MOBC to occur during VU's spring break; dates had to be shifted to accommodate students' time off. Overcoming these types of obstacles requires both flexibility and commitment to CBPR principles on the part of both university researchers and community partners.

Ensuring Rigor: Collecting Quality Data

From a CBPR perspective, an essential component of rigor is to ensure the engagement of community members from traditionally underrepresented populations throughout the research process (Benish-Weisman & Torre, 2010; Cahill, 2007). However, rigor is more closely associated with a set of "gold standard" methods, such as random sampling and randomization (Song & Herman, 2010). Although we sought to maximize both ideals of rigor, limited time and resources required a more pragmatic approach. We carefully weighed the often competing imperatives of the two ideals and sought to balance them in our decisions related to sampling strategy, choice of research personnel, and strategies for ensuring data quality. For example, when developing the sampling strategy, an overview of surveys conducted by other PNs indicated that a convenience sample was often the default. However, our NPN partners, in consultation with the VU research team, decided on a more rigorous strategy based on a stratified geographic sampling approach to provide information needed to inform implementation strategies, but the cost of adhering to random sampling at the household level was prohibitive in terms of both time and budget. Instead, we compromised by using random sampling at the block level. This decision allowed us to collect data within a four-week time period, remain within a limited budget, and collect a geographically representative sample.

A second aspect of rigor concerns data quality. We employed a two-part strategy to mitigate potential threats. First, to counter threats to reliability, all enumerators received training by the VU research team. During training, we discussed the purpose of the NPN, the role of the CNA, and the means by which data would be analyzed, interpreted, and included in future plans for the development of a NPN. During that session, all data collectors were introduced to the CNA survey to create familiarity with the document and the multiple formats in which questions were presented. With the exception of two exploratory questions, the survey consisted of closed-end responses (e.g., Likert scales), which simplified the data collectors' task. In addition to training, enumerators had access to members of the research team during the data collection process. A second part of the strategy included use of an electronic data collection system in which data collected on mobile devices were linked to Research Electronic Data Capture (REDCap), a web-based application for building and managing online surveys and databases. This approach helped eliminate data collection errors because it eliminated the conversion of the data from paper to an electronic database (Harris, Taylor, Thielke, Payne, Gonzalez, & Conde, 2009). Although the training and support system and the use of mobile devices to collect data mitigated threats to data quality, there was little we could do to monitor the process in the field and relied upon post facto audits to ensure data quality. Thus, to achieve rigor, as defined by both traditional and CBPR paradigms, additional steps were required to ensure data quality.

Fostering and Facilitating Collaborative Work

Although tensions can sometimes exist between academic and community partners, bridging the research-to-practice gap is most effectively done when authentic collaboration is achieved. In this chapter, we have described a case study and the resultant lessons learned when "doing" community-based research. The "Getting Started!" table provides supplementary guidance to readers who may be exploring projects that are inclusive of community members as co-researchers. The suggestions include instructions across the spectrum of teaching, research, and practice such that they may act as a framework for persons just getting started.

Chapter 6: Getting Started!
Conducting Research on Comprehensive Community Development Initiatives: Balancing Methodological Rigor and Community Responsiveness

---

Action Item 1: Engage in public and academic writing . . . hand-in-hand.
Scholars in the academy often feel the pressure of "publish or perish" and acutely understand how academic expectations around writing might be in contrast with those of our more community-oriented partners. However, we suggest working with community partners to produce dual products that address the same subjects—ones that can be published in a scholarly outlet (for example, a journal or as a book chapter) and ones that might be published in a more publicly accessible outlet (for example, a blog post, an editorial, or as a report). Engaging in research that has both academic and applied dimensions can serve to help meet personal and professional needs and objectives.

Action Item 2: Discuss the challenges of CBPR research in action-oriented classes and workshops.
In classes that are focused on CBPR or community-engaged research classes, be honest about the inherent challenges and tensions of community-based research. Devote a significant portion of class time to discussing the challenges with students in order to brainstorm possible solutions to increase the chance of a positive, productive experience.

Action Item 3: Seek multiple paths for expanding community participation.
Include community members as survey volunteers or create a community advisory committee to provide oversight of research activities. Include such partners at both the institutional (i.e., organizations) and individual level so there is authentic community participation regardless of the barriers presented.

(continued)

Chapter 6: Getting Started! (continued)

Action Item 4: *Compromise to meet both academic and community goals.*
Explicitly decide ahead of time, preferably during the research planning process, the expectations for all partners. If expectations diverge, make a commitment to compromise that could include utilizing alternative sampling procedures that meet both community and academic ideals about rigor or completing research activities on a schedule that works for academic and community schedules.

Action Item 5: *Address power dynamics head on.*
Avoid letting power dynamics seep into research activities by having unambiguous conversations with all partners about possibly unspoken research goals. Examples include having discussions up front about authorship (order of authorship, division of labor related to writing), the type of products to be developed, and who will tackle different tasks. Make lists, engage in dynamic writing (via interactive tools such as Google docs) and always keep lines of communication open.

Conclusion: The Dance of Collaborative Methods

Collaborative research that brings together university and community partners to engage in participatory research methods offers an exciting opportunity to actively engage social justice issues and create sustainable approaches to community change. Dewey (1916) envisaged individuals working collaboratively to solve problems via communities of social, participatory inquiry that included an understanding of the social context that surrounds any given issue. In creating dynamic partnerships between researchers, community organizations, and residents, action research methods seek to break down overarching power structures in academia through a jointly agreed upon research agenda. In the example presented in this chapter, we explored diverse tensions that result from attempts at collaboration with multiple community entities as well as opportunities and resources that may facilitate such partnerships. Throughout the collaborative process, it is important for all invested stakeholders to be aware of and honor the diverse roles and contributions of participating partners. "Community partners" can take many forms—from MOBC and NPN administrators to community residents—and there are important situational undercurrents that inform how and when different stakeholders are involved in the research process.

In this chapter, we reference a grant-driven university-community partnership to examine tensions surrounding definitions of "expertise," institutional academic barriers, and expectations of "scientific rigor." Through such results-based evaluation requirements, many third-party funders have emphasized the importance of community needs assessment and similar collaborative research activities, reinforcing the benefits of community-based research. Given the nature of this type of research, the principles of CBPR and PAR do not provide a set of clear instructions on how to proceed; rather, they offer important guidelines to help inform design and data collection. Without careful considerations about how to adapt the principles of participatory research to third-party funding requirements, resident involvement may become tokenistic as we perform research "on" rather than "with" them.

This case study highlights the challenges and possibilities of community-engaged research and makes a practical contribution to research practice. First, it speaks to the contextual realities that make it difficult to realize CBPR's ideal of full participation. In particular, our experience suggests that power differentials, such as those rooted in ethnicity, race, gender, and class, must be a central consideration for researchers who seek to foster authentic participation. In our research partnership, such explicit conversations were often overlooked because of restricted timelines, even though participation was a shared value among partners. Second, the case study demonstrates that participation of diverse stakeholders, even when it does not reflect the CBPR ideal, can benefit the research process and contribute to the community's social change agenda. We found that bringing together a diverse team that included community residents, professionals from local community organizations and schools, and university faculty and students broadened the pool of experts and contributed to collective learning and knowledge (Dewey, 1916). Specifically, the participation of diverse stakeholders in the CNA process facilitated our understanding of the community context in ways that would not have been revealed by analyzing secondary data alone. Through our interactions with our partners—community residents and NPN organizational members—we learned about the lived experiences of Cayce Homes residents, which informed our research practice. Based on this experience, we learned that when engaging stakeholders in the research process, it is essential to develop realistic avenues for participation that meet their needs, attend to their interests, and leverage their skills and expertise. We believe doing so is required to ensure that the right questions are posed, the data result in effective and culturally competent interventions, and power differentials between multiple partners do not derail the productivity of the collaboration.

Finally, our experience suggests that the process of securing partner buy-in, from both residents and affiliated organizations, at the most preliminary stages of a collaboration will likely be essential to its long-term success because such relationships will form the foundation of sustainable efforts at poverty alleviation and community-level change. For NPN, the CNA was the first visible step in this process. Moreover, the way that the CNA was developed, executed, and reported back to the community has lasting implications for the future of the initiative. In future collaborative endeavors, it is important to reflect intentionally and continuously on how, in our role as a university partner, we can either facilitate or hinder the expansion of traditional notions of rigor and the inclusion of multiple forms of expertise. We have the opportunity to learn from the major obstacles we encountered in these early stages to consider how to proceed to build greater levels of meaningful participation. The often conflicting demands of the institutional contexts in which university and community partners are embedded require a flexible, collaborative approach that seeks creative solutions to inevitable setbacks and remains focused on the shared goals and values for community change.

References

Al-Kodmany, K. (2002). GIS and the artist: Shaping the image of a neighbourhood through participatory environmental design. W. J. Craig, T. M. Hines, & D. Weiner (Eds.). *Community participation and geographic information systems* (pp. 320–29). London: Taylor and Francis.

Appadurai, A. (2006). The right to research. *Globalisation, Societies and Education, 4*, 167–77.

Arthur, M. W., & Blitz, C. (2000). Bridging the gap between science and practice in drug abuse prevention through needs assessment and strategic community planning. *Journal of Community Psychology, 28*(3), 241–55.

Benish-Weisman, M., & Torre, M. E. (2010). PAR on the couch: A discussion between disciplines. *International Review of Qualitative Research, 3*, 479–91.

Bess, K. D., Prilleltensky, I., Perkins, D. D., & Collins, L. V. (2009). Participatory organizational change in community-based health and human services: From tokenism to political engagement. *American Journal of Community Psychology, 43*(1–2), 134–48.

Bonilla-Silva, E. (2006). *Racism without racists: Color-blind racism and the persistence of racial inequality in the United States.* Lanham, MD: Rowman & Littlefield Publishers.

Billings, J. R., & Cowley, S. (1995). Approaches to community needs assessment: A literature review. *Journal of Advanced Nursing, 22*, 721–30.

Bronte-Tinkew, J., Allen, T., & Joyner, K. (2008). Institutional Review Boards (IRBs): What are they, and why are they important? Part 7 in a series on practical evaluation methods. Research-to-Results Brief. Publication# 2008–09.*Child Trends.*

Cahill, C. (2007). Repositioning ethical commitments: Participatory action research as a relational praxis of social change. *ACME: An International E-Journal for Critical Geographies, 6*(3), 360–73.

Cammarota, J., & Fine, M. (2008). Youth participatory action research: A pedagogy for transformational resistance. In J. Cammarota and M. Fine (Eds.), *Revolutionizing education: Youth participatory action research in motion.* New York: Routledge.

Chaskin, R. J. (2001). Building community capacity: A definitional framework and case studies from a comprehensive community initiative. *Urban Affairs Review, 36*, 291–323.

Craig, D. V. (2009). *Action research essentials.* San Francisco: Jossey-Bass.

Dewey, J. (1916). Democracy and education: An introduction to the philosophy of education. New York: Macmillan.

Duncan-Andrade, J. M. R., & Morrell, E. (2008). The art of critical pedagogy: Possibilities for moving from theory to practice in urban schools. New York: Peter Lang.

Fine, M. (2009). Postcards from metro America: Reflections on youth participatory action research for urban justice. *The Urban Review, 41*, 1–6.

Geller, J., Doykos, B., Craven, K., Bess, K., & Nation, M. (2014). Engaging residents in community change: The critical role of trust in the development of a Promise Neighborhood. *Teachers College Record.*

Hall, B. L. (1992). From margins to center? The development and purpose of participatory research. *The American Sociologist, 23*, 15–28.

Harris, P. A., Taylor, R., Thielke, R., Payne, J., Gonzalez, N., & Conde, J. G. (2009). Research electronic data capture (REDCap)—a metadata-driven methodology and workflow process for providing translational research informatics support. *Journal of Biomedical Informatics, 42*(2), 377–81.

Hesse-Biber, S., Leavy, P., & Yaiser, M. (2004). Approaches to research as a process: Reconceptualizing epistemology, methodology and method. In S. Hesse-Biber & M. Yaiser (Eds.), *Feminist Perspectives on Social Research.* UK: Oxford University Press.

Israel, B. A., Schulz, A. J., Parker, E. A., & Becker, A. B. (1998). Review of community-based research: assessing partnership approaches to improve public health. *Annual review of public health, 19*(1), 173–202.

Kidd, S. A., & Kral, M. J. (2005). Practicing participatory action research. *Journal of Counseling Psychology, 52,* 187–95.

Lentz, B. E., Imm, P. S., Yost, J. B., Johnson, N. P., Barron, C., Lindberg, M. S., & Treistman, J. (2005). Empowerment evaluation and organizational learning: A case study of a community coalition designed to prevent child abuse and neglect. In D. Fetterman & A. Wandersman (Eds.), Empowerment evaluation principles in practice (pp. 155–82). New York: Guilford.

Lipman, M. (2003). *Thinking in education.* (2nd ed.). Cambridge: Cambridge University Press.

Minkler, M., & Wallerstein, N. (Eds.). (2008). *Community-based participatory research for health.* San Francisco: Jossey-Bass.

Minkler, M., Blackwell, A. G., Thompson, M., & Tamir, H. (2003). Community-based participatory research: Implications for public health funding. *American Journal of Public Health, 93*(8), 1210–13.

Montenegro, M. (2002). Ideology and community social psychology: Theoretical considerations and practical implications. *American Journal of Community Psychology, 30,* 511–27.

Oakes, J., & Rogers, J. (2006). *Learning power: Social inquiry, grassroots organizing and educational justice.* New York: Teacher's College Press.

Reason, P., & Bradbury, H. (Eds.) (2006). Handbook of action research (concise paperback edition). London: Sage.

Rodriguez, L. F., & Brown, T. M. (2009). From voice to agency: Guiding principles for participatory action research with youth. *New Directions for Youth Development, 123,* 19–34.

Song, M., & Herman, R. (2010). Critical issues and common pitfalls in designing and conducting impact studies in education: Lessons learned from the What Works Clearinghouse (Phase 1). *Educational Evaluation and Policy Analysis, 32*(3), 351–71.

Stoecker, R. (1999). Are academics irrelevant? Roles for scholars in participatory research. *American Behavioral Scientist, 42,* 840–54.

Tennessee Department of Education. (2012). 2011 TCAP Results [Data File]. Retrieved from http://tn.gov/education/data/tcap_2011.shtml.

Warren, M., & Mapp, K. (2011). *A match on dry grass: Community organizing as a catalyst for school reform.* London: Oxford University Press.

Watts, R. J., Williams, N. C., & Jagers, R. J. (2003). Sociopolitical development. *American Journal of Community Psychology, 31,* 185–94.

Wilson, P.A. (1997). Building social capital: A learning agenda for the twenty-first century. *Urban Studies, 34*(5–6), 745–60.

Part III: Academic Structures That Foster Synergy, Collaboration, and Courses

Adopting and adapting Dewey's approach to lifelong learning described in Part I of this volume as well as performing the type of university-community engagement work detailed in Part II would not be possible without institutional and departmental structures and processes undergirding such efforts. Part III of this text focuses on this topic. Just as each chapter in this volume was made possible only through collaboration between faculty, students, and community partners across a variety of disciplines, action-oriented academic work is only possible when a myriad of individual, groups, processes, courses, programs, and resources are strategically aligned to make it happen. Departmental ideas and theoretical frames must be systematized and organized to ensure appropriate usage. Instead of merely transmitting knowledge through methods such as lectures, constructivist learning is espoused and encouraged in HOD to challenge students to concertedly participate as active members of the teaching/learning process. This approach does not imply that teachers do not have expertise to impart but rather that exchange, active dialogue, and participatory learning tend to be more effective classroom models than those provided by "traditional teaching" (Dewey, 1916, 1925/1958, 1938; von Glaserfeld, 1995).

Faculty are encouraged to promote experiential learning through cooperative problem solving groups that students can then use in their everyday professional and personal lives throughout the life course. HOD is presented as one possible model. Cumulatively, the authors do not suggest that this model is the only approach to accomplish action-oriented instruction. Instead, the templates presented in the four chapters of this section reflect one model to consider. Readers are also encouraged to contemplate whether and how dynamics in HOD could be selected and replicated in their specific environments as well as the types of human, economic, and/or structural resources required to accomplish such a goal. Like Dewey

(1916, 1938, 1939), the authors in this section describe some of the "how tos" associated with bringing about educational reform across institutions of higher education and its correlates to subsequent community reform.

In Chapter 7, "The Field School in Intercultural Education as a Model for International Service-Learning and Collaborative Action-Research Training," the field school experience is presented as a model that combines intellectual training and service learning in culturally diverse spaces. The chapter describes three structured programs of intercultural immersion in New Mexico; Guangxi Zhuang, China; and Cape Town, South Africa, as well as the civic engagement, student professional development, community improvements, and personal learning that resulted. Following Dewey's (1916) ideals of democratic, participatory education, the chapter details the people, processes, and programs at each site; university-community partnerships that necessitated each experience; expectations, outcomes, cultural challenges, and student experiences; and strategies to implement and sustain such endeavors for interested readers. Moreover, the chapter illustrates how useful knowledge can be created in real time that results in capacity building for both students and community members.

Chapter 8, "Creating a Mosaic of Religious Values and Narratives: Participant-Researcher Roles of an Interfaith Research Group Seeking to Understand Interfaith Organizations," considers a specific area of inquiry, religion, from which reflexive inquiry can occur. Interfaith practices and conflict provide a contemporary context to assess how academicians can transform themselves as they strive to eliminate religious intolerance. Although constructionist work broadly discusses the potential influence of religion, this chapter extends Dewey by focusing on inter-group dynamics for Christians, Muslims, and individuals who are religiously neutral (Ariyanto, Hornsey, & Gallois, 2009). The Vanderbilt University Interfaith Project is presented as an action research project to systematically examine inter- and intra-group religiosity and improve interfaith relationships through consensus-building communication, cooperative problem solving, and grassroots engagement. Activities, reflections, strategies, and the various forms of knowledge that emerged illustrate the benefits and problems associated with building community across differences.

The HOD internship experiences are considered mainstay models of academic structures informed by a constructivist approach (Dewey, 1916,

1938, 1939; von Glaserfeld, 1995). Chapter 9, "Internship: Situated Learning in the Department of Human and Organizational Development," describes the overall ideology, key processes, and courses for the HDC graduate counseling and HOD undergraduate capstone internships. Other chapters in this section document the beneficence of HOD programs as exemplars of university-community partnerships. This chapter is unique as an example of how HOD impacts the professional and personal lives of undergraduate and master's students and the organizations in which they intern. Both programs are informed by experiential learning, situated learning, and reflective practice to build capacity among undergraduates, in general, and graduate students pursuing careers in counseling, in particular. The chapter also provides real-world examples, course descriptions, administrative processes, and alumni comments about the useful knowledge they acquired as interns.

Chapter 10, the final work of the volume, focuses on the two graduate professional programs in HOD, Community Development and Action (CDA) and Human Development Counseling (HDC). In "Can Synergy Across Theory, Pedagogy, and Practice Guide Professional Education?" the authors illustrate how both HDC and CDA intentionally and strategically cultivate teaching, learning, and active dialogue between academe and non-academic organizations. Their emphasis on both human and professional development, informed by scholars such as Dewey (1897/2010, 1896, 1908) and Kohlberg (1972, 1975), provide students with the knowledge, practical skills, and the reflexive ability to actively participate in individual, group, and community change. Whether emphasizing counseling skills or community empowerment, both programs charge students as burgeoning practitioners to identity and hone personal strengths via a constructivist approach to learning. Experiential learning and interdisciplinary teaching are also key such that students are trained to work in conjunction with other individuals and groups to solve real-world problems. Such professional development provides students with a bevy of skills and expertise to understand and negotiate various contexts as practitioners. In addition to program descriptions, the chapter includes suggestions to incorporate aspects of both programs in existing departments and how to develop such programs.

Although each chapter in Part III addresses distinct structural dynamics in HOD that prepare students to solve problems for the common good, together they suggest that individuals have the unique ability to understand and address their own problems and self-improve—and in doing so, transform their environments. The departmental processes and structures help facilitate this knowledge and corresponding acumen among students that they can subsequently share with society members they serve. The four chapters also challenge readers to become reflexive practitioners and to thoughtfully integrate these practices in every dimension of their lives.

References

Ariyanto, A., Hornsey, M. J., & Gallois, C. (2009). Intergroup attribution bias in the context of extreme intergroup conflict. *Asian Journal of Social Psychology, 12*(4), 293–99.

Dewey, J. (1896). The reflex arc concept in psychology. *The Psychological Review, 3*(4), 358–70.

Dewey, J. (1897/2010). My pedagogic creed. In K. Ryan, J. M. Cooper, & J. M. Cooper (Eds.), *Kaleidoscope: Contemporary and classic readings in education* (pp. 215–21). Belmont, CA: Wadsworth, Cengage Learning.

Dewey, J. (1916). *Democracy and education*. New York: Simon & Schuster.

Dewey, J. (1925/1958). *Experience and nature*. New York: Dover.

Dewey, J. (1938). *Education and experience*. New York: Touchstone, Simon & Schuster.

Dewey, J. (1939). "Creative democracy—The task before us." (Cited in Fielding, M., & Moss, P. (2012) *Radical democratic education*. Presentation at the American Sociological Association, August 17, 2012, Denver, CO.)

Dewey, J., & Tufts, J. H. (1908). *Ethics*. New York: Holt.

Kohlberg, L. (1975). The Just Community School: The theory and the Cambridge Cluster School experiment. In *Collected papers from the Center for Moral Education*. (Chapter 29, pp. 1–77). (ERIC Document Reproduction Service No. ED 223 511).

Kohlberg, L., & Mayer, R. (1972). Development as the aim of education. *Harvard Educational Review, 42*(4), 449–96.

von Glaserfeld, E. (1995). *Radical constructivism: A way of knowing and learning*. London: Falmer.

7 The Field School in Intercultural Education as a Model for International Service-Learning and Collaborative Action-Research Training

HOLLY L. KARAKOS, BENJAMIN W. FISHER, JOANNA GELLER, LAUREL LUNN, NEAL A. PALMER, DOUGLAS D. PERKINS, NIKOLAY MIHAYLOV, WILLIAM L. PARTRIDGE, AND SHARON SHIELDS

Democracy means the belief that humanistic culture should prevail.
—John Dewey, 1938

No culture can live if it attempts to be exclusive.
—Mahatma Gandhi, 1936

The Department of Human and Organizational Development (HOD) recognizes that many of its students need to develop skills that will allow them to successfully navigate research and/or practice across cultures.[1] Our attempt to train students and utilize our core principles to address social concerns around the globe takes the form of an experiential learning model we have termed the "Field School in Intercultural Education." Previous HOD field schools have taken place in Ecuador, Argentina, China, the southwestern United States, and South Africa. Although the potential benefits of such work are vast, so too are the risks of reinforcing stereotypes of the "other" and exacerbating historical patterns of paternalistic and unsustainable international development. In this

---

1. This chapter reflects the efforts of a first author (Karakos), a team of second authors (Fisher, Geller, Lunn, Palmer, and Perkins), and a team of third authors (Mihaylov, Partridge, and Shields). Each person contributed equally within his or her respective group. Names are listed in alphabetical order within each group.

chapter, we describe the field school program, including its theoretical foundations and history, and the experiences of community partners and student participants, comparing experiences across settings and expanding on themes that have been observed consistently. Throughout our discussion, we address the complexities of simultaneously meeting the personal and professional needs of students while working with communities in ways that align with the ideals of empowerment, reciprocity, intercultural respect and learning, participatory research, and sustainability.

Design of the Field School in Intercultural Education

The concept of a "field school" in which students engage in "hands-on" learning at a site beyond the bounds of the classroom or university campus is not new.[2] Field school programs are designed to provide students with experience and skills relevant to their chosen disciplines, research topics, or professional practices; they are opportunities to apply academic concepts to a "real-world" setting. The practice of the HOD field school provides an illustrative case study to consider some of its challenges and complexities.

Former Vanderbilt Professor William Partridge designed the HOD field school to work toward specific goals aligned with the department's mission, focusing on the integration of research and action around social justice issues. In much of the world, poverty and oppression prevent people from participating in their country's or community's development as a result of their exclusion from educational opportunities, systems of justice, security of person and property, health services, financial institutions, and political representation (Partridge & Mejia, 2013). The field school provides students with opportunities to empirically investigate the obstacles that poor and socially excluded people must face to access the major institutions of society while working with community partners to develop the needed resources to sustain independent efforts to minimize or eliminate those obstacles. Our conviction is that immersing students in communities will facilitate a systematic understanding of how such obstacles

2. The work described in this chapter was funded in part by a U.S. Department of Education Fulbright-Hays Group Project Abroad award #P021A110033 and in part by Peabody College of Education and Human Development, Vanderbilt University.

often operate in people's lives and enable students to better understand how to devise projects, programs, and policies that can include the excluded. Although this vision cannot always be fully realized, each successive field school strives toward immersion, investigation, and action with the overarching goal of working toward a socially just world.

Although HOD field schools have differed over the years, they generally take the form of a supervised, collaborative research project conducted in a less-developed country or area of the United States for a period of six to twelve weeks. Participating students, supervising faculty, and host community partners discuss potential projects identified by the partners and choose those that show the most promise of: (1) addressing a pressing social issue and need as defined by the community; (2) being manageable in the timeframe of the field school; (3) matching the interests of student participants; (4) using existing skills and knowledge of participants; and (5) developing new skills and knowledge for students and community partners. Participants work in teams with community members and academic partners from host countries to implement service-learning projects to develop or improve social programs, or engage in primary data collection, refining skills such as participant observation, focus group management, survey administration, and preliminary data analysis. The experience is designed for students from masters and doctoral programs but can accommodate advanced undergraduates. When and where a field school is offered depends on funding sources and the availability of community partners in the host site. Students must complete at least two semesters of relevant course work, often including material about the host country and issues relevant to the partner communities. The field school also provides students with academic course credit and may count toward other program requirements such as practicum hours. Student admission to the field school is competitive and based on fit with field school needs and goals.

Although the field school bears some similarity to traditional study abroad programs, it is distinct in a number of ways. One distinction is its emphasis on development of both the university students and the community partner (versus solely the education of university students). Another is its emphasis on both research and action. Unlike study abroad, in which individual students may travel, enroll, and study on their own, collaborative team-based projects are a critical part of the HOD field school.

Moreover, study abroad programs are typically administered through agreements between U.S. colleges, host universities in a foreign country, and sometimes third-party sponsors; thus, students' experiences are largely defined by the administrative and academic routines of partnering institutions. In contrast, the HOD field school program varies annually and site-to-site depending on the specific interests and connections of supervising faculty, students, local partners, and funding sources. Thus, the field school program is distinct from study abroad programs and the HOD field school meets particular departmental goals.

Theoretical Foundations of the Field School

It is useful to preface our discussion of specific field school examples with the theoretical lens that frames them. Here, we consider civic education and service-learning—including the potential for extending Dewey's (1916) ideas on the role of education in democratic civic learning and engagement not only into the twenty-first century but internationally, international development and collaboration, participatory research, learning theory, cross-cultural adjustment and communication, and international education and study abroad programs (Crabtree, 2008). Key questions raised by each of these literatures are displayed in Table 7-1. Together, they address both student and community outcomes of international service-learning (ISL). Although the field school has a greater focus on research than most traditional service-learning experiences, the ISL literature aligns closely with our work. Consistent with the HOD department's ethos, Crabtree's (2008) framing of ISL reflects a transdisciplinary approach, in which scholars bring different disciplines together to jointly create new theories, methods, or applications, to understanding effective ISL and considers outcomes at multiple ecological levels (Christens & Perkins, 2008).

The recent proliferation of service-learning on university campuses likely results from increased public demand for institutions of higher education to serve the public good (Burkhardt & Merisotis, 2006; Combs & Schmidt, 2013) and the accumulation of research demonstrating the academic, social, and civic benefits of experiential learning (Eyler & Giles, 1999). However, service-learning without adequate preparation, critical reflection, and strong community input can reinforce existing stereotypes and further divide universities and communities. According to Crabtree

Table 7-1. Key Literatures and Questions to Consider Within International Service-Learning Programs

Literature	Key Questions
Civic education and service-learning	To what extent do communities benefit from service-learning? What are the long-term student and community impacts of service-learning?
Development and collaboration	To what extent does ISL address root causes of social problems? To what extent do communities participate in project design, implementation, and assessment?
Participatory research	How can communities be involved in all stages of the research process? How does participatory research improve both student and community outcomes?
Learning theory	How does experiential learning influence students differently from traditional classroom learning? What is the role of critical reflection in transformational learning?
Cross-cultural adjustment and communication	How do cross-cultural experiences influence students? What factors facilitate such positive impacts?
International education and study abroad	How has globalization impacted the ability of students to immerse themselves fully in another culture?

(2008), this risk is exacerbated in international contexts, where students may be unprepared for comprehending vast social inequities and understanding different cultural norms and practices. Further, prior experiences with externally driven development may predispose communities to regard foreign students with elevated skepticism or optimism. This risk is exacerbated when possibilities for a sustainable university-community relationship are limited by time and distance. Crabtree's (2008) research focuses on the experiences of undergraduate students (or younger). Our work extends previous research by describing the unique advantages and challenges of engaging graduate students in such work.

Literature suggests that student and community outcomes should be synergistic. When students benefit, so too should communities, and vice versa. Service-learning literature typically positions student- and community-level outcomes as competing interests, perhaps because institutions of higher education are focused on student learning (Cruz & Giles, 2000). Crabtree (2008) states, "attention to community-level concerns is underwhelming at best" (p. 23). She suggests principles from participatory action research (PAR) and feminist research may guide ISL. Both PAR and feminist research stress that researchers must consider their positions of power, avoid conducting research that reproduces patterns of social injustice, and most importantly, collaborate with communities during all stages of the research process. The strong, trusting, reciprocal relationships that result will often benefit communities and enhance the transformational learning experiences of students. This same scholar offers three questions that have guided her own experience with ISL and bear directly on our experiences with HOD field schools. How do ISL and field school programs: (1) balance student learning with community improvement, working toward "sustainable improvements and meaningful social change," (2) empower all participants, neither "reinforcing nor exacerbating the social distance among them," and (3) avoid becoming paralyzed by social problems that seem too vast and overwhelming to address responsibly in a short period of time (p. 29). These questions raise important issues that have emerged in nearly every HOD field school. The reader is challenged to bear these questions in mind and join us in working to meaningfully explore them.

History of HOD Field Schools

Professor William Partridge organized the first three field schools during the summers of 2003, 2004, and 2005 in the Ecuadorian cities of Riobamba, San Lorenzo, and Otavalo among Quichua and Afro-Ecuadorian peoples. They centered on the impacts of programs aimed at building human and social capital in minority communities through grants provided to bright but poor young people to finish high school, university, or postgraduate studies. Funders included Vanderbilt's Peabody College of Education and Human Development (2003–2007) and the Research Institute for the Study of Man in New York (2004–2005). Professor Isaac Prilleltensky led a field school in Buenos Aires in 2006, focusing on poverty in "villas miserias," or "misery villages" as they are known in Argentina.

Students partnered with governmental and local grass roots organizations to understand residents' challenges and contribute to community organizing.

Professor Douglas Perkins organized the 2007 field school in Guangxi Zhuang Autonomous Region, an interior area of southern China with a large ethnic minority population. Chinese university students and faculty worked with eleven Vanderbilt students to design and implement four projects local organizations needed and welcomed. In one project, students and a local hospital and center for disease control collected data on the changing dietary habits of youth and associated health trends. A second project identified educational resource and quality disparities in rural versus urban schools and assisted English language instruction. Community needs and assets assessments were also conducted in a small city near Vietnam and in a poor rural area (Robinson & Perkins, 2009).

In 2009, Professor Sharon Shields spearheaded student research in a poor geographically isolated community in New Mexico to identify and enhance community resources for healthy living, healthy dietary options, and physical activity. Students and community partners from a local private hospital collected community data; students then analyzed the data and presented it to a community advisory board. This endeavor was not explicitly envisioned as a field school, and did not engage with community partners until after the identification of the research topic and study design. Instead, it emerged out of an 11-year relationship built on research, training, and service exchanges with the University of New Mexico–Gallup that facilitated a partnership with local residents. The experience reflected many field school features that are relevant here.

In 2012, Professors Douglas Perkins, Maury Nation, and Gina Frieden obtained a grant from the U.S. Department of Education Fulbright-Hays Group Projects Abroad program (along with the U.S. Agency for International Development, an excellent potential source for supporting international service-learning) to support a summer field school in Cape Town, South Africa, including educational tours of Durban, Johannesburg, and Pretoria. Participants included fifteen students from all three HOD graduate programs and two South African graduate students. Each of the three main projects included a team of students from multiple programs working in a low-income neighborhood. One team studied high school dropout dynamics in partnership with school stakeholders. Another project focused on professional development for primary school teachers and the creation of a program to foster students' social and emotional learning. The third assessed treatment adherence and stressful life events among individuals with HIV/AIDS at a local clinic. In all three projects, students provided suggestions and tools for community partners to continue the work after they left. The brief field time and ambitious goals created an intense experience as well as a wealth of lessons learned—both successes and challenges. We now discuss the experiences of community partners and student participants based on the three most recent HOD field schools in China, New Mexico, and South Africa.

Community Partners' Experiences

Each field school comprises primarily two groups: participating students and local community partners. The following sections describe the nature of the relationships cultivated with community partners, challenges managing expectations, issues around work and relationship sustainability, use of community-based participatory research methods, and challenges inherent to cultural outsiders working with local communities.

University-Community Partnerships

In each field school, the various types of partners and relationships reflect responsiveness to local settings. Community partners contributed in varying ways. Some provided local legitimacy needed for project success; others connected the university with additional partners; others helped recruit research participants; and still others worked directly with the research team during data collection and analyses. Despite efforts by field school participants and organizers toward flexibility and responsiveness to community needs and preferences, tensions between university and community partners are common. Differing expectations have been a common source of misunderstanding. Another source of possible tension arises when more than two parties are involved; other academic partners, local NGOs (non-governmental organizations), or a number of other groups might also be working with the local community around the relevant issue. For example, in New Mexico, three universities had partnered together and the inter-group values and expectations differed greatly. The number of involved parties put additional strain on the community partner to interpret inter-organizational dynamics and to reconcile the sometimes-conflicting messages from the different institutions.

The limited resources—especially time—of the local community partners can also challenge relationship building. Field school participants must endeavor to create maximally beneficial and minimally taxing opportunities for community partnerships. Such efforts must happen alongside strategies to maximize project ownership and participation by community partners. However, this balancing act can take a toll on field school participants. When soliciting approval from community agents and officials to ensure project ownership, field school participants may be unsure of how to proceed when approval is not granted or when community partners and field school participants have different priorities. For example, local officials in China blocked a rural needs assessment project and delayed an urban needs assessment project for fear of criticism and emboldening Chinese students and citizens. In New Mexico, offers from local officials to promote the project were not realized. In South Africa, some meetings with local NGO representatives were slow to materialize, possibly as a result of field school participants' arrival when many locals were traveling. In each case, field school participants lacked full understanding of the context that might have allowed them to anticipate and navigate these complications to maximize community partners' contributions. Although developing relationships is challenging, the potential benefits for both parties far outweigh the work required to overcome the challenges.

Managing Expectations

Differing inter-group expectations are a common source of misunderstanding that can create disappointment or frustration for one or both groups. For community partners, the field school is often their first opportunity to work on a research project, and members may be unclear about what this work entails, their role, and the anticipated outcomes. This misunderstanding might result in part from field school participants failing to communicate expectations to the community or naïveté about the realities of how this work might progress (for example, slower than expected, less popular than hoped). Fieldwork can be an unpredictable endeavor, and expectations from both sides must be continually renegotiated. Thus, successful partnerships require honest and open communication throughout all project stages. Managing expectations presented a major challenge in the China field school as last-minute changes required significant restructuring. Although the public health and schools projects went smoothly, the two remaining projects, assessing urban and rural community needs and assets, were considered potentially sensitive or embarrassing by local Communist Party officials in the university and city government who were not accustomed to international collaboration (Robinson & Perkins, 2009). Thus, the urban project had to change partners in the final weeks of the field school to another university and city that welcomed the project and foreign collaboration. Selecting local partners with more international experience and more local political clout could have helped avoid many barriers and improve community participation. Unfortunately, the rural project did not receive local approval until it was too late for completion, forcing students to switch to a less controversial project. The ability to be flexible in response to changing circumstances is essential to successful field school experiences.

In New Mexico, community partners initially expressed confusion over specific, concrete project deliverables after idealistic visions of the partnership during the planning phase had dissipated. Nearing the end of data collection, community members remained uncertain about whether the project had been worth their investment. Several months after completion, they acknowledged the project's usefulness for bringing together relevant stakeholders in addressing community needs because advisory groups formed as a result of the project continued to function independently. According to one community partner during post–field school interviews:

> I might even be so bold to say that the real failure or success of this past research project is coming up. [. . .] If some significant things happen over the next year, then I would consider this research project very successful. But right now, I can't tell.

Although primary project goals were not achieved, the community partners had flexible expectations. Communicating about expectations and progress helped achieve feelings of some level of project success because all parties appreciated the final outcome and were not surprised by the progress made during the field school.

Additionally, field school participants working at a local high school in South Africa worked continually to manage expectations with the school principal, teachers, coaches, local police, and other key community stakeholders. Because these stakeholders frequently met and established a clear idea of desired project deliverables, they opened lines of communication (for example, group meetings about progress and next steps). Although expected outcomes shifted, from developing a dropout prevention program to providing tools to continually address this issue as a community, effective communication meant that all partners seemed pleased with the resulting products. One community stakeholder working in the high school reported in a post–field school interview:

> The very fact that the (field school students) have been here and the processes that (were) facilitated—all the workshops and the interviews—have been such an eye-opener for me . . . because it has woken me up to the fact that . . . there needs to be a process, it needs to have structure. It's been hugely helpful, absolutely.

Expectations are almost certain to change throughout the field school. Communicating frequently and honestly about whether and how expectations align with outcomes is key.

Sustainability

It is important to intentionally provide mechanisms to maintain relationships over time such that interested community partners can continue field school work after participants depart. The challenges, opportunities, and success of such efforts have varied. Many field schools adopted a model in which community representatives are designated as liaisons between the university and community partners. Such persons typically work in other full-time capacities; thus their time and resources are already potentially strained, making sustainability of this new role difficult. For example, in the New Mexico project, an effort to promote long-term sustainability was made by designating half of the grant funding to the community partner, offsetting some of the financial burden that participation could entail. However, this mechanism did not result in a reduced workload for the primary community partner because the funding was not used for staffing but rather for anticipated future intervention costs and for other project-related costs that the grant did not anticipate. Academic partners recognized the heavy burden of the project on the community partner and attempted to minimize the time she had to spend in meetings and preparation. In retrospect, this strategy actually resulted in increased project ambiguity and disconnect, thus diminishing its sustainability over time. Thus, efforts to be sensitive to time and financial resources inadvertently caused neglect of an important dimension of fieldwork—community buy-in.

Participants in the South African field school began with the understanding that there was no sustainable source of funding for their work. Therefore, they included activities to facilitate organizational capacity building to maximize impact and project sustainability. One way sustainability was accomplished was by training community members. For example, at a township primary school, field school participants provided staff training in classroom discipline and stress management, and student training in conflict resolution and positive communication. Another student, placed at an NGO in the same township, trained parents to better understand healthy childhood development and parenting practices. At another site, field school participants created a survey and implemented a tracking system to monitor high school dropout rates that staff members could continue to use to gather new information about student risk and protective factors. Similarly, during two projects in China, sustainability was promoted by providing local partners with empirical data to inform health promotion and community development decisions in addition to teaching applied research skills so they could continue to collect new data over time. Teaching research and application skills and knowledge to community partners is one way field school participants have helped build sustainability. Project sustainability and partnerships can extend beyond the field school. For example, in South Africa, field school participants ensured that community partners were able to contact them post-project through email, phone, and GoogleDocs. Although partners demonstrated the skills and resources to utilize these tools, subsequent communication was not as frequent or substantive as participants and partners had hoped. Creative uses of time during field schools and technology afterward have enabled some degree of sustainability, although there is still much opportunity for improvement.

Community-Based Participatory Methods

Community-based participatory research (CBPR) methods align closely with the HOD ethos, combining research and service for social change (Mosavel, Simon, van Stade, & Buchbinder, 2005). One of the strengths of the South African field school was the use of CBPR methods. Participants studied potential partner schools and organizations prior to the field school. Yet final partners were selected and projects developed on-site in collaboration with community organizations. During an initial site visit, community stakeholders identified their top priority as understanding the school's high dropout rate in order to develop prevention programs. Receiving the invitation to collaborate directly from the school was an important step for at least two reasons. First, it meant that the field school group was working at the request of the community rather than imposing itself in a well-intentioned but paternalistic way. Second, it granted the field school participants access to teachers, administrators, staff, students, and community partners in a way that would not have been possible without their invitation.

After the invitation, field school participants spent time in conversation with interested stakeholders (e.g., teachers, students). Community members influenced the final products. For example, school personnel wanted to be able to track students as they progressed through high school to assess various factors potentially related to dropout. In response, participants developed a student survey and an associated web-based spreadsheet wherein information could be collected, recorded, and used by staff. Drafting the survey was an iterative process during which school staff provided feedback about wording and content. After agreeing on a final version, school members were trained to administer the survey and record the data in a format that would enable them to continue post–field school. Thus, CBPR methods facilitated an experience that was beneficial for all invested parties.

Although utilization of CBPR methods confers many benefits, this approach also presents some challenges. For example, waiting until after the start of the field school to meet and choose partners, observe settings, and plan projects leaves less time to carry out actual project work. To offset this potential problem in China, faculty and graduate students identified potential partners prior to the start of the field school and used a semester-long preparatory course to communicate with them and collaboratively plan projects via email and Skype. The study of changing youth diet and health outcomes, the most successful of the four projects in China, would not have been feasible if students had not had time to prepare and plan collaboratively with local partners in advance. Although full implementation of CBPR methods was the goal in each project, they were implemented to varying degrees based on available resources to community partners and field school participants as well as the level of group trust.

Challenges of Being Cultural Outsiders

By definition, field school participants are outsiders in their host community. This creates unique challenges for both groups (Chawla-Duggan, 2007; Young, 2005). For many community partners, the field school might be their first experience working intensively with university members who have substantial academic training but little applied community work experience. This type of interaction can easily lend itself to undesirable power differentials, especially if communication has not been honest and frequent and if community partners are unsure about expectations (Merriam et al., 2001). Some community members may also be uncomfortable with or unaccustomed to serving as community representatives. Underlying suspicion or distrust may be especially acute in communities that have participated in research projects with little benefit to them (Smith-Morris, 2007). Moreover, as cultural "outsiders" researchers may not understand the complex dynamics that operate in the community and are necessary for successful work there (Mosavel, Simon, van Stade, & Buchbinder, 2005). Pre-trip orientation to the culture and history of the site is crucial. Furthermore, the definition of project "success" may be ambiguous and the practical implications from data analyses may be unclear. One community partner from the New Mexico site revealed his concern:

> I don't think the advisory council members really understood what the implications of this research study would be. Even now, I'm not quite sure what all this means, all this data means, or what we can do with it, or what kind of policy steps we can take.

Assumptions about differing amounts of inter-group knowledge often pose challenges. Developing relationships among cultural insiders and outsiders requires careful consideration of inter-group assumptions and requires varied approaches for developing and fostering communication (Maeda, 2011). Field school participants must also remember that community partners are experts and provide invaluable information about local context. Honoring inter-group expertise is one approach to reduce power differentials between field school participants and community partners, minimize ethnocentrism, and increase cultural appreciation.

The group in South Africa bridged this gap by developing relationships with community stakeholders before fully delving into project work as well as by listening more than talking. In one community meeting, a South African pointedly asked field school participants, "Where are the coloured researchers?" Although he eventually became a key ally in supporting the project, his remark reminds us of the importance of a racially, ethnically, and culturally diverse field school team and the limitations of our team's profile and skill set in this regard. By talking directly about obvious cultural gaps, this community partner pushed the group to more open communication and greater willingness to discuss difficult topics, which helped navigate the challenges of collaborative work between cultural insiders and outsiders. Thus cultural differences present challenges but also rich opportunities for learning (Chawla-Duggan, 2007).

Student Participants' Experiences

Educators must understand how to prepare students for the field school program, manage their expectations throughout the process, and facilitate formative learning experiences. Understanding diverse student profiles can lead to an understanding of how field schools can best develop culturally responsive, committed, and highly skilled researchers and practitioners.

Preparing, Planning, and Reflecting: Cultivating Student Buy-In

The field school is designed to involve students of varying academic and professional backgrounds. It is often the first exposure some students have to poverty, community tensions, and cultural diversity. Moreover, their shocked reactions often occur in recognition of their own middle- and upper-class privilege as they examine for the first time how their own experiences and beliefs about other groups are vastly different from reality. Such experiences often lead to questions about their own communities, values, and careers. To prepare them for this intense, potentially jarring experience, field school participants are generally required to complete specific coursework. For example, before the South Africa field school, participants were required to take an intensive three-week course about the history and current cultural climate of South Africa, as well as research topics of personal interest such as HIV interventions or youth activism in impoverished communities. Although this preparation was valuable, post–field school discussions suggested the value of holding the preparatory course on site with instruction by local experts and professionals. For example, a local South African tour was an invaluable resource. The combination of localized knowledge with direct experience and cultural immersion provided an educational lesson that would be impossible to deliver remotely. In addition to context-specific education, general courses about cultural understanding and communication can provide essential training for students prior to a culturally immersive experience (for example, Schmidt & Finkbeiner, 2006).

Student schedules present another challenge to proper preparation, particularly when they are traveling to the field school from other research or project sites. This can lead to a significant gap between the preparatory course and field site arrival. In contrast, a tight timeline between preparatory course completion and the beginning of field school can make sufficient pre-field school reflection a challenge. Making time for reflection on-site can also be difficult based on time constraints. In addition, graduate students who are accustomed to more autonomy than undergraduate students may be resistant to having group reflection times dictated during their "free time." Despite field school organizers' best efforts, missed opportunities to provide preparation, planning, and reflection can be detrimental to student experiences. Time for these pre- and post- reflection activities must be prioritized to cultivate buy-in by all involved.

Managing Expectations

Student expectations around personal experiences, project work, and on-site work must be managed. Despite warnings that they were entering an unpredictable space where navigating cultural differences and negotiating the barriers of local political systems were expected, several students were repeatedly frustrated by the realities they experienced. Field school participants' flexibility and responsiveness are critical in fostering community partners' involvement in and ownership of work. This flexibility can limit the formation of clearly defined roles and expectations. Communication with students about the changing nature of a project and expectations can alleviate some of the problem; in some cases, it may not be apparent to leaders that students have disparate expectations about roles and responsibilities. For example, the New Mexico project could be more accurately described as a field *experience*—as opposed to a field *school*—because it did not emphasize student learning or devote substantial attention to student needs. Instead, the project largely involved students as study personnel in a community field setting. Many students expected more time and attention from faculty, diverse learning experiences in the field, and more direct contact with community members. The contrast of these expectations with the project reality led to disappointment and unmotivated students.

In South Africa, master's and doctoral-level students had different interests. Some students wanted practical experience and others wanted research experience. Having multiple projects with flexibility to match student interests and skills enabled community members to take full advantage of students' abilities during projects and enabled students to satisfy their own personal and professional goals. Several students were able to work directly with South African youth, teachers, and parents while others were able to conduct research in partnership with local organizations. Unfortunately, the time required to facilitate such meetings reduced student work time with community partners. Several other timing constraints in South Africa limited reflection periods during which tensions about the field school's work/immersion balance and student expectations could have possibly been addressed.

Student followup after program completion often presents an additional challenge. Meaning-making often occurs well beyond the end of field school, especially given the short timeline for the experience. Students commonly question what it means to exit their field sites, return to their community of relative privilege, and leave the host community perhaps as it had been before. A student from the New Mexico project notes:

> We don't know what the impact of our research has been, and I think that's kind of unfortunate, not just because you want to help the population, but also, as a researcher you want to feel that the work that you did and the effort that you put in and the commitment you made was for a good purpose . . . [It's not] that I'm saying nothing has happened, but it just hasn't been very transparent.

Initial preparation as well as discussion and reflection throughout and at the close of the project assists students in assessing the totality of their experiences and making meaning from them. Yet the task of reflection can be difficult. For example, in South Africa, students left the country at varying times—rendering post–field school reflections logistically impossible. Time for this had not been planned and protected in advance. Meeting all participants' expectations is an impossible task. The goal is to manage expectations, which can be accomplished through open, honest communication and continual dialogue among all parties. In addition, preparatory courses, student flexibility, post-reflection sessions, and debriefing sessions throughout the field school are important tools in managing student expectations.

Working with Academic Partners

Field schools are designed to involve a partner academic institution at the host location. This partnership enables students from a local university together with U.S.-based students to further mutual learning opportunities. Inclusion of local students has had varying degrees of success in the field schools. The China field school would not have been possible without close collaboration of local faculty and students. They facilitated agenda development, located housing for field school participants, identified partners, negotiated entrée, contributed to the design of projects and collection of data, and served as translators. In contrast, the South Africa field school did not involve a formal academic partner but included two local students who contributed significantly to the experiences of the American students and also reported a high level of educational benefit. More structured involvement from a local South African academic institution would have provided infrastructure to ensure that the work done was part of a larger, strategic initiative, thereby ensuring the continuity and sustainability deemed important by both field school members and local partners.

Another critical function of local academic partners is the provision of institutional resources. For example, many field school participants hope to gather data during their project in order to publish peer-reviewed articles. Data collection often requires Institutional Review Board (IRB) approval. Gaining IRB approval from the home institution can be especially difficult given the ever changing and often last minute planning of in-country projects. For example, two projects in South Africa necessitated IRB approval. Instead of trying to initiate a new proposal through the Vanderbilt University IRB, team members worked under the umbrella of existing approved projects from South African IRBs. These approvals facilitated opportunities to present and publish research that might otherwise not have been possible. Choosing the right academic partners is critical. For example, the Chinese field school may have proceeded more smoothly had a university with experience working with international groups been initially chosen. One of the goals of field schools is to work where the needs are greatest and students can have the most impact, so there may be some value in introducing international collaborations to partners who have not experienced them. Thus, selecting partners is a delicate balance of prioritizing places with the greatest need and ensuring selection of projects that are feasible within field school constraints. Regardless of the institution, local academic partners help ensure sustainability and community access and are critical to the success of field schools.

Facilitating a Field School Experience

The "Getting Started!" table provides suggested action items to help guide educators interested in facilitating a field school experience based on the authors' experience with prior field schools. We acknowledge that each field school and site is different; the model must therefore be adapted to tailor each action item to the needs and situation of a particular community. For example, some field schools might not have the opportunity to work closely with community partners prior to entering the site, requiring alternative, creative ways of preparing and planning for stakeholders. Other field schools might involve students with diverse interests and

Chapter 7: Getting Started!
The Field School in Intercultural Education as a Model for International Service-Learning and Collaborative Action-Research Training

Action Item 1: Update your reading list.
Assign Donald Schön's *The Reflective Practitioner* (1983) as required reading. This text will provide a baseline for students, faculty, and community partners to discuss expectations of the roles of different stakeholders. Use this common reading to define, discuss, and problematize concepts of power, professional, expertise, and action, and identify sources of power inequality that may be associated with these terms. Identify additional readings specific to the location and partners with whom you will be working to familiarize students and faculty with the language, culture, geography, and politics of the region and community.

Action Item 2: Define your vision of an excellent field school experience.
Together with all stakeholders on your project, read chapter 9, "Strengthening the Role of Service in the College Curriculum," in Eyler & Giles (1999) *Where's the service in service-learning?* Use it to identify specific metrics for how participants will identify both quality learning and service during the project. These dimensions—quality of learning and quality of service—can guide the conversation about what it means to have a community-school partnership. The chapter provides guidance on reflection as well.

Action Item 3: Begin the experience before the experience begins.
Assign students to begin taking field notes (on the planning and preparation activities leading up to the field school placement) and reflecting on their experience well before they arrive in the field. Assign reflective writing to uncover student expectations, both academic/work-related and affective/hopes and fears. These activities can serve as benchmarks to which students can return throughout the experience. Prompts and guidelines for different types of reflective journals are described in "Reflection in service learning: Making meaning of experience" by R. G. Bringle and J. A. Hatcher (Chapter 1 in the service learning toolkit, available free online).

Action Item 4: Incorporate the participatory action research model.
Use students' reflections and field notes as rich data sources from which to draw theoretical understandings about the experience. Encourage students to move through the action research model. Draw a map of the model to post in a common area and chart your progress through the model as a community. Free resources on participatory action research (including methods, tools, and prompts for scaffolding conversations to support it) can be found at the Community Toolbox (www.ctb.ku.edu).

Chapter 7: Getting Started! (continued)

Action Item 5: *Model and practice structured times for dialogue.*
Before students arrive in the field, plan ahead to set aside times to negotiate and renegotiate the role of different stakeholders. Prepare students, faculty, and community partners for the possibility that some situations may not go as planned such that they are more comfortable adjusting expectations, procedures, roles, and relationships as needed. Discuss all stakeholders' expectations on a regular basis, encouraging honest views of whether expectations will be met or need to be adjusted with time.

Action Item 6: *Provide safe space for affective responses.*
Be prepared for all participants to have a wider variety of feelings and possibly more emotional reactions than they may have in a traditional work, course, or lab setting. Experiential learning involves the whole person and this long-lasting learning typically requires greater emotional investment. Be sure to set aside time for adequate self-care (rest, exercise, and breaks) and for debriefing about difficult issues that may emerge in the field. Continue to engage in direct conversations about the concepts of power, professionalism, expertise, and action.

Action Item 7: *Consider the field experience an ongoing relationship.*
The uncertainty of an applied experience—the time required for negotiating and renegotiating relationships, working outside the traditional university power dynamic, and working in an unfamiliar culture—may mean that originally intended goals cannot be reached in the timeframes established. Understand that the field experience process itself, particularly the way stakeholders are included and conflicts are managed, may be more important than the immediate outcomes. Include unmet goals and unanswered questions in subsequent rounds of the action research cycle and encourage participants to learn as much as they can where they are each day.

professional development needs, requiring responsive mentorship and strategic planning from faculty leaders. Every attempt should be made to follow the key principles of these action items, namely: prepare thoroughly, communicate honestly, act collaboratively, and reflect continually.

Conclusions and Implications

With each new iteration, the field school program adjusts to meet the ever-changing needs of students and local community partners in a way that remains consistent with our mission. By doing so, the questions explicated by Crabtree (2008) are in constant focus—questions about the balance of student learning with sustainable community change, empowering participants without unintentionally replicating power differentials, and taking on major social problems without allowing their magnitude to overwhelm participants. Additionally, given the unique contexts of each field school, this process must cater to the specific strengths, barriers, and histories of community partners. One way we have addressed the first two questions raised by Crabtree (2008) is through the use of community-based participatory research methods. Future field schools—and other programs seeking to carry out this kind of cross-cultural, collaborative work—would benefit from instituting formal accountability measures to help participants continually evaluate communication as well as power differentials. This kind of dialogue can be difficult, especially with cultural differences in communication styles. Yet formally agreeing to continual conversations can facilitate this process and build trusting relationships. For students engaging in a field school, experiencing the lived realities of poverty and oppression can be overwhelming. With adequate preparation and reflection they can lead to important discussions and reflections about privilege, personal values, and inequality; without support they can easily lead to feelings of helplessness. Preparatory coursework and self-reflection throughout time on-site and afterwards can better prepare students. Times for group processing, reflecting, and de-briefing must be a consistent and systematic part of every field school experience. Allowing student and community member feedback also helps create a sense of ownership, facilitating more open, meaningful dialogue, and a potentially transformative experience for all involved.

Although not a panacea, we posit that field schools reflect one contemporary approach to extend Dewey's (1916, 1939) emphasis on theory and praxis outside the traditional classroom. Interested readers can pursue this form of intercultural education by seeking information and possible strategic partnerships with other institutions with greater funding or that have successfully sponsored field schools, seeking funding via sources such as the U.S. Department of Education and the Agency for International Development, tapping into social media such as Skype and GoogleDocs to interact with potential and/or existing community partners despite limited resources, initially sponsoring small-scale field schools locally and regionally that lend themselves to car or bus transport, and continuing sustained work by prior field schools.

The field school approach extends international service learning by allowing students to engage in action research using community-based participatory methods to respond to social issues together with community partners who engage continually in this work. Drawing from the principles of international service-learning *and* the values of the HOD department, the field school challenges faculty, students, and community partners to expand their thinking, diversify their toolbox of research and practice skills, and consider how their personal and professional strengths can be used to work toward community betterment. Simultaneously, it can create bridges between the university and community partners, increase the relevance of practical research, open doors to new resources, and inspire new, innovative approaches to combat social problems. Field schools provide an opportunity for students and communities to engage each other to promote partnership, collaboration, and experiential learning. Although the field schools described here have all been located far from the home institution, we propose that other groups can draw from many of the field school principals, programs, and lessons learned to implement a similar experience wherever opportunities allow, whether in their local community, a neighboring state, or a distant country.

References

Burkhardt, J. C., & Merisotis, J. (2006). An introduction. In P. A. Pasque, L. A. Hendricks, & N. A. Bowman (Eds.), *Taking responsibility: A call for higher education's engagement in a society of complex global challenges* (pp. 1–9). Retrieved from http://www.thenationalforum.org/Docs/PDF/Wingspread_Monograph_Taking%20Responsibility_2006.pdf

Chawla-Duggan, R. (2007). Breaking out, breaking through: Accessing knowledge in a non western overseas education setting—methodological issues for an outsider. *Compare: A Journal of Comparative and International Education, 37*(2), 185–200.

Christens, B., & Perkins, D. D. (2008). Transdisciplinary, multilevel action research to enhance ecological and psycho-political validity. *Journal of Community Psychology, 36*(2), 214–31.

Combs, M. B., & Schmidt, P. R. (Eds.). (2013). *Transforming ourselves, transforming the world: Justice in Jesuit higher education.* New York: Fordham University Press.

Crabtree, R. D. (2008). Theoretical foundations for international service-learning. *Michigan Journal of Community Service Learning, 15*, 18–36.

Cruz, N. L., & Giles, D. E. (2000). Where's the community in service-learning research? *Michigan Journal of Community Service Learning, 7*, 28–34.

Dewey, J. (1916). *Democracy and education: An introduction to the philosophy of education.* New York: Macmillan.

Dewey, J. (1939). *Freedom and Culture.* New York: G. P. Putnam's Sons.

Eyler, J., & Giles, D. E. (1999). *Where's the learning in service-learning?* San Francisco: Jossey-Bass.

Gandhi, Mahatma. (1936). *Harijan* (Sept. 5).

Maeda, M. (2011). Heightened awareness of a researcher's own culture through carrying out research on development cooperation. *Comparative Education, 47*(3), 355–65.

Merriam, S. B., Johnson-Bailey, J., Lee, M. Y., Kee, Y., Ntseane, G., & Muhamad, M. (2001). Power and positionality: Negotiating insider/outsider status within and across cultures. *International Journal of Lifelong Education, 20*, 405–16.

Mosavel, M., Simon, C., van Stade, D., & Buchbinder, M. (2005). Community-based participatory research (CBPR) in South Africa: Engaging multiple constituents to shape the research question. *Social Science and Medicine, 61*, 2577–87.

Partridge, W. L., & Mejía, M. C. (2013). *Socio-cultural analysis in inter-American Development Bank projects.* Washington, DC: Inter-American Development Bank.

Robinson, J., & Perkins, D. D. (2009). Social development needs assessment in China: Lessons from an international collaborative field school in Guangxi Zhuang Autonomous Region. *China Journal of Social Work, 2*(1), 34–51.

Schmidt, P. R., & Finkbeiner, C. (Eds.) (2006). *ABC's of cultural understanding and communication: National and International Adaptations.* Charlotte, NC: Information Age Publishing.

Smith-Morris, C. (2007). Autonomous individuals or self-determined communities? The changing ethics of research among Native Americans. *Human Organization, 66*(3), 327–36.

Young, J. (2005). On insiders (emic) and outsiders (etic): Views of self, and othering. *Systematic Practice and Action Research, 18*(2), 151–62.

8 Creating a Mosaic of Religious Values and Narratives

Participant-Researcher Roles of an Interfaith Research Group Seeking to Understand Interfaith Organizations

HASINA MOHYUDDIN, MARK McCORMACK, PAUL R. DOKECKI, AND LINDA ISAACS

> The truth is not fully free when it gets into some individual's consciousness, for him to delectate himself with. It is freed only when it moves in and through this favored individual to his fellows; when the truth which comes to consciousness in one, extends and distributes itself to all so that it becomes the Common-wealth, the Republic, the public affair.
>
> —John Dewey, 2008

> Religion is both an awareness of the sacred and concrete action arising out of that awareness.
>
> —Thomas Moore, 2014

Introduction

Religious diversity and prejudice have been and continue to be persistent features of the United States religious landscape, with various minority religious groups at different points in U.S. history serving as targets of derision and discrimination for a majority American Christian population (Beneke & Grenda, 2011; Eck, 2001). In the years following the September 11, 2001 terrorist attacks in particular, interest in religious diversity in the United States and in religious prejudice targeting the minority American Muslim population has grown (McCarthy, 2007; Wuthnow, 2005). Such increased interest has been accompanied by increased focus on effective methods for improving interfaith relations in communities (Roozen, 2011). Recent initiatives and developments, such as the nationally renowned Interfaith Youth Core, President Obama's Interfaith and

Community Service Campus Challenge, and the Islamic Society of North America's Office for Interfaith and Community Alliances, are examples of these increasing interests in the general American public. Yet there is limited empirical research about how interfaith work effectively reduces religious prejudice and subsequently improves interfaith relations.

Eboo Patel (2012), visionary founder of Interfaith Youth Core and in many ways the figurehead of the American interfaith movement, recently lamented the dearth of evidence-based practice on these topics. The purpose of this chapter and the project described herein is to begin to answer Patel's call for evidence-based interfaith practice and advance current understandings of the processes and mechanisms that lead to reduced prejudice through interfaith practice. This query will be considered within the context of Vanderbilt University's HOD department, consistent with the department's core values of social justice and community-based participatory research, and will pay special attention to the epistemological and methodological concerns that inevitably emerge in the implementation of an interfaith action research project. Of particular interest will be how the utilization of an interfaith research team impacts research on interfaith organizations. That is, although the research on interfaith organizations itself is still in the formative stages, the implication of this *process* of interfaith research on deepening understanding is equally important. Specifically, for scholar activists who are interested in being embedded in their phenomenon of study, we believe our research method provides a unique model for understanding and engaging in participatory research.

Interfaith Conflict and Work in the United States

Our approach to religious prejudice and interfaith programming is strongly rooted in the theoretical traditions of intergroup relations and social psychology. Here, interfaith conflict can be understood as emerging out of social psychological processes in which social groups construct boundaries of common identity and belonging around themselves, while also constructing boundaries of common identity and "otherness" (or nonbelonging) around social groups that exist outside their own group (Marty, 2005; Pettigrew & Tropp, 2011). These group constructions typically create "us/them" relations between groups, subsequently leading to inter-group competition, fear, and animosity. Recent work in behavioral immune systems has framed these processes in terms of health behaviors and "contagion" avoidance: Social groups seek to preserve a strong sense of group identity and survival by avoiding "contamination" by other social groups, typically manifested through social conservatism and out-group prejudice (Terrizzi Jr., Shook, & McDaniel, in press).

This understanding of the intergroup process is philosophically rooted in the classic works of such theorists as Martin Buber, whose *I and Thou* (Buber, 1958/2000) helped to explicate the human subject's objectification of the human (and divine, for Buber) "Other." More relevant to this chapter, intergroup research has examined intergroup processes and conflict between various religiously defined groups, such as Catholics and Protestants (Tausch et al., 2011); Christians and Muslims (Ariyanto, Hornsey, & Gallois, 2009); and Muslims and Hindus (Tausch, Hewstone, & Roy, 2009). For example, Tausch, Hewstone, and Roy (2009) find that Hindus in India (the majority religion in that context) tend to perceive Muslims (a minority religion in that context) as "symbolic threats" to Indian nationality and cultural values, while Muslims in turn tend to perceive Hindus as "realistic threats" to access to economic and community resources. Similar perceptions of minority religious out-groups have been a regular feature in the U.S. religious landscape. In the nineteenth century, Catholic immigrants were demonized by a largely Protestant American population as undemocratic, un-Christian, and dangerous to U.S. society (Griffin, 2004). Similarly, in the nineteenth and twentieth centuries, members of the Church of Latter Day Saints (or "Mormons") were collectively viewed as intellectually inferior, sexually depraved, and violent (Givens, 1997).

More recently, Muslims, atheists, and pagans have borne the brunt of American Christian group processes of "othering," with Muslims in particular suffering negative out-group assessments and conflict (Merino, 2010; Edgell & Tranby, 2010; Putnam & Campbell, 2010). Edgell and Tranby (2010) find that American Christians tend to perceive Muslims, more than any other social group, as "un-American" and opposed to important American values such as freedom and democracy. Similarly, Merino (2010) finds that American Christians are less willing to include

Muslims in American community life than they are any other social group. Ecologically, then, religious tensions reflect not just present day, local conflicts but transcend national and international boarders and are deeply impacted by historical, generative narratives. As such, this work reflects a trans-disciplinary framework in order to appropriately address these complex, multi-faceted issues.

Along with these persistent tensions between religious groups, various forms of interfaith work have steadily emerged in an attempt to improve interfaith relations. Religion scholars and religious leaders in recent decades have sought to quell interfaith conflict through theological statements of religious plurality and tolerance (Hick, 1995; Knitter, 2002; McClaren, 2012) and clarion calls to greater interfaith understanding and cooperation (Eck, 2003; Numrich, 2009; Wuthnow, 2007). Accordingly, there has been an upsurge of community responses to interfaith tensions, most commonly in the form of interfaith dialogue forums, interfaith political coalitions, and interfaith community groups and organizations (McCarthy, 2007). American congregations have become increasingly involved in interfaith efforts at the local community level as well, especially since the September 11th attacks and in light of the potentially negative implications of those events for the American Muslim community (Roozen, 2011).

Despite upward trends in interfaith work, there remain questions about the actual effectiveness of interfaith initiatives in alleviating interfaith tensions. McCarthy (2007) notes the limited scope and effectiveness of interfaith initiatives in general, while Roozen (2011) and Wuthnow (2005) both contend that, despite recent increases, American congregational involvement in interfaith work remains relatively limited and leaves much room for growth and improvement. Thus the project described here is rooted at the intersection of these two critical problems facing the American interfaith landscape: (1) persistent tensions between certain religious communities and (2) limited effectiveness of interfaith efforts in alleviating those tensions. After a brief description of this project, our discussion will move to epistemological and methodological issues for action researchers engaging in such a project. While we feel work in interfaith phenomena certainly presents some unique issues, it is our hope that this discussion of our methodology will be relevant and potentially implementable across a variety of topics and fields of inquiry.

Vanderbilt University Interfaith Project

Our project began in 2010 in direct response to religious conflicts in New York City and Murfreesboro, Tennessee surrounding the proposal and construction of new Islamic centers. We were initially struck, not only by the tragedy of these conflicts as they unfolded and eventually erupted into violence and sustained litigation (in Murfreesboro, in particular), but also by the seeming lack of attention to interfaith conflict and issues within our own discipline of community psychology. Therefore, we formed a research team to reflect on how an action research project on interfaith conflict might be developed. Early stages of the project focused on local interfaith organizations as a potentially fruitful avenue for examining and improving interfaith organizations; we decided to develop a sample of interfaith organizations across the United States to better understand these phenomena.

The first interfaith organization selected for our project, Women of Faith, was formed in direct response to the tensions in Murfreesboro and was, at the time, the community's most visible and sustained effort to improve local interfaith relations in the wake of the above-mentioned mosque controversy. Subsequently, we have broadened our scope to examine other U.S. communities similarly facing persistent interfaith tensions, resulting in the inclusion of four other interfaith groups: (1) Haven Interfaith Parents in Fort Wayne, Indiana, comprised of parents of students at a private middle school; (2) Sons and Daughters of Abraham in Sewanee, Tennessee, an interfaith collaboration between Christian, Jewish, and Muslim youth groups; (3) Vanderbilt University Interfaith Council in Nashville, Tennessee, a student-led group facilitating interfaith activities and events on the Vanderbilt campus; and (4) Interfaith Mission Service in Huntsville, Alabama, a congregation-based interfaith organization focused on collaborative community service and education initiatives.

We have been able to represent a group of distinct organizations, each with a unique organizational model, community context, and set of concerns and goals. We believe that these groups each foster the spirit of twenty-first century Deweyism, as their very existence challenges dominant notions of who can participate and who has valid knowledge (Dewey, 1927/1954, 1938). In order to understand how their members connected with these principles and other issues germane to interfaith collaborations, we are conducting in-depth interviews with key leaders and members and observing monthly meetings and community service and/or engagement activities. A survey is also being designed and implemented for measuring individual-level psychological processes (for example, one's psychological sense of community), as well as religious attitudes, beliefs, and behaviors. Importantly, our study is grounded in the discipline of community psychology, fundamentally interested in "action research" and participatory methods. The project undertakes, through a community-based approach, research that is in part guided by the lived experiences and distinct community contexts of each of the groups mentioned earlier and tailored to address their unique issues and challenges as they define them. At this point in the research process, 30 in-depth interviews have been conducted as well as direct observation of several meetings and events. Preliminary findings are shared here within the context of the epistemological and methodological issues that arise when utilizing an interfaith group to study interfaith organizations. Again, the hope is that this example will be valuable not just to those interested in interfaith research, but also to any scholar-activist interested in being embedded in their research sites to promote social justice on a wider scale.

The Interfaith Research Team

The original team, comprising a Catholic (Paul), a Methodist (Mark), and a Muslim (Hasina), reflected on how our own traditions and communities responded to religious conflict, as well as on other indications of such challenges in the United States and abroad. In considering interventions that countered religious prejudice and conflict, we believed that interfaith organizations are at the forefront of such efforts. Further, we recognized that our own research team (reflecting a variety of faith traditions) mirrored many interfaith organizations, and deliberately incorporated our intra-group dialogue into the research process. Such dialogue is grounded in the works of Buber (1923/1996) and Marty (2005), and framed as a method to engage in interfaith efforts to understand the religious "Other." We then asked a fourth member with expertise in organizational consulting (Linda) to join the group to facilitate documentation of the group dialogue process and its impact on research. Her decision to join the team also reflected her interest in participating in interfaith dialogue as a person who is spiritual and knowledgeable about a variety of religious traditions.

Efforts to effectively engage community members pose an ongoing challenge for researchers (Israel et. al, 2008), especially when considering questions of race and ethnicity (Baca Zinn, 2001; Chavez et al., 2008), gender (Cornwall, 2003), sexual orientation (Clements-Nolle & Bachrach, 2008), or other marginalized voices (Cooke & Kothari, 2001). The distance between insiders (the study participants) and outsiders (researchers) is often magnified when participants face issues of discrimination and/or stigmatization given the inherent power differentials that typically exist in the research context (Chavez et al., 2008). One method for minimizing the insider/outsider dichotomy has been to utilize participant observation (Baca Zinn, 2001). The idea of the researcher being fully embedded in the group under study has played a significant role in challenging traditional positivist paradigms of objectivity by arguing that reducing the distance between community members and researchers allows for greater authenticity in understanding the lived experience of others. Collins (1990), in particular, utilized her position as an African American woman to center the voices of impoverished African American women in research. However, even as greater numbers of minority group members become researchers, there often remains a distinction between the roles of researcher and community member participant, even within the participatory research paradigm (Baca Zinn, 2001; Delgado-Gaitan, 1993). Although individuals may be "insiders" by virtue of race, ethnicity, sexual orientation, religion, or a variety of "other" categories, the inherently privileged position of being a researcher remains. This privileged position, based on a differential in knowledge, is critical to explore.

Departing from the traditional definition of participant observation, we are simultaneously studying our *own* processes as an interfaith research team in addition to our work with interfaith organizations. Although participatory research does pay attention to the subjectivities that researchers bring into the process, rarely do researchers subject themselves to the research process even when they themselves can be considered "insiders." Thus, our interfaith research team provides us the unique opportunity to be both *participant observers* as well as *research participants*. Each of us is interested in interfaith organizations not just as researchers but also as people who believe that such organizations can help ameliorate religious conflict and for whom the reduction of religious prejudice and conflict is a personal priority. As Moore (2014) suggests, echoing Dewey before him, religion is not just an appreciation of the sacred for us but also an inspiration for concrete action. We remain mindful of our dual roles as researchers and participants, and acknowledge that each role necessarily impacts the other. In consideration of these dual roles, two fundamental questions emerge: (1) As participants, how do we assess the effectiveness of our efforts? and (2) How does our role as participants impact our role as researchers?

Park (2001) provides a useful framework for considering both questions. He suggests that three types of knowledge can emerge from participatory research: representational, relational, and reflexive knowledge. Representational knowledge is concerned with the ability to define and derive meaning from a phenomenon (pp. 85–87); relational knowledge is the ability to bond with others through shared dialogue, as well as through the sharing of feelings and experiences (pp. 87–89); and reflexive knowledge results from the consideration of actions taken, including the emotional and empowering aspects of engaging in change efforts (pp. 89–91). A specific type of power emerges from each of these three types of knowledge—the power of competence, connection, and confidence. Wallerstein and Duran (2008) note:

> As people engage in dialogue with each other about their communities and the larger social context, their own internal thought patterns and beliefs about their social world change; their relationships to each other become strengthened; and, ultimately, they enhance their capacities to reflect on their own values and make new choices. (p. 33)

It is our hope that through our own increased competence, connection, and confidence, we may become more effective research partners with the interfaith organizations with whom we engage.

Interfaith Activities of the Research Team

Our interfaith participatory action project consists of three distinct activities: ongoing weekly meetings with the project team, individual experiences with interfaith activities, and participation in a focus group and an in-depth interview. The first method that fosters interfaith dialogue *within* the research team is ongoing weekly meetings. Typically lasting 60 to 90 minutes, these meetings provide a forum for our roles as both participants and researchers. As participants, we discuss relevant literature, current events highlighting religious conflict or cooperation, and reflections on group processes. As researchers, the weekly meetings also provide an official space to discuss project progress, data collection, and fieldwork experience. These meetings provide the primary vehicle for sharing insights from each religious tradition, as well as for considering ways in which our roles as participants and researchers intersect and influence each other.

Research team members also have personal experiences with the interfaith groups in the study, as well as with other interfaith efforts in the Nashville, Tennessee area. Mark and Hasina, in particular, have been involved in a variety of interfaith groups and events as participant observers. Mark has developed an interfaith class at his church and is also a member of the North American Interfaith Alliance. Hasina is a member of Women of Faith and is on the planning committee of a Joint Interfaith Scriptural Study (JISS) between Christians, Jews, and Muslims. In addition, both have helped plan and have attended a number of interfaith events, including interfaith speakers and panels, events supporting the Islamic Center of Murfreesboro, and a variety of academic and social events geared toward promoting religious pluralism.

Finally, to provide greater insight into the research process from a participant's perspective, we all participated in a focus group and conducted in-depth interviews with each other. The focus group was facilitated by a colleague from our department and included the research group members and a spiritually seeking fellow graduate student. The protocol for the focus group mirrored the process utilized for interviewing study participants. It included questions on individual spiritual journeys, current involvement within our own faith traditions, and the impact of interfaith dialogue in our lives. In addition to the focus group, Mark conducted in-depth interviews with Paul and Linda. Mark and Hasina also engaged in what might be described as an "interactive interview" process, in which participants "act as both researchers and research participants" (Ellis, 2004, Kindle Locations 1908–1909). Through the interactive interview process, we reflected on how our participation in the interfaith dialogue has impacted us personally as well as the impact it has had on the research process.

These activities might be described as autoethnographic—which Ellis (2004) describes as, "start[ing] with my personal life and pay[ing] attention to my physical feelings, thoughts, and emotions. I use what I call 'systematic sociological introspection' and 'emotional recall' to try to understand an experience I've lived through" (Ellis, 2004, Kindle Locations 319–320). In a sense, we utilize autoethnographic techniques in order to enhance our participatory research methodology. Cumulatively, this process eliminated the wall between us as researchers and our research sample because we asked ourselves a similar line of questions. In this way, we endeavored to connect with twenty-first century Deweyism by linking a democratic process to each step of our approach to research (Dewey, 1927/1954, 1938).

Representational Knowledge and the Power of Competence

Park (2001) posits that participatory research enhances representational knowledge because the ability to know, define, and understand the meaning behind a phenomenon "requires that a knower come as close to the known as possible" (p. 85). We contend that the process of participation has increased our representational knowledge in three key ways. First, it has resulted in greater insight into the language of interfaith organizations as a means of creating an interpretive lens by which to frame research. Second, it has allowed us to consider how our own religious and interfaith experiences may resemble—and differ from—the experiences of study participants. And last, it has increased our awareness of both the strengths and challenges inherent in conducting interfaith work on a visceral, emotive level.

Understanding the language of interfaith organizations is a critical outcome of being a participant in interfaith activities because it provides the interpretive lens through which our research is framed. Becker (1996) suggests that even as researchers attempt to give voice to "actors," they are doing so from their own interpretive lens. To provide greater credibility, it is important to spend time learning the language of respondents to be able to understand their viewpoints—in this case, the language of interfaith groups. In *Truth and Method*, Gadamer (1960) foreshadows Becker

(1996) and notes that all "truth" is interpreted, and that we only "know" through our biases. As such, researchers are challenged to reflect on who we are and how that influences what we know, an activity absent from the majority of traditional research activities. By being participants as well as researchers, we may experience a privileged position of knowing. Our weekly meetings on interfaith literature and current events allow us to better understand the language in the field, as well as to be more aware of how issues may be discussed from our own religious traditions and the traditions of fellow research team members. As Moore (2004) notes, understanding the perspectives of other religious traditions often enables us to deepen the understandings we have of our own traditions.

Moreover, our personal experiences and shared stories help us better understand where we stand in terms of interfaith work, and allow us to more accurately define the lens through which we work with study participants. For example, within the context of interfaith work, a number of different terms emerge to describe and understand that work—such as interreligious, multi-religious, and multi-faith. For some, these terms are used interchangeably, as noted by the President's Advisory Council on Faith Based and Neighborhood Partnerships (White House, 2010). Others, such as Heckman (2013) from Religions for Peace, USA, argue that words like "interfaith" have become "plastic" and often ignore the growing number of people who have multiple religious affiliations or no affiliation at all. In our own research, working with organizations such as Haven Interfaith Parents, which has wrestled with both the theoretical and practical implications of using one word ("multi-faith") instead of another ("interfaith") in describing its work, we have learned what specific terms mean to different persons or groups and have developed a heightened awareness of using those terms in the field.

Participatory research also provides greater understanding of the relationship between our own religious perspectives and experiences and those of study participants. For example, in describing her personal spiritual journey, Linda discussed how the Women's Rights Movement influenced her to question the very conservative gender roles upheld in her religious tradition. She characterized her quest to learn about other religious traditions as a result of questions about those roles and highlights the impact of a larger social movement on her spiritual journey. Similar stories of how social movements have impacted their spiritual journeys are reflected in the interviews of a number of participants. Most notably, several members of Interfaith Mission Services (IMS) recount how the organization grew out of the interfaith effort to support the Civil Rights Movement. Hearing Linda's story thus provides an important frame of reference with which to more fully understand the experience of study participants—that is, the importance of connecting spiritual journeys to the corresponding historical context.

Participation in interfaith efforts has also nuanced our understanding of potential strengths and challenges faced by interfaith organizations. Study participants often articulated the need to increase participation within interfaith organizations, especially with minority religious groups such as Muslims. In her experience with the JISS planning committee, Hasina personally experienced the frustration of this challenge. The JISS consisted of three separate events that participants signed up to attend. In the third event, only two of the scheduled twelve Muslim participants attended. Although through the process of working with the local Imam, the total number of Muslim participants eventually increased, it highlighted a difficulty that may occur when engaging members of minority religious traditions in interfaith work. In another example, Mark faced a challenge with speakers in his interfaith class based on delivery style or command of the English language. Students in the class had a more difficult time understanding and connecting with presenters who had a dry presentation style or spoke with heavily accented English. Although we may hope such contextual factors will not actually impact interfaith understanding, practically we must find ways to deal with these situations as they arise. We posit that although researchers can empathize about challenges study participants may face, actually living through similar challenges provides greater ability to effectively partner with respondents to consider remedies for such situations.

However, it is as important to recognize strengths inherent in interfaith organizations. Indeed, Kretzman and McKnight (1993) argue that traditional "needs-based" approaches that focus on challenges often reinforce a deficit mentality when defining a community by its problems. In response, there has been a growing appreciation for strengths-based approaches in research. In the JISS example, because newer members recruited for the third event enjoyed their experience, they expressed the desire to engage in interfaith efforts in the future. Similarly, in Mark's interfaith class, a positive experience interacting with Muslim presenters led church members who openly expressed their reluctance to interact with Muslims to rethink their prior conceptions about this religious group. The increased competence achieved through greater representational knowledge has influenced our work as researchers in a number of ways. First, it allowed us to ask more nuanced questions during semi-structured interviews and in questionnaires as we became more aware of possible meanings behind language used by study participants. Second, it aided in the refinement of study procedures as we became more attuned to the similarities and differences between our processes and the processes of study participants. Finally, we have become better resources for our research partners as we gain valuable experience in appreciating the strengths and addressing the challenges of interfaith work.

Relational Knowledge and the Power of Connection

Although it is closely associated with representational knowledge (knowing a person through an interpretive lens), relational knowledge is a separate dynamic. Park (2001) suggests "relational knowledge comes from connecting and leads to further connection" (p. 88). In actuality, much of interfaith work is predicated upon building relationships. All groups within the research study actively incorporate dialogue as a way of understanding the "Other," and learning about different religious perspectives. Some seek to connect and build friendships primarily through service-learning and social gatherings such as Sons and Daughters of Abraham and Interfaith Mission Service; others more deliberately incorporate dialogue into their interactions, as in the case of Haven Interfaith Parents, Vanderbilt's Interfaith Council and Women of Faith. However, all groups acknowledge the importance and actively pursue the attainment of relational knowledge. Two aspects of relational knowledge are particularly pertinent to enhancing the connection between our roles as researchers and our roles as participants: the ability to "rehearse" difficult conversations and the ability to connect to study participants outside the realm of research.

One aspect of relational knowledge we gained from interfaith participation is the ability to more effectively handle difficult conversations that we often keep private. Chavez et al. (2008) suggest that even as researchers attempt to build relationships with community members within a CBPR process, often they will "have access only to what is considered public" (p. 96). Scott (1990) further posits that there are often *hidden transcripts* within communities that are not discussed with outsiders. Indeed, some interfaith discussions are hard to share with others on a personal level and require significant amounts of trust to discuss. However, establishing safe spaces makes it easier to discuss those issues. O'Brien (2011) notes how Muslim youth utilize "backstage rehearsals" as a safe way to discuss how they and others have handled or may handle difficult conversations or situations. Similarly, our engagement with one another provided a safe space to address uncomfortable situations. For example, Mark reflected on the difficulty of broaching the subject of interfaith efforts with his conservative Christian family and friends. Similarly, Hasina has discussed challenges associated with having conservative Muslim views while interacting with more progressive members of other faiths. Providing a safe space to discuss these issues allows us to consider multiple ways of communicating difficult information while remaining true to our values and beliefs. Moore (2014) notes that being able to wrestle with these types of questions actually help us to deepen our faith. Further, in *Thinking Points*, Lakoff (2006) suggests that to connect to others, one must be able to present their own values in an authentic way that builds trust and with which others can identify. Thus this relational aspect of our interfaith research group has a broader impact on our ability to interact with others and establish the trust and authenticity needed to connect within study participants.

It is also important to realize that relational knowledge is enhanced by the opportunity to interact with others outside the realm of "research." One of the criteria for effective intergroup contact is the ability to engage in relationship building activities outside of the target area of contact. Being members of the same academic department has allowed the research team to maintain sustained, ongoing contact that has developed into friendship. Team members care for and trust each other. As Mayeroff (1971) notes, as individuals care for others and are cared for in return, the process establishes importance in both persons' lives. Similarly, by engaging in interfaith efforts outside our study, we have an opportunity to interact with participants in non-research, collegial contexts. LeCompte (1997) suggests that shared experiences can lead others to feel more confident to confide their stories because they feel connected to someone who is also "in the trenches" (p. 9). In addition to building relationships, such connections can facilitate the collection of deeper, more meaningful data. Through intra-team relationship building during the research process, we are able to foster greater trust and empathy with organizations and individuals in the study. We have experiences sharing our thoughts and feelings with each other, making us better equipped to do so with others. Furthermore, rehearsing answers to difficult questions in dialogue within safe spaces enables us to feel more able to have those conversations with others. Finally, we are able to interact with study participants outside the realm of "research" to build bonds of friendship and trust.

Reflexive Knowledge and the Power of Confidence

A final source of knowledge resulting from a multipart, participatory research process is reflexive knowledge. As stated earlier, reflexive knowledge results from the consideration of actions taken and may include certain emotional and empowering aspects of those actions. In the context of our interfaith study, the reflective process has primarily taken the form of group reflection in team meetings and personal reflection in field journals. As a team, we regularly discuss our field experiences, the emotional responses to these experiences, and potential implications of these experiences and emotions for generating knowledge in service of the larger project. For example, Mark and Hasina have jointly reflected on the experience of engaging in an interfaith prayer with one of the project groups—a common interfaith practice of collectively reciting a "generic" prayer that ostensibly expresses a sense of religiosity that can cut across multiple religious traditions without referring to specifics of those traditions. They both experienced feelings of discomfort in witnessing this activity, as it seemed to impose religious ideas on the group with which every member of the group may not agree. This experience and accompanying emotional response, as well as the intentional process of collective reflections, helped generate knowledge about the diversity of experiences that may exist within interfaith settings (not all of them positive) and has led the team to focus more directly on the tendency in the interfaith movement to strive toward consensus or universality and its related challenges.

Several team members have also engaged in personal field journaling as a method to capture personal experiences, reactions, and reflections as we participate in and observe various interfaith events and activities in the field. Journaling exercises and the processes of reflecting both personally and collectively on them have served as another avenue to generate knowledge that is then directly applied to the ongoing study. A personal journal entry by Mark helps to illustrate this point. Here, he journals about being told by the cofacilitator of his interfaith class that certain members of his church were responding negatively to the prospect of hosting a class on the topic of Islam:

> Anthony (pseudonym) came up to me after the class and told me "several" people in the church have told him that they would not be attending our class on Islam next month. This didn't surprise me at first, and I knowingly nodded my head when Anthony told me this, but the more I thought about it the angrier and more hurt I became. Do people in the church have a negative perception of what we're doing in our class? . . . This left me worried that people are beginning to have a negative reaction to us even having this class, that maybe the church would regret letting us do this, if they end up getting some negative feedback from church members. What if they end up asking us to discontinue the class?

In addition to working through this experience in his journal, Mark also shared the experience with the research team and shared his thoughts and emotional responses. While this journal entry illustrates some of the frustrations and anxieties that accompany the work of facilitating an interfaith class, these personal and collective reflections also provided us with insight into some of the social and institutional supports often required to successfully lead interfaith efforts. Consistent with the ecological focus of the HOD department, through these reflections (and others), we have come to view interfaith groups as situated within various systems of support (for example, faith communities, families, friends, public policies) that help shape both the scope of their activity and their effectiveness in carrying out certain efforts. These insights, gained primarily through reflective processes, have directly helped shape our interview and survey questions.

Finally, these reflective activities have enabled the research team to live out the importance of being reflective-generative practitioners, defined by

Dokecki, Newbrough, and O'Gorman (2001), as "an ethically grounded form of relational practice through which one intends to develop community as a generative social group and, thus, to develop and empower people to be self-efficacious, socially competent, and active participants in social life, and to have a psychological sense of community" (p. 503). Through continued participation in interfaith dialogue, team members reflect on our own social contexts and histories and how they shape the way we approach research on interfaith groups with the explicit intention of helping to foster their growth. In other words, interfaith activities within the research group help team members feel empowered and equipped during the research process both professionally and personally.

Strategies for Participant-Researchers

There are similarities between our processes and those of ethnographic participant observers and reflective practitioners. We have attempted to straddle the two traditions to both improve our own understanding of interfaith organizations (as participant observers) as well as to improve our own interfaith participation (as reflective practitioners). It is our belief that doing so enhances our ability to be both more effective participants and more effective researchers. Figure 8-1 illustrates the interplay between the two roles. In this cycle, collecting and analyzing the data as "participants" helps us refine our research process. Similarly, although the goal is ultimately to disseminate our findings, analysis of data collected as "researchers" allows us to improve our participation in interfaith efforts. Although we have been considering this iterative process in the interfaith context, it may also be useful as a model for similar studies in which researchers are active participants in the phenomenon of focus.

Engaging in Interfaith Collaborative Work

With evidence of increasing rates of religious diversity in the United States, interfaith collaborations open the doors to a wide range of exciting opportunities for research and practice across many social domains. Scholarly work that takes an interfaith approach creates spaces for enhanced understanding across religious groups; however, doing this work is far more complicated than assembling a research team encompassing

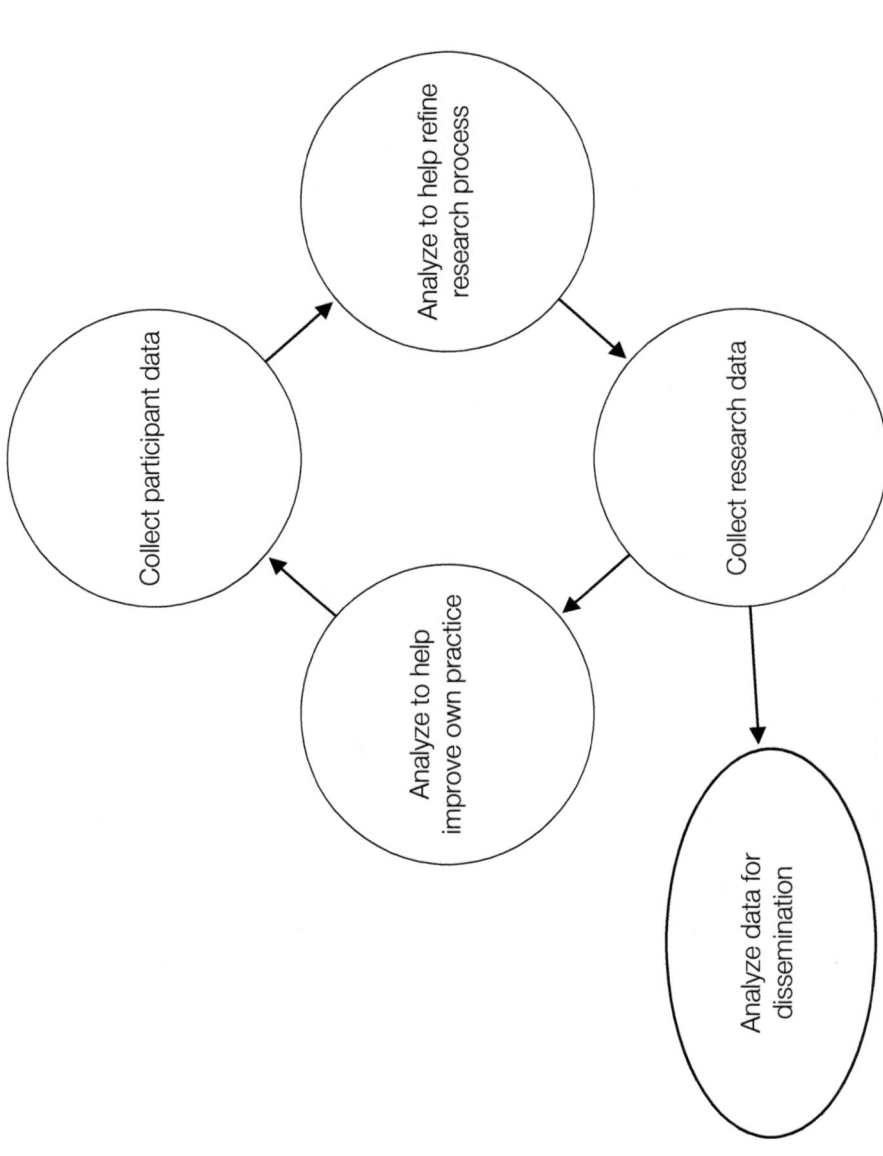

FIGURE 8-1. Participant-researcher data cycle

diverse faith orientations. The present chapter highlights the experiences of one interfaith research group. The members of the research team learned a number of important lessons about distinct facilitators and barriers to conducting and analyzing such research. One of the most important strategies that we identify highlights the importance of taking a process-oriented approach, allowing for continuous discussion and individual and collective reflection. With a more responsive and flexible approach to research, the work is able to respond to the emergent needs of both researchers and participants. The "Getting Started!" table summarizes five suggestions to consider when engaging in interfaith, collaborative work.

Conclusion

Increasing religious tension in the United States, and more precisely the religious conflict in our own Middle Tennessee community, provides the impetus for our study of interfaith organizations. Although there are numerous issues and complexities in studying and engaging this topic, here we focus on the intentional awareness of our own identities as religious/spiritual people, and our collective identity as a sort of "interfaith organization," as indispensable to our ability to engage in the roles of both participant and researcher. We contend that by cultivating representational, relational, and reflexive knowledge, we have been able to more accurately understand and more effectively engage interfaith phenomena. Epistemologically, we have attempted to understand these dynamics, primarily by participating in them. Methodologically, the distinction between our internal process and our study remains clear. In this way, our efforts embody the values of participation and reflective practice espoused by the department of HOD, we experience the beneficence of participation in the process, and we are able to translate the acquired knowledge into more meaningful partnerships with interfaith participants and organizations. Through this reflexive process, where we serve as both researcher participants and facilitators, we are forced to analyze our findings in a comprehensive, ongoing away. As such, we consider participatory action projects such as ours and the processes that guide them to embody the essence of twenty-first century Deweyism (Dewey, 1927/1954, 1938).

Chapter 8: Getting Started!
Creating a Mosaic of Religious Values and Narratives: Participant-Researcher Roles of an Interfaith Research Group Seeking to Understand Interfaith Organizations

Action Item 1: *Clearly define goals.*
As with any study, it is important to clearly define the research goals. However, in this model there are personal as well as research goals to consider. Some personal and research goals may overlap; others may not. Understanding and defining both sets of goals helps balance the two roles. For example, in our own study, the primary research goal is to understand the impact of interfaith organizations, whereas our personal goals focus more on the amelioration of religious conflict. Although there is significant overlap between these two goals, there are also distinct differences.

Action Item 2: *Set participant/researcher boundaries.*
Once the goals have been defined, it is also important to consider boundaries. As an individual who is personally interested in the phenomenon, it is important to understand your own boundaries and the boundaries of the research project. Actions that might be acceptable as a participant may negatively impact a research study. For instance, Mark and Hasina have been active participants in Women of Faith and Interfaith Mission Service. The impact of their involvement in these organizations is discussed during research meetings to ensure the integrity of the overall research project.

Action Item 3: *Consider impact on relationships.*
Although you may have clearly defined goals and boundaries, those involved in your research study may not. Being able to communicate clearly and honestly with others about your dual roles is important in developing and maintaining relationships. Given the nature of interfaith work, many of the participants within the study also collaborate on projects outside the study scope. Being able to maintain those relationships helps ensure the validity of research data, as well as the successful outcome of joint interfaith efforts.

Action Item 4: *Call in "outside" researchers.*
As participants, we had colleagues take on more traditional "researcher" roles, such as focus group facilitator or evaluator of weekly group meetings. Abdicating these traditional researcher roles enabled us to more fully immerse ourselves in the role of participant and gain a deeper understanding of what it felt like to be participants.

Action Item 5: *Reflect, reflect, and reflect.*
Given the dual roles, reflection is a central component to the participant-researcher model. Both individual reflection via journaling as well as group reflection via weekly discussions were key components to be able to analyze and utilize participant and research data.

References

Ariyanto, A., Hornsey, M. J., & Gallois, C. (2009). Intergroup attribution bias in the context of extreme intergroup conflict. *Asian Journal of Social Psychology, 12*(4), 293–99.

Beneke, C., & Grenda, C. S. (2010). *The first prejudice: Religious tolerance and intolerance in early America.* Philadelphia, PA: University of Pennsylvania Press.

Buber, M. (1923/1996). *I and thou.* New York: Simon & Schuster.

Collins, P. H. (1990). *Black feminist thought: Knowledge, consciousness, and the politics of empowerment.* New York: Routledge.

Dewey, J. (1927/1954). *The public and its problems.* Chicago: The Swallow Press.

Dewey, J. (1938). *Education and experience.* New York: Touchstone, Simon & Schuster.

Dewey, J. (2008). *The early works, 1882–1898: 1893–1894. Early essays and the study of ethics.* (Edited by Jo Ann Boydston). Illinois: Southern Illinois University Press.

Eck, D. L. (1993). *Encountering God: A spiritual journey from Bozeman to Banaras.* Boston, MA: Beacon Press.

Eck, D. L. (2001). *A new religious America: How a "Christian Country" has become the world's most religiously diverse nation.* New York: HarperCollins Publishers.

Edgell, P., & Tranby, E. (2010). Shared visions? Diversity and cultural membership in American life. *Social Problems, 57*(2), 175–204.

Ellis, C. (2004). *The ethnographic I: A methodological novel about autoethnography.* AltaMira Press. Kindle Edition.

Givens, T. L. (1997). *The viper on the hearth: Mormons, myths, and the construction of heresy.* New York: Oxford University Press.

Griffin, S. M. (2004). *Anti-Catholicism and nineteenth-century fiction.* Cambridge, UK: Cambridge University Press.

Halevy, N., Chou, E. Y., Cohen, T. R., & Bornstein, G. (2010). Relative deprivation and intergroup competition. *Group Processes & Intergroup Relations, 13*(6), 685–700.

Hick, J. (1995). *A Christian theology of religions: The rainbow of faiths.* Louisville, KY: Westminster John Knox Press.

Knitter, P. F. (2011). *Introducing theologies of religions.* Maryknoll, NY: Orbis Books.

Marty, M. E. (2005). *When faiths collide.* Malden, MA: Blackwell Publishing.

McCarthy, K. (2007). *Interfaith encounters in America.* Piscataway, NJ: Rutgers University Press.

Mead, N., & Maner, J. (2012). When me versus you becomes us versus them: How intergroup competition shapes ingroup psychology. *Social and Personality Psychology Compass, 6*(8), 566–74.

Merino, S. M. (2010). Religious diversity in a "Christian nation": The effects of theological exclusivity and interreligious contact on the acceptance of religious diversity. *Journal for the Scientific Study of Religion, 49*(2), 231–46.

Moore, T. (2014). *A religion of one's own: A guide to creating a personal spirituality in a secular world.* New York: Gotham Books.

Numrich, P. D. (2009). *The faith next door: American Christians and their new religious neighbors.* New York: Oxford University Press.

Patel, E. (2012). *Sacred ground: Pluralism, prejudice, and the promise of America.* Boston: Beacon Press.

Pettigrew, T. F., & Tropp, L. R. (2011). *When groups meet: The dynamics of intergroup contact.* New York: Psychology Press.

Putnam, R. D., & Campbell, D. E. (2010). *American grace: How religion divides and unites us.* New York: Simon & Schuster.

Roozen, D. A. (2011). American congregations reach out to other faith traditions: A decade of change 2000–2010. Report for The Hartford Institute for Religion Research. Retrieved from http://faithcommunitiestoday.org.

Tausch, N., Hewstone, M., & Roy, R. (2009). The relationships between contact, status, and prejudice: An integrated threat theory analysis of Hindu-Muslim relations in India. *Journal of Community & Applied Social Psychology, 19*(2), 83–94.

Tausch, N., Hewstone, M., Schmid, K., Hughes, J., & Cairns, E. (2011). Extended contact effects as a function of closeness of relationship with ingroup contacts. *Group Processes & Intergroup Relations, 14*(2), 239–54.

Terrizzi, J. A., Shook, N. J., & McDaniel, M. A. (2012). The behavioral immune system and social conservatism: A meta-analysis. *Evolution and Human Behavior.*

Wuthnow, R. (2005). *America and the challenges of religious diversity.* Princeton, NJ: Princeton University Press.

9 Internship: Situated Learning in the Department of Human and Organizational Development

HEATHER L. SMITH, VICTORIA J. DAVIS, MARYBETH SHINN, AND STEPHANIE ZUCKERMAN

> Give the pupils something to do, not something to learn; and the doing is of such a nature as to demand thinking; learning naturally results.
>
> —John Dewey, 1922[1]

> We have a powerful potential in our youth, and we must have the courage to change old ideas and practices so that we may direct their power toward good ends.
>
> —Mary McLeod Bethune, 1953[1]

For thousands of years, some of the great thinkers of the times acknowledged that experience is a source of powerful learning. In addition to the preceding noted quotes, in about 500 BCE, Confucius said, "I hear and I forget, I see and I remember, I do and I understand." In about 400 BCE, Sophocles noted, "One must learn by doing the thing, for though you think you know it, you have no certainty until you try." In the 1880s, Isadora Duncan, posited, "What one has not experienced, one will never understand in print." According to Albert Einstein several decades later, "The only source of knowledge is experience." As these thoughtful quotes suggest, in American higher education, experiential learning is a common strategy to engage students and achieve a higher level of learning.

Literature reveals considerable variability in the definition of experiential learning, however, including: "learning from experience or learning

---

1. Dewey, J. (1922) *Democracy and education: An introduction to the philosophy of education*, New York: MacMillan Press, p. 181; and Mary McLeod Bethune: *Building a better world: Essays and selected documents*, edited by A. Thomas McCluskey and E. M. Smith, 1999, Bloomington: Indiana University Press, p. 61.

by doing" (Lewis and Williams, 1994, p. 5); "a philosophy and methodology in which educators purposefully engage with learners in direct experience and reflection to increase knowledge, develop skills, and clarify values" (Association for Experiential Education, 2010, p. 1); and, "a direct encounter with the phenomenon being studied rather than merely thinking about the encounter or only considering the possibility of doing something with it" (Keeton & Tate, 1978, p. 2).

Even within the Department of HOD, experiential learning can mean everything from using interactive data collection tools in a large lecture, to a case study in the classroom, to a semester-long field experience. This chapter will focus on the field experience element of the spectrum, more specifically the Human Development Counseling (HDC) master's internship and the HOD Undergraduate Capstone Internship (HOD UGCI). We posit that these experiences embody the deepest meaning of experiential learning: a learning experience situated within a professional context. We will highlight the foundational learning theory upon which the two internships are built and illustrate how the department of HOD has constructed and achieves learning objectives in these two very different internship experiences. Moreover, we will focus on ways to leverage and exploit the potential learning that is situated within the professional context of the workplace.

The educational philosophy of the department of HOD is informed by constructivist developmental and social learning theories, most directly influenced by the teachings of John Dewey and Lev Vgotsky as well as by defining contributions of Kohlberg (1981), Perry (1998), Kegan (1998), and Kolb and Kolb (2008). This constructivist philosophy is operationalized through active involvement of and shared responsibility with learners, building upon and linking learning throughout the curriculum, interaction that leads to communities of learning, and situated and experiential learning that relies on authentic activities that embody theories, abstract concepts, and best practices. The HDC internship and the HOD UGCI are grounded in constructivist theory and built upon foundational concepts from the bodies of work on situated learning and reflective practice. They serve as examples of academically sound, well-designed experiential learning within a research university setting.[2]

---

2. In the United States, two types of accreditation exist: institutional, requiring evaluation of the entire institution, and specialized, requiring evaluation of professional

Although ample research supports the value of both situated and experiential learning, such learning experiences are often met with resistance in traditional academic settings. This resistance can be exacerbated by failure to build experiential learning courses upon a solid educational foundation and/or a failure to integrate experiential learning effectively into a comprehensive curricular design. Even Dewey understood that experience alone is inadequate in shaping education. In *Experiences and Education* (1938/1998) he explains, "The belief that all genuine education comes through experience does not mean that all experiences are genuinely or equally educative. Experience and education cannot be directly equated to each other. For some experiences are mis-educative" (p. 13). For experiential learning to be effective, educators must ensure a close alignment of learning objectives with field experiences and provide a structured and intentional process to allow learners to construct meaning. Experience without this underlying educational foundation and curricular design is similar to sailing a ship on the ocean without navigation: Luck might land the ship on a lovely, tropical island, but few of us would be willing to take that risk. Educators should not take that risk either. To ensure effective experiential learning, the educational design and practices of the HDC master's internship and HOD UGCI have been carefully and consciously constructed upon the framework of the department's underlying constructivist philosophy.

---

preparation programs within institutions. The Council for Accreditation of Counseling and Related Educational Programs (CACREP) is the specialized accreditation for master's and doctoral counseling degree programs. Since 1981, CACREP has been accrediting programs and providing recognition that the content and quality of graduate professional programs have been evaluated and meet standards set by the profession of counseling. The HDC program was first accredited by CACREP on March 1, 1983, and has achieved continuous reaccreditation since that time. The standards serve as the basis from which the HDC program and 261 (185 public; 77 private) other institutions engage in self-assessment and evaluation of their programs, are held accountable for educational activities, and construct student-learning assessments (CACREP, 2012). The internship processes and requirements described in this chapter adhere to CACREP standards. Refer to http://peabody.vanderbilt.edu/departments/hod/hod-undergraduate-program/internship_program/ for additional information on the two internships described in this chapter.

The M.Ed. Human Development Counseling Internship

The Human Development Counseling (HDC) internship has been in existence since 1983 and, today, retains much of its experiential learning pedagogical roots. In the sections that follow, a discussion of intentional internship design and local community impact of situated learning in counseling is discussed within the context specific to the pedagogical values of the HDC program. Learning objectives and teaching methods throughout the program curriculum and beginning in the first semester rely on developmental, constructivist, and experiential approaches to provide the frameworks and contexts for action, reflection, and learning. The internship serves as the capstone experience that requires students to integrate learning throughout the curriculum, including enacting the competencies related to skills, professional ethics, and personal growth. The consistent and intentional course design encourages what Kolb and Kolb (2008) called *integrative* learning. Kolb added to the work of Dewey (1938/1998) and Kohlberg (1981) by describing an experiential learning cycle model for teaching and learning. According to Kolb (1984) four conditions—concrete experience, reflective observation, abstract conceptualization, active experimentation—are necessary for significant construction of learning. A learner enters the cycle at any point and learning occurs in either direction (see Figure 9-1).

Concrete experience appeals directly to the senses. This type of experience occurs in counselor education when students in their first semester pair with fellow students to engage in role-play (assuming roles of counselor and client) *prior* to practicing counseling skills in professional roles. Students are encouraged to participate fully and openly. From this experience, instructors encourage and model reflective observation, which occurs when the learner steps back from the role-play (concrete experience) and asks, "What did it mean when the client stated s/he didn't understand my question?" Instructors might ask the client during role-play, "How was this interaction helpful to you?" and "What was not as helpful to you?" The goal of these experiences is to help counselors-in-training learn to make sense of the interaction (reflective observation) from the perspective of both the client and counselor. Abstract conceptualization occurs when counselors-in-training begin to realize that *a pattern exists to what is helpful.* Active experimentation occurs when they

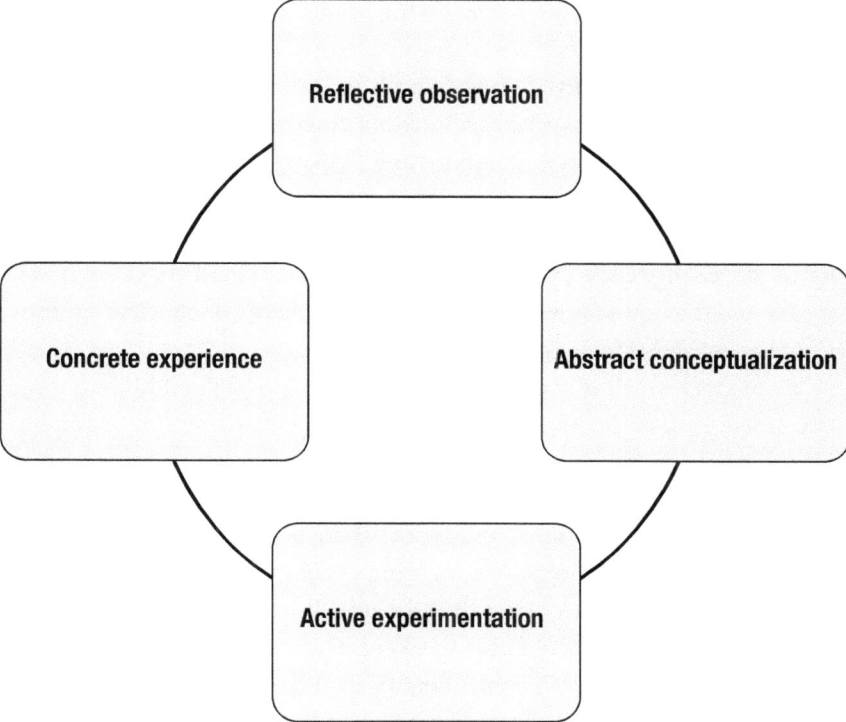

FIGURE 9-1. Kolb's (1984) experiential learning model. Four stages of learning construction.

enact a theory of therapeutic relationship based on a conceptualization of what is helpful to guide concrete interactions with clients.

Kolb's experiential learning model is well-suited for training counselors who must be able to take multiple perspectives. Thus, consistent practice reflecting upon one's own behavior and interactions with others in hypothetical role-play is imperative. When interacting with clients (either in role-play or in real life), counselors must view a situation as the client sees it, consider how pertinent others might view the situation, and consider what is known in helping relationships, including professional standards of practice. Counselor education, therefore, provides instruction on and experience with tolerance for uncertainty, deep listening skills, cultural relativism, and ethical and legal ways of working. Per Kegan's (1982) theory of adult cognitive development, growth processes depend on connections, and these processes occur perpetually within a context.

Students with different ways of knowing need different forms of support and challenge from their surrounding contexts in order to challenge their own thinking and build upon their skill sets as counselors. These surrounding contexts are defined as "holding environments" (Kegan, 1982, 1994). Counselor education programs and field experience settings create holding environments for counselors-in-training, wherein they develop the ability to engage in meta-level thinking, feeling, and behaving, all while attending to the present moment. The creation of these environments and the development of the mental complexity of effective professional counselors are not small tasks.

To support students' ability to think complexly, Kolb and Kolb (2008) encourage instructors to move from registrative learning (for example, traditional lecture courses) to interpretive and integrative learning by asking students to reflect upon case scenarios, work in teams to form abstract conceptualizations, and report their team's process and ideas for moving forward. Integrative learning occurs in the cycle when students' counseling work during their internship replaces case scenarios, role-play, and the stories of guest speakers. The internship class provides structure to reinforce each component of the learning cycle model. During weekly internship class, students are asked to reflect upon and communicate their experiences with clients using each component in the model. They are also asked to use the same process to construct meaning of their experiences of supervision. Interns are taught what to expect from supervision, the basics of supervision theories, and best practices in supervision. Instructors guide them through discussion about their supervision experiences, to reflect upon the purpose, possible intentions, and theories guiding their supervisors, and encourage them to begin to construct their own ideas for supervision.

Integration is supported when students are asked to evaluate and apply theories, research findings, standards of practice, and classroom understandings to their work as interns. The work of counseling requires cognitive complexity (Choate & Granello, 2006). Using Anderson and Krathwohl's (2001) Bloom's Revised Taxonomy for framing thinking, for example, students remember, understand, and apply information in courses such as ethics and theories. During internship they become responsible for distinguishing between relevant and irrelevant information (analyzing), making clinical judgments (evaluating), and engaging in the construction of goals with clients for interventions (creating). For students who want to fulfill requirements for state licensure and the ability to practice clinical mental health counseling independently, cognitive complexity and situated learning must continue during the 2–3 years (3,000 hours) of full-time post-master's supervised experience. The following example demonstrates situated learning in the HDC internship, with structure for fostering integration of learning and achievement of cognitive complexity. Identifying information has been removed to protect confidentiality.

Background. Isabel is a counseling intern through the Vanderbilt Center for Integrative Health (VCIH). Griffin is a Licensed Professional Counselor–Mental Health Service Provider (LPC-MHSP) at the VCIH who provides weekly supervision for her. Isabel also participates in weekly group supervision with five other interns and a faculty supervisor, Dr. Olivia. Isabel meets with Dr. Olivia several times throughout the semester for individual supervision. Much of Isabel's internship consists of counseling clients referred by physicians at the Vanderbilt Eskind Diabetes Clinic (VEDC). VEDC formed a partnership with VCIH several years ago in an effort to improve overall patient care. The diabetes medical care model puts patients at the center of their disease management; patients, however, don't always have the personal resources necessary for self-management. VCIH provides support services and supervises interns in mental health counseling for patients of the VEDC. During the first few weeks of internship, Isabel is immersed in VCIH work. She is oriented to its mission of integrative health and complementary and alternative medicine as well as to staff, practitioners, resources, services, and programs. Next, Isabel begins orientation to VEDC. She meets physicians, nurses, and allied health professionals; forms an understanding of their roles, basic processes, and commonly prescribed medications; and forms an abstract conceptualization of her specific role. As she experiments actively communicating what she is trained to do, Isabel uses listening and relationship-building skills to build trust with practitioners, resulting in referrals.

Concrete experiences at the internship site. Isabel receives referrals for counseling and quickly has her first contact with clients. During initial sessions, she uses the active listening skills and person-centered theory learned in the classroom and in practice with her peers to build rapport and trust with clients. She concentrates on client presentations and known data to build a hypothesis for working with clients. As her clients begin to demonstrate trust through expanding descriptions of their current functioning, Isabel considers appropriate intervention modification and the use of culturally responsive therapeutic interaction. Isabel demonstrates skill in conducting intake interviews, mental status evaluations, biopsychosocial histories, mental health histories, and psychological assessments including screens for addiction, aggression, harm to self or others, and co-occurring mental disorders.

Concrete experience during internship class. Isabel participates in class by sharing her concrete experiences and active experimentation at VEDC. She shares her new working knowledge of diabetes care and a struggle to engage a client, Emma, during the initial counseling interview. The faculty supervisor, Dr. Olivia, asks Isabel and a peer to engage in role-play and set up a similar scenario. Isabel enacts the role of Emma-the-client while her peer plays the role of a counselor. During the process Dr. Olivia stops the role-play and prompts discussion toward reflective observation.

Reflective observation. Isabel reflects and then states that she now realizes how frightening it must be to have diabetes and how well her peer-playing-the-counselor during the role-play explained what Emma-the-client could expect. Other peers reflect upon how the peer-playing-the-counselor worded her assessment questions pertaining to self-harm and suicidal risk. Another class member brings up a recent situation at his site. He asks the group to help him think about how the American Counseling Association's (ACA) *Code of Ethics* guides the situation. Later, Dr. Olivia asks the class how Isabel might have inquired more deeply to assess Emma's possible use of other substances. Through these reflections, Isabel and her peers recognize some of their individual strengths as well as improvement areas based upon their own self-monitoring and supervisory feedback.

Abstract conceptualization during faculty supervision. Dr. Olivia begins individual faculty supervision with Isabel by reviewing the purpose of their supervision, including the methods, models, and practices she uses for supervision. Isabel asks questions of Dr. Olivia and formulates questions for her site supervisor in order to get the most out of supervision at her internship site. Dr. Olivia scaffolds early faculty supervision sessions to assist Isabel in using her understanding of coursework to create working hypotheses based on initial meetings with the client. Isabel develops a conceptual/theoretical frame for understanding her client's world, including a discussion of short- and long-term goals and developmental constructs: stage, style, and tasks. Dr. Olivia's supervision also provides a holding environment for Isabel to increase her awareness and discern how her cognitive and affective reactions during a counseling session relate to her own personality style and life experiences so as not to interfere with her working relationship with the client.

Abstract conceptualization during site supervision. Isabel meets with Griffin, her site supervisor, and shares her reflections on her work with various clients. Griffin assesses Isabel's understanding of a variety of roles, research findings, and theories related to clinical mental health counseling, particularly as they apply to her work with clients. Isabel formulates an abstract conceptualization of one client, Michael. Michael was an electrician for ten years before sustaining a work-related injury. Since that time, he has been unable to work and has been diagnosed with type-2 diabetes mellitus. Griffin and Isabel discuss the potential impact of trauma on Michael, including what is known about his biopsychosocial history, mental health history, and medical history.

Active experimentation. Isabel practices current record-keeping standards related to clinical mental health counseling, including documentation formats of clinical assessment and treatment planning. She compares her new understanding of VEDC's electronic records system and experiments on paper with what she thinks is most appropriate. Moreover, Isabel seeks outs feedback from Griffin, who makes recommendations for her record-keeping. Although Isabel learned multiple common formats during her practicum class, every clinical site has different and nuanced expectations. Isabel reviews ethical and legal standards for record-keeping and consults with a physician on basic diabetes terminology, medicines, and complications. She experiments with appropriate use of her new understanding of the connections between diabetes self-management and her conceptualizations of professional counseling.

Concrete experiences at the internship site. Isabel begins working with James, a 65-year-old man who lives five hours from VEDC in a remote area of a neighboring state. He came to receive specialized diabetes care available only at VEDC. During initial interactions, Isabel hypothesized that James did not seem comfortable talking about himself with strangers, based, in part, on her initial attempts to engage him in casual conversation, which produced one- and two-word responses. She noted from his clinical record that he had been assessed with normal cognitive functions despite having had a brain tumor removed several years ago. Quickly moving through the entire learning cycle, Isabel formed a conclusion that her expectations for counseling might need to change. Expectations to engage James in counseling sessions—to identify and express his feelings to develop new behaviors to decrease stress and reduce his blood glucose levels—would not be respectful of his life situation or culture. During their second session, James briefly shares that meeting Isabel reminded him of an Asian-American friend he knew during "the war." Isabel decides to engage in a bit of appropriate self-disclosure by sharing brief facts about her own Asian background. She uses this self-disclosure to continue to build rapport and trust with James and reminds herself that it is her responsibility to discuss issues of difference with her clients, encouraging discussion on how her clients perceive the impact of differences on the process of professional counseling. By doing so, Isabel maintains ethical standards while demonstrating the ability to adapt to appropriate modification and use of culturally responsive counseling.

Community impact. Broader acceptance of situated and experiential learning approaches in the academy could be promoted by understanding the impact such experiences have not only for the students who engage in them but also for the surrounding community. Reporting the impact of a counseling internship can be hindered by, among other issues, concerns for the confidential nature of counseling work, difficulty in objectively measuring outcomes of therapeutic relationships and interventions, and a traditional academic focus on advancing student learning outcomes. However, the sheer amount of services HDC practicum students and interns provide is impressive. Students in the School Counseling (SC) track serve children and adolescents in elementary, middle, and high school. Students in the Clinical Mental Health Counseling (CMHC) track serve children, teens, and adults in a wide variety of settings, including cancer and diabetes centers, college campus counseling centers, employee assistance programs, homeless shelters, charter schools, large multi-level mental health service agencies, substance abuse treatment and recovery centers, prisons, and transitional living programs. During the 2011–2012 academic year, practicum and internship students in CMHC and SC tracks provided more than 7,000 hours of face-to-face services with clients in

53 different organizations, agencies, and schools in greater Nashville, Tennessee.

Information gathered from faculty site visits with site supervisors, supervisor evaluations of interns, intern evaluations of sites, and community advisory boards communicates the value of the HDC internships. Common site supervisor feedback can be summarized by the comments of two site supervisors "We really value your interns; they are so bright, responsible and challenge us with new information and ways of thinking" and "They are professional with all of the logistics, and it's obvious they have been practicing relationship-building skills, so we can focus more on the meanings they are constructing in their learning."[3] Site supervisors evaluate CMHC students on general counseling skills, general professional characteristics, specific counseling tasks, ethical conduct, and personal characteristics related to professional work. This information is then incorporated into the formal evaluation of intern competencies as well as the HDC program's comprehensive learning assessment system.

Concurrently, HDC interns express the value of situated learning in relation to their own growth and development. Interns provide feedback on thirteen areas addressing their ability to participate in service delivery and treatment planning and twenty-three areas about quality of supervision and training environment. Analysis of this student feedback of site experiences can then be used to inform HDC faculty when communicating experiential education needs with community internship partners and university administration. Additionally, the program periodically conducts an anonymous survey of HDC alumni. The most recent survey, conducted in 2012, showed a historic trend of alumni feedback about the utility of the internship. Of the 97 respondents, the mean response (1 = not prepared to 5 = very well prepared) to the statement, *my internship training was helpful in preparing me for my first professional position*, was 4.68.

The work of professional counseling requires thinking systemically, creatively, and ethically to make decisions under often uncertain conditions, in which knowledge of the client and context may be incomplete or evolving. The legal and ethical protections for members of the public in counseling situations place additional responsibilities on those who

---

3. These comments were made by supervisors at sites with which HDC has partnered for at least eight years and five years, respectively.

provide training. Counselor educators and supervisors carry the responsibility for professionally endorsing graduates beyond successful completion of coursework. As Lee Shulman (2005), past president of the Carnegie Foundation for the Advancement of Teaching, stated, "Professionals rarely can employ simple algorithms or protocols of practice in performing their services . . . professional education is about developing pedagogies to link ideas, practices, and values under conditions of inherent uncertainty that necessitates not only judgment to act, but also cognizance of the consequences of one's action. In the presence of uncertainty, one is obligated to learn from experience" (pp. 18–19). Situated learning represents an example of academics in action that is informed by this perspective.

The HOD Undergraduate Capstone Internship

What do these scenarios have in common?

- A program that increased hospital hand-washing compliance from 58 percent to 93 percent
- A Ford Foundation benchmark Metropolitan Schools Executive Board training and engagement program
- A hospital group contract analysis that exposed contract overlaps and netted $60,000 savings
- An ESL tutoring program to help integrate recently resettled refugees into the community
- An accounts receivable process that reduced time required for an international manufacturing firm to document and deposit payments by as much as 36 hours

The preceding projects were the culminating assignments undertaken by students completing the HOD UGCI. These projects, the result of coursework requirements, had considerable positive impact on the organizations in which they were conducted as well as the surrounding community. The UG Capstone internship is built upon the same underlying constructivist and experiential models that guide the learning process in the HOD Department. By situating learning within a professional context and carefully constructing the experiential learning framework, the HOD

UGCI, like that in HDC, advances this constructivist meaning-making process. The key learning objectives of the HOD UGCI coursework are scaffolded to help students construct meaning and develop the core competencies of the undergraduate degree: understanding and solving human problems in organizations and communities. As students situate the core competencies in the complex social environment of the workplace, they develop a professional worldview that shapes their thinking and guides their future actions. As in the HDC internship, the Kolb learning cycle is employed to facilitate meaning-making and advance student learning. The HOD UGCI results in a synergistic relationship between the university and the community, similar to that fostered by the HDC internship. However, the HOD UGCI experience employs a different educational design from that of HDC.

Traditional internships rely on the master/apprentice model. An apprentice (intern) works under a master (supervisor) situated within a profession/practice, and through interactions with and lessons from the master, the apprentice (intern) masters the knowledge, skills, and attitudes (KSAs) of that profession. In this model, the workplace supervisor assumes the educator role. By contrast, the HOD UGCI is constructed upon a model in which learning does not rely upon the supervisory relationship between intern and supervisor. Instead, the internship coursework is designed to provide the opportunity for students to apply their organizational problem-solving skills, situated in the complexity of a workplace setting. An action research model is used to explicitly outline the key organization and community problem-solving processes. The UG capstone internship both promotes and assesses students' ability to use this model and demonstrate that they can indeed understand and solve problems in organizations and communities. The instructional design and assignments of the accompanying weekly seminar provide the structure for the combined learning and assessment process. It is important to note that this is not a consulting or research internship model; students do the work of the organization in the same way a traditional intern would.

The difference lies in how the coursework of the capstone internship requires students to situate and apply concepts from earlier HOD courses as they attempt to understand and then add value to the internship organization. The examples of organizational impact described earlier were the result of the structure provided by the coursework. Students diagnose the effectiveness of the organizational system and select and implement an intervention that improves the system's overall performance. Within this model, then, an internship organization is not simply an experiential classroom but rather a living case study in which students both analyze and work to improve. The following quote, collected by a faculty member from an internship supervisor[4] during mid-semester site visits, is typical of the community response to the HOD UGCI: "We prefer HOD interns over other interns, even [other departments' and universities'] master's level interns. I really value the academic component of this internship. It makes the interns engage more deeply so I can trust them with more demanding projects." An internship that ensures that students add value as a requirement of the experience helps to create a positive reputation in the community, which, in turn, benefits the HOD department and the university in broadening their connections to and impact upon their community.

Unlike more traditional internship arrangements, the HOD department does not have to rely on the site supervisor as master/educator, and as a result, faculty retain control over the depth and quality of student learning. Accordingly, the industry/field competencies students learn on site may be of great interest to the student personally but are not learning objectives or evaluated as part of the internship experience. By situating the key theories, philosophies, and practices of the HOD degree in a workplace experience, the internship allows students to learn organizational problem-solving within contexts they will likely confront in future workplaces. The learning becomes real and relevant and deeply integrated into the student's worldview, where it can be accessed for future experiences. In the words of a past intern "The HOD internship was the most valuable, applicable, and interesting part of my HOD experience. Being given the opportunity to apply all that I have learned in the classroom to real-life business practices proved to be the most effective education."

---

4. Although she had supervised numerous interns from other schools over the last ten years, she had only recently worked with our interns. Her comments were prompted by her experience with this academically grounded internship experience, and she credited the internship structure for the difference in the quality of the internship experience. During the site visits, internship supervisor feedback is collected and then analyzed and used to adjust the coursework of the internship and the HOD undergraduate degree.

The HOD UGCI provides an opportunity for faculty to transform inert knowledge from earlier coursework to the upper levels of Bloom's (1956) taxonomy of learning: application, evaluation, and synthesis. It supports the developmental and academic goals of higher education while at the same time addressing the site-specific individual vocational learning goals of students. It also helps students develop confidence and provides a portfolio of success that demonstrates actual versus potential performance. Although an educational program may claim to be effective and valuable without actual "proof," both comments and survey ratings from graduating seniors and five-year alumni surveys provide corroborative evidence of these features of the HOD UGCI.

Alumni Comments from Former HOD Undergraduates

"Definitely the career development class and internship together [most valued aspect of degree]. . . . I wouldn't have been able to get the job with Bank of America without my internship experience and resume/interviewing skills. It's extremely hard getting a job right out of school in the area you are interested in because you lack 'experience.' So an internship is crucial to give Vandy students a leg up searching for a job in a tight market." (Class of 2003)

"The internship was key. It was practical experience applied to theory." (2004)

"The internship [. . . was most valuable]. I did my internship in Uganda and it turned into a three-year international career with various organizations in various countries." (2006)

"Having the internship experience to use to talk to future employers. I was able to use that experience and talk about the class that I took in conjunction, as well as show my tangible work products to make myself a better candidate when looking for my first job." (2007).

Comments from Graduating Seniors in HOD

"The HOD internship was definitely the most valuable part of the HOD experience. It provided insight into the world of work and how to handle it. However, the internship experience would not be as beneficial without the prerequisite courses leading up to it." (2010)

"I think the internship was the most valuable part. It was a culmination of everything that I had learned and made all of the course work useful." (2010)

"My HOD internship was unquestionably the most valuable part of my HOD experience. My internship experience completely changed my plan of what I was planning on pursuing in the future—thankfully!" (2010)

"Synthesizing key information from the past courses in HOD internship courses was highly valuable because it enabled me to remember what I had learned and apply those lessons in real-world scenarios." (2011)

In addition to the preceding quotes, survey statistics in Table 9-1 illustrate the benefits of the internship experience.

In addition to the benefit to student learning, the HOD internship model also provides immediate and ongoing feedback about the effectiveness of the HOD curriculum. Weak theoretical grounding and missing/weak skill sets become readily apparent when they have to be employed in support of an internship experience. Learning gaps and trends inform the curriculum development process to improve the quality of coursework and learning outcomes. Increasingly, cost-conscious educational consumers are demanding evidence of learning claims and looking for a return on investment. The evidence of organizational impact and student abilities that result from the HOD UGCI coursework are critical in answering these demands and supporting accreditation processes.

The HOD UGCI learning design. So how does this unique internship achieve these learning outcomes? The HOD UGCI is built upon a sophisticated instructional design framework to provide structure for students

Table 9-1. Percentage Indicating the Internship Was Very or Extremely Valuable

Graduating Senior Survey		5-Year Alumni Survey	
Class of 2012	79.2%	Class of 2007	86.6%
Class of 2011	77.4%	Class of 2006	86.2%
Class of 2010	79.6%	Class of 2005	79.2%

as they seek to understand their internship organizations to meet course objectives. The coursework aligns with and makes explicit the steps of the action research model to guard against reactive interventions and a short-term focus on symptoms rather than root causes.

The action research model has two distinct phases—diagnosis and intervention (see Figure 9-2). In the diagnostic phase, internship coursework focuses on systemic data gathering, analysis, and formal organizational

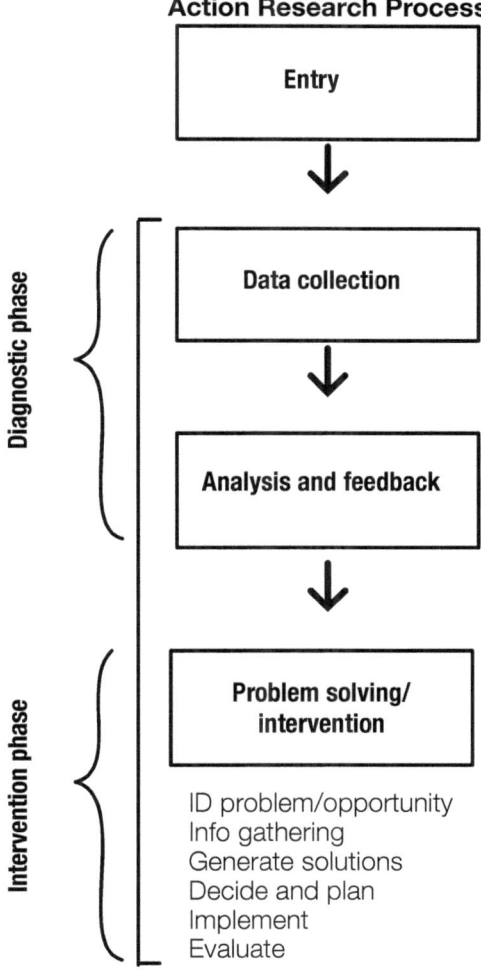

FIGURE 9-2. The action research model

feedback processes. Because students are simultaneously engaged in work within their organizations, these processes are not executed as a researcher or a consultant but as a participant-observer. The diagnostic phase of the process culminates in an organizational Strengths, Weaknesses, Opportunities, and Threats (SWOT) analysis and report. The intervention phase proceeds from the SWOT analysis. Informed by the feedback diagnosis, students select an organizational need they believe they are most equipped to and interested in addressing, building upon strengths, addressing a weakness, realizing an opportunity, or guarding against a threat. They then apply professional project planning techniques and tools to manage their intervention, from convincing their supervisor about the idea to the final evaluation of organizational impact.

The 15-credit-hour academic internship. Interns participate in a weekly three-hour seminar designed to execute the action research process, process their learning experiences through the stages of Kolb's learning model, and facilitate the transition to the workplace. They enroll in four courses, earning 15 credit hours overall (12 hours for the summer semester). Tuition (and financial aid) associated with the courses pay for the faculty who teach the courses as well as the operation of the internship office. Academic credit is awarded for coursework that accompanies the internship and each course has specific learning objectives and requirements:

Internship in Human and Organizational Development (6 credit hours, pass-fail and 3 credit hours during the summer). This includes the credit awarded for onsite internship performance.

Advanced Internship Seminar (3 credit hours—graded). This course assesses the ability to apply self-directed learning skills in an organizational learning situation and to use key theories of human and organizational behavior to understand, evaluate, and respond to personal work experiences.

Theoretical Applications (3 credit hours—graded). This course assesses the ability to demonstrate competencies associated with the analysis portion of the action research process.

Senior Project (3 credit hours—graded). This course assesses the ability to demonstrate problem solving and project management competencies associated with the action research process.

Each course has a foundational and culminating assignment (deliverables) with several supportive assignments. The assignments provide assessment of student learning, but more importantly, they also serve as learning tools. The assignments help students integrate concepts, techniques, and tools from multiple courses and situate the learning in the more complex and ambiguous workplace setting. By the end of the semester, students have a portfolio that demonstrates highly valued workplace competencies and the confidence to make a difference and add value in organizations. A 2003 graduate summarized the experience:

> I talk about my coursework and internship all the time (specifically in interviews where I can easily sell myself as someone who has been working 5.5 years plus another 4 from undergrad because HOD was such an application-based major). In addition, I have been able to take on numerous projects that no one else felt qualified for, and oftentimes, I created projects because I saw opportunities within an organization. I credit the ability to analyze situations, see opportunities, work with many different types of people and be comfortable in a number of settings to the innovative HOD coursework and program design.

Internship administration. The HOD Department has created formal HOD UGCI programs and hired and trained internship faculty in several cities beyond Nashville to allow students to pursue internships that may lead to post-graduation employment. These locations have shifted over the years as employment patterns have shifted; currently, HOD UGCI programs exist in six cities: Chicago, New York City, San Francisco, Washington D.C., London, England, and of course Nashville.

Each year the HOD undergraduate program supports approximately 200 total interns across the spring, summer, and fall semesters. The flexibility of the degree and academic nature of the internship coursework allows students to choose internships from a wide variety of industries and fields. In any given semester, students participate in a wide range of internships, including advertising, marketing, public relations, national and local non-profit community and service organizations (for example, Make-a-Wish Foundation, YMCA, the Nashville Martha O'Brien Center), national and local financial firms, both profit and non-profit healthcare, law and justice, music and film, news and sports broadcasting, publishing, international and local commercial real estate, entrepreneurial start-ups, policy research, insurance, government (city, state, and national), and educational institutions (for example, KIPP Academy, charter schools, university student life, international students, and athletic departments).

HOD students choose their own internships, as opposed to being placed by staff; thus, the internship search mirrors the job search process. Students contact organizations, market themselves, receive offers, and choose the internship experience that best meets their personal learning goals. The HOD UGCI staff maintains a networking database of pre-approved internship sites, which streamlines students' internship search process, although sites not in the current database may also be selected with proper approval by the program. Students are also allowed to petition for the opportunity to pursue an internship in a city other than those sponsored by HOD. In such cases, coursework is completed online. However, these alternate-city experiences are limited to special circumstances, given that students' academic learning experience in these cases is diminished by the lack of accompanying classroom discussion and interaction (Lave & Wegner, 1991). Examples of approved alternate experiences include an HIV orphanage in Uganda; the International Chamber of Commerce in Brussels, Belgium; a school in South Africa; Disneyworld; a dolphin therapy center in Key Largo; a film production facility in Los Angeles; General Electric Aviation in Cincinnati; and a summer program for high-risk youth run by an individual state.

Challenges. The HOD UGCI achieves the intended learning goals and provides a rich, situated learning experience for the students. It is not without its challenges, however. When combined with the multidisciplinary nature of the HOD degree, the internship must often be defended as a legitimate academic experience to college and university administration, parents, and even some faculty. Several forms of evidence answer these frequent challenges, including extensive feedback from students and internship supervisors; clearly written purpose, alignment, and flow rationale statements to explain each week of the internship semester coursework; a purpose statement and objectives linked to the published HOD undergraduate degree objectives for each assignment; and academic research that explains and supports the value of situated and experiential learning. The biggest challenge of the HOD internship experience is helping students navigate and balance competing objectives. Students choose their internships based on vocational and/or personal interests and may lose sight of the academic focus or resent the time required to complete coursework. To overcome this potential barrier, instructors must continuously reinforce the steps of the action-research process, demonstrate the alignment and linkage among the individual assignments, and communicate relevance of the coursework to students. Coaching and collaboration from instructors ensure that students keep academic and personal objectives in balance.

Situated Learning in the Department of HOD

This chapter focuses on the field experience component of experiential education. We present two examples of university-based internships, an academic internship at the undergraduate level and a professional counseling internship at the graduate level. The chapter offers a description of both internships, highlighting the unique objectives, challenges, and strengths of each, while demonstrating a shared commitment to best practices in experiential education. It may serve as a model for readers interested in developing their own professional or academic internships situated within a professional context. An accompanying website (previously footnoted) is also included that provides more detailed information about the internship experiences. The "Getting Started!" table provides additional suggestions and guidelines for developing an internship component within an academic environment and creating the kind of intentional learning experience espoused by Dewey (1938).

Conclusion

This chapter details two different HOD internships. We concede that significant economic and human resources are needed to maintain them. Readers interested in developing similar programs are encouraged to refer to the website listed in the endnotes and consider which modules or aspects are applicable to their environments as well as the challenges associated with implementation. Both the master's-level HDC and the undergraduate HOD capstone internships reflect the underlying constructivist philosophy of the department and a belief in the value of experiential and

Chapter 9: Getting Started!
Internship: Situated Learning in the Department of Human Organizational Development

Action Item 1: Determine the purpose and desired learning outcomes.
Before integrating a practicum and/or internship component into an academic program, the director(s) and creator(s) of these components should identify the overall purpose and desired learning outcomes that are expected to result from these experiences. Central to this clarification is the consideration of how these experiences foster degree/program learning outcomes and how a related curriculum that ensures these connections might be articulated and sequenced. These efforts ensure that students have a situated learning experience that is purposeful and linked to academic goals. We consider intentional design to be the critical action item that guides all those that follow, including the rationale needed to gain stakeholder buy-in.

Action Item 2: Ensure buy-in and support.
Before proceeding to incorporate a field experience, carefully consider the stakeholders whose approval and buy-in will be needed to obtain crucial resources and support. They may include university personnel (for example, deans, chairs, faculty), community leaders (for example, potential sites and supervisors), and even students and their family members (for example, parents/caregivers). Some practica and internships, especially those embedded in graduate and professional programs, are required for licensure or other certification and are part of an accredited program of studies. The task of ensuring buy-in for such experiences may be small, but identifying community stakeholders for community support and site availability/need will be critical. In contrast, establishing an undergraduate academic internship may require convincing university administrators and faculty of its academic merit and, if needed, conveying that merit to parents and students who may not comprehend its place and value in liberal arts education. Identifying and soliciting buy-in from appropriate stakeholders is essential to the eventual success of these immersive, situated learning experiences.

Action Item 3: Prepare students throughout the curriculum and prior to the internship.
Prepare students with the experiential learning, reflective practice competencies, and other competencies (knowledge, skills, and attitudes [KSAs]) needed for success. These competencies should be identified prior to the field experience and infused within the appropriate coursework. For example, prior to the graduate counseling internship, the HDC coursework includes instruction about key counseling competencies and incorporates role-play exercises that replicate anticipated counseling situations and hypothetical dilemmas with site supervisors. Reflective of Kolb's experiential learning cycle, these role-plays allow students to accumulate concrete experience and develop experiential learning and reflective practice processes under the guidance and support

Chapter 9: Getting Started! *(continued)*

of an instructor. Additionally, team exercises and activities that promote group cohesion should be included in the preparatory coursework. As illustrated previously, instructors should also consider developing courses that are devoted to skills related to fieldwork placement success.

Action Item 4: *Develop appropriate internship site relationships.*
The task of arranging appropriate internship sites should begin, at a minimum, with a needs assessment in the community in which the internship will occur. Needs of various sites and available opportunities should be assessed and appropriate onsite supervisors identified (and trained if needed). In addition, faculty expectations for learning objectives and suitable experiences should be communicated to and accepted by the potential internship sites. Skills training (for example, reflective listening) or review of pertinent research and theory (for example, developmental theories) can be offered to supervisors, such that students gain the most from the internship and supervisors remain aware of what knowledge students may bring to their fieldwork. In addition, once the internship begins, faculty site visits allow the opportunity to observe the intern in action and help build support and community among site supervisors and sites.

Action Item 5: *Maintain a database of available sites.*
A searchable database should be created as a resource for future internships and ongoing management of site relationships that includes details about the site, supervisor contact information, organizational needs, student evaluations of their experiences on site, and other information to help ensure an optimal fit between student and organizational needs. This database can also be a source of valuable information about student interests and needs/issues confronting the field or discipline that may inform the internship curriculum.

Action Item 6: *Develop the internship seminar/course that accompanies fieldwork.*
A classroom component that occurs simultaneously with the internship and links the onsite experience to desired learning objectives should be developed that encourages students to integrate pertinent concepts, competencies, and KSAs from earlier coursework into a coherent body of knowledge that can be accessed on site. The instructor can ensure that students move through the experiential learning cycle, support them through insecurities and difficulties on site, and challenge them to reconcile situations when reality and theory do not align. As in courses prior to the internship, specific exercises (for example, role-plays, group work) and coaching can be integrated, but now in response to actual onsite situations, helping students troubleshoot and further integrate academic learning in real-life experiences. The classroom can also provide valuable program feedback, as the instructor observes student strengths and weaknesses, onsite expectations, and emerging field/discipline issues that can be useful to improve the program.

(continued)

Chapter 9: Getting Started! *(continued)*

Action Item 7: Develop appropriate documentation and feedback processes.
These documentation processes and forms will differ depending on the purpose and level of the fieldwork experience and might include time logs, supervisor evaluations, student evaluations, site assessments, faculty visitation reports, and other records that appropriately document the internship experience. Key here is the appropriate use of information. In addition to providing feedback on student performance and learning or site viability, useful program feedback can also be generated that may reveal common issues, misunderstandings, or unrecognized student or site needs. This information can uncover learning deficiencies that suggest curriculum and coursework changes, new field/discipline issues to consider, and instructor effectiveness trends.

Action Item 8: Reinforce lifelong, self-directed learning.
Meaningful closure of powerful learning experiences is critical in order to ensure that learning is transferred into future experiences. This closure may be accomplished through a reflective process that helps students focus on the personal changes that have occurred and the development of action plans for future learning. Specific assignments may also be developed that incorporate these reflective processes explicitly. For example, in the HOD UGCI, students begin the semester with an individual development plan (IDP) that identifies their specific learning objectives. Meaningful closure is assisted via the development of a professional portfolio that consolidates evidence of their learning (content and process) and the creation of a future IDP that bridges from their current experience into the future, thereby reinforcing lifelong, self-directed learning.

Action Item 9: Access available information and support via professional organizations.
Professional organizations, such as the National Society for Experiential Education (NSEE: http://www.nsee.org/) and the Cooperative Education and Internship Association (CEIA: http://www.ceiainc.org/home.asp) provide useful resources for students and educators. The National Association of Colleges and Educators (NACE) has an extensive body of internship resources. Organizations and local chapters of the professional organizations related to your field or discipline are also useful, both as sources of professional development materials and contacts about possible internship sites.

---

situated learning. Moreover, both programs reflect and advance Peabody College of Education and Human Development's reputation in the community through the positive impact interns have upon the organizations they work with. In this way, internships are prime examples of academics in action.

References

Anderson, L. W., & Krathwohl, D. R. (Eds.). (2001). *A taxonomy for learning, teaching and assessing: A revision of Bloom's Taxonomy of educational objectives: Complete edition*, New York: Longman.

Association for Experiential Education. (2010). *AAE fact sheet*. Retrieved on May 5, 2013 from http://www.aee.org/about/

Bloom, B. S. (1956). *Taxonomy of Educational Experiences, Handbook 1: The Cognitive Domain*. New York: David McKay Co, Inc.

Chi Sigma Iota Counseling Academic & Honor Society International. (2013). *What Is CSI?* Retrieved on June 5, 2013 from http://www.csi-net.org/

Choate, L. H., & Granello, D. H. (2006). Promoting student cognitive development in counselor preparation: A proposed expanded role for faculty advisors. *Counselor Education and Supervision, 46*, 116–30.

Council for Accreditation of Counseling and Related Educational Programs. (2012). *CACREP 2012 annual report*. Retrieved on May 5, 2013 from http://www.cacrep.org/detail/news.cfm?news_id=74&id=9

Dewey, J. (1938/1998). Experiences and education (60th anniversary edition). Indianapolis, IN: Kappa Delta Pi.

Granello, D. H. (2000). Contextual teaching and learning in counselor education. *Counselor Education and Supervision, 39*, 270–83.

Keeton M. T., & Tate, P. J. (Ed). (1978). *Learning by experience—what, why, how*. Jossey-Bass, San Francisco, CA.

Kegan, R. (1982). *The evolving self: Problems and process in human development*. Cambridge, MA: Harvard University Press.

Kegan, R. (1998). *In over our heads: The mental demands of modern life*. Cambridge, MA: Harvard University Press.

Kohlberg, L. (1981). *The philosophy of moral development: Moral stages and the idea of justice*. San Francisco: Harper & Row.

Kolb, A. Y., & Kolb, D. A. (2005). Learning styles and learning spaces: Enhancing experiential learning in higher education. *Academy of Management Learning and Education, 4*, 193–212.

Kolb, D. A. (1984). *Experiential learning: Experience as the source of learning and development*. Englewood Cliffs, NJ: Prentice-Hall.

Lave, J., & Wegner, E. (1991). *Situated learning: Legitimate peripheral participation*. New York: Cambridge University Press, 16th printing.

Lewis, L. H., & Williams, C. J. (1994). Experiential learning: Past and present. *New Directions for Adult and Continuing Education, 62*, 5–16.

Perry, W. G. (1999). *Forms of intellectual and ethical development in the college years*. New York: Holt, Rinehart & Winston.

Shulman, L. S. (2005). Pedagogies of uncertainty. *Liberal Education, 91*, 18–25.

10 Can Synergy Across Theory, Pedagogy, and Practice Guide Professional Education?

The Community Development and Action and Human Development Counseling Graduate Experiences

ANDREW FINCH, OLUCHI NWOSU, GINA FRIEDEN, EMILY HENNESSEY, CRAIG ANNE HEFLINGER, ALLISON McGUIRE, SARAH V. SUITER, EMILY BURCHFIELD, NINA C. MARTIN, LINDA ISAACS, LAUREN BRINKLEY-RUBENSTEIN, PAUL SPEER, ABBEY MANN, SHARON SHIELDS, NEAL PALMER, BETHANY PITTMAN, AND SANDRA L. BARNES

The most important factor in the training of good mental habits consists in acquiring the attitude of suspended conclusion . . . To maintain the state of doubt and to carry on systematic and protracted inquiry—these are the essentials of thinking.

—John Dewey 1910[1]

Education is the most powerful weapon which you can use to change the world.

—Nelson Mandela[2]

The two professional development programs in the department of Human and Organizational Development, Community Development and Action (CDA), and Human Development Counseling (HDC) repre-

---

1. Dewey, J. (1910). *How we think.* Lexington, MA: D. C. Heath & Co. Publishers, p. 14.
2. Nelson Mandela, S. K. Hatang, Sahm Venter (Eds). (2012). *Notes to the future: Words of wisdom.* New York: Atria Books, p. 101.

sent examples of informing theory with practice at its best.[3] Both efforts are firmly undergirded by foundational theoretical frameworks; both reflect the centrality of being able to put such models to the test. The two subsections that follow present a brief history of the respective programs, key scholarly figures, instructional processes, and examples of how coursework is translated into skills and experiences that graduate students can use in their roles as reflexive practitioners (Schön, 1983). CDA and HDC prepare students to proactively understand, examine, and solve real-world problems based on a constructivist approach. In doing so, students are creating useful knowledge to transform the lives of individuals, groups, communities, and the broader society (Dewey, 1988).

Community Development and Action

Community Development and Action (CDA) is a 30-hour master's degree program with a substantial field practicum requirement. As a professional practice program, CDA is challenged to integrate the desire for practical skills among students with the theoretical and research perspectives of faculty. The following subsection describes CDA's conceptual model and curriculum alignment, provides strategies for possible implementation in other departments, presents student and faculty experiences, and illustrates how CDA reflects twenty-first century Deweyism.

CDA Purpose and Conceptual Program Model

As active and ethical agents of change, CDA students are prepared to take the role of community organizer or to assume managerial and advocacy positions within human service organizations, private foundations, advocacy groups, educational institutions, global non-governmental organizations (NGOs), or government agencies. It is the shared focus of community building and human development to collaboratively solve complex problems

---

3. This chapter reflects the collaborative efforts of three teams of authors. This includes a team of first authors (Finch, Frieden, Heflinger, and Nwosu), a team of second authors (Barnes, Burchfield, and Hennessey), and a team of third authors (Brinkley-Rubenstein, Isaacs, Mann, Martin, McGuire, Palmer, Pittman, Shields, Speer, and Suiter). While names are listed alphabetically here, each author contributed equally within his or her respective team.

that distinguishes CDA from master's programs within public administration, social work, and not-for-profit management. The main program tenants—active community participation, inquiry into social problems, group learning, and effective communication—are based upon Dewey's four contextual conditions for the emergence of community and democracy: participation, learning and education, inquiry, and communication (Dewey, 1988: also refer to Chapter 1).

The CDA program model is based on three key domains—philosophy, theory, and practice—linked through an active pedagogy (see Figure 10-1). Dewey's pragmatism (1988) grounds the program. Social-ecological systems theory informed by Bronfenbrenner (1977, 1994) contributes a broad framework for a multidisciplinary orientation to pragmatic problem setting and solving. The reflective-generative practitioner model introduced by Schön (1983) and expanded upon by Dokecki (1996, this volume) is the program's practice model. And finally, a pedagogy informed

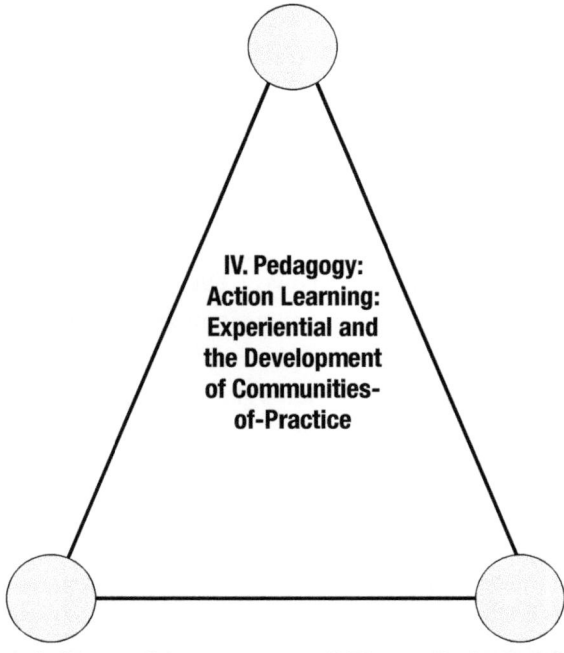

FIGURE 10-1. CDA's conceptual program model

by an active and social orientation to learning is employed to link the three domains and represents the intellectual content, performance expectations, and basic values and presuppositions espoused by the program.

Philosophy: The Pragmatism of John Dewey

Although a detailed account of Dewey is provided in Chapter 1, several points are germane here. Dewey (1988) suggested that citizenship within a democracy requires *participation* to the extent of each person's capacity as well as the intentional inclusion of all citizens to recognize and further the common good. Viewing community and democracy through a participative and educative lens suggests that maximum inclusion and participation are essential parts of public problem solving; exclusion from this process becomes an issue of social justice. The centrality of this premise is evident in the following comment by a first-year CDA student: "I have been able to learn how issues can be viewed using multiple perspectives and learn what constitutes effective change . . . the program offers unique perspectives on current issues facing our society." Moreover, participation is also linked to *learning and education* that is often more local and geared toward specific problems and that offers a space to learn and increase one's capacity. Finally, Dewey was concerned about *communication* and the dissemination of findings offered by social science and community groups. Thus, problem-focused inquiry brings people together to enable learning while building community that can improve overall quality of life.

Orienting Program Theory: Social-Ecological Systems

Bronfenbrenner (1977, 1994) provides the cornerstone of the community theory foundations of this program. Students are encouraged to focus on social issues on multiple levels, considering factors in the microsystem (individual, family, peers), mesosystem (interactions among microsystem members), exosystem (communities and community organizations), and macrosystem (culture and policy) as well as interactions between levels. For example, students often discuss the influence of policy on organizations, groups, and individuals; the influence of individuals and groups on policy decisions; and the relationships between community organizations and individuals. According to one faculty member:

Our graduates are hugely intelligent . . . they are knowledgeable about how communities work, how families work, how individuals work. We understand systems at the micro, meso, and macro levels and we . . . and . . . they also have some real practical appreciation for how to solve problems in the real world. (Professor in HOD for four years)

An examination of power dynamics in research and practice and reflection on one's own role in reinforcing or changing existing dominant paradigms in communities, organizations, and classrooms is central to the CDA experience.

Program Practice Model: The Reflective-Generative Practitioner

Informed by Dewey's belief in the relationship between participation and learning, Schön (1983) posited that professionals learn within rich contexts of challenge while in partnership with others to address everyday problems using a type of knowing-in-action or epistemology of practice. Schön utilizes the metaphor of a "swamp" to capture the ambiguity, uncertainty, stakeholder multiplicity, and complexity presented to professionals in practice and distinguishes it from the often more decontextualized world of a positivistic researcher or the rational technical practitioner. Inquiry, such as action research, is embedded in the role of the *reflective-generative practitioner*. Such intense focus on the problem aspect of professional work may have led Schön to recognize and acknowledge the centrality of problem-setting (the ability to structure or frame and sometimes re-frame problems) as a characteristic of an experienced reflective practitioner. For CDA students, this equates to an understanding of the historical, political, and socioeconomic context in which problems exist and multiple factual aspects and stakeholders in a given situation (Dewey, 1988; Dokecki, 1996; Innes, 2006, 2007). The reflective-generative practice model offers students a way of thinking, valuing, relating, and acting that connects their actions to broader organizational and social policy networks and change efforts (King, 2000).

Program Pedagogy

This section summarizes program pedagogy—its classroom orientation, community activities, and expectations, as well as steps for implementation by readers (Dokecki, 1996; Gherardi, 2009).

Professional education. Professional schools have come under increasing scrutiny because students are now expected to have skills to solve complex problems, communicate effectively, and collaborate rather than merely acquire static knowledge. The desired outcome of a CDA education is the ability to take well-informed and effective action within the context of community development and capacity building. As community practitioners, CDA students are asked to develop community partnerships, engage in active group problem setting and solving, develop and manage programs, evaluate policies, design and facilitate change initiatives, and provide leadership within these same areas. In a way we contend is different from other more traditional management or public administration programs, students are not being taught *what to do;* rather they are learning *how to learn* and *how to reason what to do* to create positive change, then *how to evaluate* what they have done, *how to learn* from both the intended and the unintended consequences of their interventions, and *how to begin again*. This skill set becomes invaluable as students are challenged in "swampy" real-world situations:

> I have become acquainted with foundational theories that, to my surprise, have articulated the values I have developed and the frustrations I have encountered in working with communities. These authors have suggested viable pathways and tactics for pushing through or circumventing these obstacles. (First-year CDA student, M.Ed. candidate)

The merging of theory, context, values, and skills within authentic practice spaces is what distinguishes CDA's professional education; all elements are required.

Performance competencies. Competency refers to the ability of a professional practitioner to make intentional choices from a variety of options, across varied situations, and in contexts that are often complex. Competencies include engaging in practice and addressing the inevitable questions when confronted by new ideas and theoretical material: What am I to do with this? How exactly does this *work or look* in practice?"[4] Each competency (see Table 10-1) is linked with and supported by the program's philosophy, theoretical frameworks, and/or the reflective-generative practice model. Measures to assess learning outcome were

---

4. Refer to the departmental website for the six core learning outcomes and twelve competencies desired for CDA.

Table 10-1. CDA Program Learning Outcomes and Competencies, 2012

Learning Outcomes	Competencies*
1. Develop an understanding of the interdisciplinary complexity and systemic nature of embedded social problems.	A. Community assessment and evaluation
2. Gain an understanding of the challenges of community development work as practiced within a professional context.	B. Communication C. Critical thinking and judgment
3. Develop an understanding and a basic proficiency in observation and reflection skills necessary to become a reflective generative practitioner.	D. Collaboration (and consultation) E. Reflective-generative practice
4. Develop proficiency in one of the following: participatory action research, case studies, community research methods and/or policy program evaluation.	F. Interdisciplinary practice and perspective G. Applied research H. Organizational assessment
5. Master analytical skills suitable for collaborative, multidisciplinary community development work.	I. Problem solving J. Group process K. Capacity building
6. Demonstrate solid competence in the ability to apply theoretical knowledge to specific social problems and professional dilemmas within the field of community development.	L. Life-long learning

*The competencies are applied toward each of the learning outcomes.

developed and data are collected for program review in alignment with the university's accreditation process (Commission on Colleges, 2012).

Core learning activities. Core learning activities include those activities that are evident throughout the program and on which the pedagogy of active social and experiential learning depends. They are provided via participation within authentic contexts, group work or team based learning, reflective writing (observation, reflection, and questioning), and dialogue.

Participation in authentic contexts. A defining characteristic of the CDA pedagogy is an emphasis on experiential learning to develop students' professional judgment and expertise. Students are presented with multiple possibilities for constructing meaning within specific community situations. Students participate in the classroom community, the program, and the wider community at a practicum site. Following these experiences, student observations, questions, and reflections are brought into the classroom to understand the various perspectives that surfaced. Community partners also realize its benefits:

> Partnering with Vanderbilt University has been an essential component to the [group name] initiative. The initiative is dedicated to having research-informed and evidence-based outcomes . . . and using local-level data to help us determine community-specific strengths and vulnerabilities. In order to get that very local-level data and community voice involved in the programming and planning for an initiative that is large scale and long-term, we need an academic research partner . . . Our work right now is about documenting that [systemic problems] so that we can then have a collective voice to say we know that we can do this, and we need to change some of the systems and structures that are barriers right now. (Program Director of a local center)

As illustrated in the above comment, the academic-applied emphasis in CDA results in partnerships that inform and empower local communities.

Group work or team-based learning. For community change agents, the setting and solving of community problems occurs within the context of groups such as advocacy groups, neighborhood groups, task forces, and fundraising subcommittees that present opportunities for community development and capacity building. Another CDA student comments, "I've been able to partner with a community organization doing significant community development work . . . which has provided me with a great parallel to my academics." Dewey (1988) suggested that education for a democratic society include the skills necessary for joint work in community problem solving. As evidenced by the student's experiences, groups often do the everyday hard work of framing and addressing problems, building coalitions, conducting action research, and developing and evaluating community programs.

Reflective writing. Framing chaotic situations into actionable problems requires that students learn to notice the myriad and important details within a given practice situation. Learning to think-in-action and to reflect-on-action, as described by Schön (1983), assumes that students know what to observe and how to reflect deeply. Reflective writing assignments emerged from Kolb's (1984) orientation to experiential learning that includes the four quadrants of concrete experience, reflective observation, theoretical conceptualization, and active experimentation. These writings support the central practices of observation, reflection, and question drafting and framing to understand a specific situation. Learning to frame questions encourages students to clarify their own thinking while attempting to clarify "messy" practice situations while asking questions such as: What do I know about this situation? How do I know this? What more do I need to know? Whom can I consult to discover alternatives?

Dialogue. Communication is both a program goal (a skill to be developed) and a core learning strategy taught through ongoing dialogue, discussion, and debate around issues central to human, organizational, and community development. Providing opportunities to reframe and revise work after receiving feedback from peers and instructors furthers the process of shared reflection and joint learning. Students can also reflect deeply and question key assumptions and personal theories of action (Argyris & Schön, 1996) as well as the systems in which they are working and embedded. Fostering dialogue requires honing one's written and verbal communication skills; gaining an awareness of the ways inequalities inhibit, enable, and shape communication; and developing strategies for promoting diverse and dissenting voices in all of the communities in which we work. The practitioner is not an expert but rather is always in the process of learning alongside and with community partners. The goal of communication in such a relationship is to learn rather than to convince the other party to alter the outcome of a situation (Dokecki, 1996).

Bringing the Curriculum Together: Thumbnail Descriptions of the First Semester

Three first-semester required courses form the CDA foundation and subsequent community work: Community Development Theories, Community Inquiry, and Proseminar. Each is summarized in the text that follows (also refer to the HOD website) along with two broader processes central to the program's success. Furthermore, course faculty work regularly to: (1) identify logical points where the three curricula can be coordinated and support one another across experiences, assignments, and timing; (2)

ensure that core readings are incorporated in all courses but reading redundancy is eliminated, and (3) continuously improve this process and the rubric to assess a skill identified by all instructors as an area for student development in presentations.

Community Development Theories. This course is designed to explore the complexities and less-than-obvious aspects within embedded and complex social problems. It includes a range of theories including structural, political process, and agentic theories, focusing on community development and change. This course stresses how political, cultural, and economic conditions shape these theories, as well as how these theories explain the interaction of multiple forces that influence communities and residents; it complements the methods and practice courses.

Community Inquiry. This course focuses on systematic inquiry. The learning outcomes include: (1) a personal framework for the relationship between researcher and the "researched" in a community; (2) belief that there should be a fit between ideas/questions, theory, methods used, and the social context; and (3) realization that research is not a linear and fixed process, but often cyclical, dynamic, complex, and "messy." Quantitative and qualitative approaches, various data collection methods, and community-participatory and ethical principles that underlie research are presented (Israel et al., 1998).

Proseminar. A first-semester Proseminar and subsequent Practicum courses link philosophy and theory to practice. During a practicum experience, students observe and reflect on the practices, processes, and cultural norms within a particular organization. First they read extensively in the areas of organizational culture, structure, power, and learning and are introduced to a systems orientation to organizational analysis through the work of Morgan (2006). Cooperative learning groups are also used extensively within classroom activities and community assignments. A final semester project contains many of the essential elements of an action learning project (Marsick & O'Neil, 1999; Revans, 1982) and integrates theory and inquiry skills from the other two courses.

Kolb's (1984) learning cycle (observation, reflection, and questioning) and problem setting and problem solving. Students are specifically directed toward their group's process and are often, during the professional seminar, provided time at the end of class for reflection. Most importantly, they are asked to notice and to describe the contexts of their early community assignments and to extend their observations beyond what is simply stated within a situation or the documentation of those present. Reflective writing assignments help guide student observation and reflection; they also serve as diagnostic tools to provide feedback and encourage reflections from different system levels. Case studies and films augment participant observations and enable the class to think together and frame a problem out of a conversation. Once students begin their practicum, these case studies become more meaningful and their discussions deepen in complexity. And for students with little work experience, case studies are essential for understanding abstract concepts and thick description of ethical, political, structural, economic, and intellectual challenges present within real situations (Geertz, 1973; Schön, 1983).

Learning to learn. Scholarship suggests that the over-arching goal of professional education is significant learning that endures well beyond the end of a course or a master's program. Practitioners must be able to meet new challenges within a constantly shifting professional work place, use new technology, and anticipate its consequences on building and sustaining community. The foundational skills of observing, reflecting, and questioning can be recognized as grounding for the more difficult challenges of reasoning and critical thinking and the strategies of interpersonal communication embedded within the program's key competencies. Learning to learn from experience within ambiguous and confusing circumstances is a theme repeated within all other core learning strategies. Overall, what distinguishes the CDA program is its insistence that students develop these critical skills for lifelong learning.[5]

Conclusion: CDA Synergies Across Theory, Pedagogy, and Practice

The cornerstones to ensuring a balance of theory and practice in CDA are (1) implementation of a triangular program model that emphasizes aptitude in three key domains—philosophy, theory, and practice—linked through an active pedagogy; (2) grounding of the program in a pragmatic, progressive educational ethos advanced by Dewey (1988); and (3) commit-

---

5. Vanderbilt University is accredited by the Southern Association of Colleges and Schools (SACS) Commission on Colleges (2012).

ment by individual faculty to support the first semester and work collaboratively despite barriers in the academic culture. As noted by the following CDA student's testimony, faculty and students work collaboratively to this end: "I have met some faculty that are really engaged in helping their students succeed. Here, I'm not just a student but also a colleague, researcher, and leader." The main tenants of the program—active community participation, inquiry into social problems, group learning, and effective communication—are based upon Dewey's four contextual conditions for the emergence of community and democracy (Dewey, 1988). The desired outcome is the ability to take well-informed and effective action within the context of community development and capacity building as community practitioners. CDA students are asked to develop community partnerships, engage in active group problem setting and solving, develop and manage programs, evaluate policies, design and facilitate change initiatives, and provide leadership within these same areas. We posit that it is this shared focus of community building and human development, within an active context of problem solving, that distinguishes CDA from other master's programs in this field. It is the intentionality to develop a reflective-generative practitioner that distinguishes the CDA graduate in the profession.

Human Development Counseling: Creation and Program Development

The following brief history of the Human Development Counseling (HDC) program is provided to help readers appreciate its evolution and understand how the HDC culture came to be imbued with a developmental framework. HDC was created in 1974 by faculty from diverse disciplines, including community psychology, humanistic counseling, and human development. The program was designed for implementation both overseas and on the Peabody campus (then the George Peabody College for Teachers) and within an innovative overseas extension program (P. Dokecki, personal communication, September 28, 2012). In 1974, John Dunworth became the new President of George Peabody College. While at Ball State University, he had designed a master's degree program in counseling that was sold to the Department of Defense and was offered on various military bases in Europe. Larry Weitz, director of counseling psychology at Peabody, and Richard Percy and Ken Anchor, also Vanderbilt faculty members, created the title "Human Development Counseling" (R. Percy, personal communication, November 24, 2012). Later meetings with faculty members Ray Norris (of the Vanderbilt Psychology department), Jules Seeman, and Paul Dokecki (of the Peabody Psychology department) determined program details, which included both a master's and doctoral degree in counseling.[6]

Roger Aubrey was hired to become the first director of the Peabody HDC on-campus program in 1977 (Briddick, 1997). For twenty years, he incorporated the ideas of Hobbs and Dewey in crafting his vision of a counseling profession that would utilize developmental theory in an integrated and applied manner (Dewey, 1988; Hobbs et al., 1984). Soon after arriving at Peabody, Aubrey (1980) published an article emphasizing the multidimensional nature of counseling and calling for a rapprochement across sectors rather than a narrowing of the field:

> The bedrock of counseling is meager at best. It can ill afford to ignore or deny significant findings in related professions/sciences that could contribute to its own development. (p. 319)

Specifically, since its inception, HDC has called for counselors to embrace social and behavioral sciences, the humanities, and philosophy. Coursework is designed to provide students with the skills and competencies necessary to work with a variety of clients in a multitude of settings (R. Percy, personal communication, November 13, 2012). Originally designed with a developmental emphasis, the program has embraced the traditions of a "learning organization" (Cannon & Edmonson, 2005), including the willingness to examine what is not working, allow experimentation, and embrace changes, which has helped ensure HDC's relevance and resilience across the years. In 1983, HDC became one of the earliest CACREP accredited programs.[7] In 1995, the program became just

---

6. In the fall of 1974, Dunworth presented the new HDC model to the U.S. Department of Defense (DOD), which signed a contract to offer the program at seven European bases, to be directed initially by Norris and later by Percy. One of the DOD's requirements was that Peabody could not offer a program overseas that was not also offered on campus.

7. An early example of this resilience came with the closing of the overseas program in 1981 and the merger of Peabody College and Vanderbilt University. The campus program remained intact, becoming part of the larger Vanderbilt University system,

the seventh program to earn the "Outstanding Chapter Award" from Chi Sigma Iota, the international counseling honorary.[8]

How HDC Differs from Other Counseling Programs

From the program's founding as a community counseling and school guidance graduate program in the 1970s through its evolution to a fully accredited program today, a prominent objective of the HDC program has been to teach students the skills and practices essential to promoting positive human development in individuals, families, and communities. Students of the program are expected to develop the knowledge, skills, and attitudes needed to respond effectively to contemporary social demands and to address these challenges in part by drawing upon the knowledge base of human developmental theory.

The HDC faculty strives to provide students with conceptual frameworks of human development that will ultimately inform approaches of counseling and therapy unique to individual clients' needs. For example, a second-year HDC student described the "collaborative family approach that the program has adopted." Professional development requires being able to add value to non-academic spaces in ways that are professionally and personally rewarding. According to another HDC student in the School Counseling track, his time in HOD is providing broad-based training for systemic change: "Of the more noteworthy experiences, I've really enjoyed an understanding of the role of sound policy-making . . . I look forward to functioning as an advocate." The interdisciplinary scope of the program prepares students as counselors with numerous lenses to solve complex problems. Furthermore, students feel that faculty members

---

which had merged with the George Peabody College for Teachers in 1979 (P. Dokecki, personal communication, September 28, 2012). Because both Vanderbilt and Peabody had their own Psychology departments at the time of the merger, HDC's Doctor of Education program was gradually phased out in the 1980s (R. Percy, personal communication, April 19, 2013). According to counseling historian Mark Pope (2013), the Council for Accreditation of Counseling and Related Educational Programs was formally established by ACA Governing council resolution in 1981, and that year, 106 programs were formally accredited out of a possible 350.

8. According to the Chi Sigma Iota website (2013), the Outstanding Chapter Award was first given in 1988.

are invested in their professional and personal development, regardless of their diverse backgrounds and future aspirations:

> As someone who made an academic shift from Chemistry and Secondary Education to a Mental Health and Counseling program, I feel grateful for the guidance and assistance of the faculty and cohort members in helping me adjust to the academic and social expectations of this program. (Second-year HDC student)

These responses, coupled with those in the previous subsection on the CDA experience, illustrate a strong connection between HOD's interdisciplinarity, academic rigor, and the instructional processes. Overall, faculty are committed, using their varied perspectives and approaches, to respond to community and student needs as well as to provide the rigorous mentoring, guidance, and support students will ultimately require to successfully navigate a complex society upon program completion (Dewey, 1988).

The HDC Philosophy

The social and educational philosophies of both Nicholas Hobbs and John Dewey have shaped institutional and instructional approaches significantly at Peabody College and in the HDC program, in particular. Additionally, the legacies of Kehas, Mosher, Sprinthall, Kohlberg, Piaget, and the Harvard school flow through the HDC curriculum. As the field has developed, so too have the developmental aspects of the program, which now incorporate more recent theoretical frames including constructivism, neuroscience, attachment, and social-ecology. HDC also remains true to Aubrey's (1980) vision that "counseling could expand its horizon and strengthen its resolve" (p. 326); HDC's home within such a diverse academic department as HOD leaves it well positioned to continue carrying out these ideals. Both HOD and HDC have multidisciplinary faculty, yet "Human Development" is in the titles of both programs, which represents a common thread that binds the overall departmental culture. Themes emphasized by HDC align well with the HOD philosophy, including an emphasis on *the social community and active learning,* a focus on *personal strengths and the process of "becoming,"* the centrality of *human development,* and the development of *self-in-relation.* This philosophy is apparent in the experiences of a second-year HDC student in the School Counseling track: "We're all working together for solutions to issues that outweigh our personal differences." Furthermore, according to a long-time faculty member:

> I can't imagine now working in a single-discipline department. I think that it would feel constraining to me. What I have really appreciated is that sometimes I realize that my own perspectives have been limited. I have become a much more open person to considering other perspectives. . . . to see that individuals in the community bring such rich experiences and perspectives.

Across CDA and HDC programs, students observe shared social justice goals that accommodate diverse approaches to problem solving (Bronfenbrenner, 1977; Dewey, 1988). This characteristic undergirds the sustainable provision of resources such as networks, community partnerships, and research projects that students may have difficulty accessing otherwise. Thus interdisciplinarity is crucial to promote the exchange of ideas and approaches within and outside of the academy.

Structure of HDC Programs: Connecting Theory and Practice

The HDC curriculum has evolved through the years to include specialty courses in each of the program areas—School Counseling and Clinical Mental Health Counseling. Students acquire diagnostic and assessment skills within the context of a proactive, client-centered, and strength-based curriculum. Accordingly, students are trained to nurture personal strengths and conceptualize diagnostic codes and labels through a developmental rather than pathological framework. The HDC program trains students from the ground up, focusing first on the comprehension and application of individual and group counseling skills before transitioning into an analysis of the social and systemic forces that influence development. Another HDC student describes personal and professional challenges and benefits of inter-group diversity:

> The biggest endeavor for me has been to observe, recall, and reflect upon my outlook and worldview. This program pressures you to do that, and finding a healthy sense of identity has certainly been a cornerstone of my time here. . . . However, the personal resistance and

conditioning that are in-built serve as consistent barriers. Scaling those walls and navigating those densely clouded elements of the personal worldview are truly difficult, yet rewarding activities.

Courses are sequenced the first semester to include developmental and counseling theories classes as well as an applied counseling skills class. The overarching theme of these courses is to connect knowledge gleaned during the developmental and counseling theories courses to the acquisition and development of the skills needed to perform individual counseling in the counseling skills class. The second semester introduces specialized classes needed for each program area.

In the second year, both School and Clinical Mental Health Counseling students take a course in Counseling Diverse Populations (CDP) that introduces them to the breadth and depth of multicultural competencies and skills needed to be culturally competent counselors. This course is taken at the beginning of the second year once initial multicultural content has been introduced in first-year classes. Students begin to notice the synergistic way multiculturalism and life span development shape meaning—whether the work is counseling an individual client or advocating for change in social policies. The CDP course advances the idea of working in a social ecological environment to promote social justice and ways to confront oppression on multiple contextual levels. Students continue to integrate this knowledge through applied projects such as an advocacy assignment during their second internship experience and during the final year in the program. An Advanced Developmental course for Clinical Mental Health Counseling track (CMHC) students includes case conceptualization and counseling methods that bridge developmental theories with applied counseling practice. This conceptual framing is then incorporated into ongoing case discussions during field placements.

Practicum and Internship

Both the fieldwork and classroom experiences of students in the HDC program reflect the belief that individuals thrive through active learning. Dewey asserted that individuals do not exist in a vacuum and that human development is qualitatively affected by the social contexts to which individuals are exposed (Newbrough, 1973). Individualized learning connected to practicum and internship experiences occurs in small group seminars and individual supervision with site and faculty supervisors. Classes that are not connected to field experiences incorporate case studies and personal reflections.

The practicum is a 100-hour experience that typically takes place during the spring semester prior to the internship year. The internship takes place during the final year of the student's academic program and includes a 600-hour experience with 240 hours of direct counseling services provided to specific populations. The commitment to personal and professional development is reflected in student training. Every student must complete six sessions of personal counseling before beginning an internship field experience. During supervision and small group seminars, students examine how their understanding of clients reflects the ongoing co-constructed process of meaning making as well as how personal biases can undermine treatment. Each seminar incorporates a case conceptualization presented by a student or students on active cases. These cases are examined using multiple frameworks that reflect biological, psychological, and cultural influences on development. Learning through multiple frameworks in a peer-centered environment also hones critical thinking skills, which form the basis of sound service delivery. Such intentional instruction reflects academics in action as students learn how to incorporate class work and training to respond to actual scenarios.

HDC and Dewey in the Twenty-First Century: Synergies Across Theory, Pedagogy, and Practice

The idea of "deliberate psychological education," based on the Deweyan principle that education should promote the development of students to their full potential as individuals and as responsible citizens, is reflected in the current HDC mission statement and was central when the program was initially founded (Mosher & Sprinthall, 1971; Sprinthall & Mosher, 1978). Additionally, in the spirit of Deweyan thought, the HDC program supports the idea that counselors endeavor to become self-reflective individuals willing to undergo genuine introspection and achieve understanding and acceptance of themselves—with the ultimate aim of teaching their clients to do the same (Newbrough, 1973). Psychological education, now often referred to as promoting social emotional development in school and community contexts, is the bedrock of healthy human development.

The premise that lifespan development should be the epistemological foundation for the HDC program and the profession of counseling remains central to the mission of the program.

In essence, the HDC philosophy that exists today is a synthesis of client-centered humanism, constructivist human development, human ecology, and active learning. As such, HDC is preparing students for a professional identity that has diverged from traditional psychology or education programs in its emphasis on wellness and human development and the depth of its understanding of human development. This focus continues to be borne out in surveys from alumni and employers that show that HDC students understand how to apply these principles in practice. The HDC program continues to grow in ways that reflect the current zeitgeist of new ideas and processes to address ever-changing counseling needs. At the same time, students are challenged to understand the "nuts and bolts" of developmental theory as well as how the *application* of this body of knowledge can shape counseling approaches in school and clinical contexts that are individualized and constructed for clients with myriad realities, worldviews, and experiences.

Developing Synergies Across Theory, Pedagogy, and Practice

The "Getting Started!" table lists six action items that can support other programs striving to develop synergy across their theoretical groundings, pedagogy, and practice. Building on Dewey's pragmatism (1988), as discussed previously for both master's programs, action items include updating student readings, using proseminars and subsequent coursework to build upon core concepts, and teaching and using deliberate communication models and intentional pedagogical tools, all toward building a learning community that reflects democratic educational practices.

Conclusion

Professional programs are continually challenged to remain relevant to the needs of current and future clients. Programs such as CDA and HDC must continue to thoughtfully incorporate theories, methods, approaches, and processes to provide appropriate prevention and intervention strategies for a plethora of problems. The tasks may seem daunting, but they

Chapter 10: Getting Started!
Can Synergy Across Theory, Pedagogy, and Practice Guide Professional Education?
The Community Development and Action and Human Development
Counseling Graduate Experiences

Action Item 1: Update your reading list.
Assign Dewey's *The Public and Its Problems* (1988) as required reading to all incoming students. Ask them to identify Dewey's four conditions of democracy as outlined in this piece (participation, learning/education, inquiry, and communication) and to begin a journal they will keep throughout their first year; in the first journal entry, ask them to define what these four conditions of democracy mean to them.

Action Item 2: Use a proseminar to introduce core concepts.
Organize the core concepts to be introduced in the first semester around Dewey's conditions of democracy. Use student journals to focus on personal strengths and challenges in the process of "becoming" as well as for group experiences and reflections on class work to reinforce the connections between Dewey's notion of democracy and the core competencies of your discipline.

Action Item 3: Practice communication with advocacy and inquiry.
Assign Argyris's "Ladder of Inference" (Argryis & Schön, 1996). Teach this model as a tool for uncovering and understanding our own biases as well as understanding other people's perspectives more deeply. Intentionally and explicitly use the "ladder of inference" as a tool for negotiating difficult conversations inside and outside the classroom. This common language will help reinforce advocacy and inquiry as a norm in your learning community, bolstering Dewey's conditions of inquiry and good communication.

Action Item 4: Be intentional and explicit about pedagogy.
Using your syllabus and initial class sessions, let your pedagogy reflect your commitment to Dewey's democracy. Resist the urge to perfectly structure every learning opportunity for students, but be explicit that the goal is to provide them with an experience to work in authentic contexts. Reserve more time for classroom discussion than lecture and be sure to point out that you want them to practice their communication skills and develop methods of inquiry rather than being passive recipients of class material. Incorporate fieldwork to reflect the belief that individuals thrive through active learning.

Action Item 5: Use subsequent coursework to build upon core concepts.
Encourage students to link advanced coursework back to the conditions of democracy. How do the ethics of counseling link back to participation? To communication? Why might statistical training be important to Dewey? Help students evaluate their increasing skill sets in terms of how they help increase participation, learning, inquiry, and communication.

(continued)

Chapter 10: Getting Started! *(continued)*

Action Item 6: *Build a learning community.*
Case studies, jigsaw classrooms (where students teach other students), and group efforts to solve common problems will help students practice their skills of dialogue in authentic contexts. For more information about how to structure peer teaching in college classrooms, see www.apa.org/research/action/jigsaw.aspx. Interdisciplinary group work can also help students from disparate fields find common ground as they have foundations in the basic Deweyan tenets.

---

become more tenable when students are prepared with sound theoretical and practical tools provided by faculty with broad-based educational backgrounds, training, and experiences. Such comprehensive preparation means, as the two quotes that opened this chapter suggest, students are best trained to think proactively, effectively solve problems, and ultimately do their parts to change the world.

References

Argyris, C., & Schön, D. A. (1996). *Organizational learning II: Theory method and practice.* Reading, MA: Addison-Wesley.

Aubrey, R. F. (1980). Technology of counseling and the science of behavior: A rapprochement. *The Personnel and Guidance Journal, 58*(5), 318–27.

Briddick, W. C. (1997). Twenty years since and beyond: An interview with Roger Aubrey. *Journal of Counseling and Development, 76*, 10–15.

Bronfenbrenner, U. (1977). Towards an experimental ecology of human development. *American Psychologist, 32* (7), 518–21.

Bronfenbrenner, U. (1994). Ecological models of human development. In M. Gauvain & M. Cole (Eds.), *Readings on the development of children.* (pp. 37–43). New York: Freeman.

Commission on Colleges. (2012). Principles of accreditation: Foundations for quality enhancement. Decatur, GA: Southern Association of Colleges and Schools (SACS).

Dewey, J. (1988). *The later works of John Dewey: Volume 2, 1925–1927 essays, reviews, miscellany, and the public and its problems.* J. A. Boydston (Ed.). Carbondale, IL: Southern Illinois University Press.

Dokecki, P. R. (1992). On knowing the community of caring persons: A methodological basis for the reflective-generative practice of community-psychology. *Journal of Community Psychology, 20*(1), 26–35.

Dokecki, P. R. (1996). *The tragi-comical professional: Basic considerations for ethical reflective-generative practice.* Pittsburgh: Duquesne University Press.

Geertz, C. (1973). *The interpretation of cultures.* New York: Perseus Books Group.

Gherardi, S. (2009). Introduction: The critical power of the "practice lens." *Management Learning, 40* (2), 115–28.

Hobbs, N., Dokecki, P. R., Hoover-Dempsey, K. V., Moroney, R. M., Shayne, M. W., & Weeks, K. H. (1984). *Strengthening families.* San Francisco: Jossey-Bass.

Innes, R. B. (2006). What can learning science contribute to our understanding of the effectiveness of problem-based learning in groups? *Journal of Management Education, 30* (6), 751–64.

Innes, R. B. (2007). Dialogic communication in collaborative problem solving groups. *International Journal for the Scholarship of Teaching and Learning, 1* (1), 1–19.

Israel, B., Schulz, A., Parker, E., & Becker, A. (1998). Review of community-based research: Assessing partnership approaches to improve public health. *Annual Review of Public Health, 19* 173–202.

King, P. M. (2000). Learning to make reflective judgments. *New Directions for Teaching and Learning, 82,* 15–26. doi: 10.1002/tl.8202.

Kolb, D. (1984). *Experiential learning.* Englewood Cliffs, N.J.: Prentice-Hall.

Marsick, V. J., & O'Neil, J. (1999). The many faces of learning. *Management Learning, 30* (2), 159–76.

Mosher, R. (1988). Larry Kohlberg: A personal tribute. *Counseling and Values, 32,* 201–7.

Mosher, R., & Sprinthall, N. A. (1971). Deliberate psychological education. *Counseling Psychologist, 2*(4), 3–82.

Newbrough, J. R. (1973). Community psychology: A new holism. *American Journal of Community Psychology, 1*(3), 201–11.

Revans, R. M. (1982). *The origin and growth of action learning.* London: Chartwell Bratt.

Schön, D. (1983). *The reflective practitioner.* New York: Basic Books.

Conclusion: Academics in Action—Bridging Principles and Practice!

> If we teach today's students as we taught yesterday's, we rob them of tomorrow.
>
> —John Dewey [1]

> One of the great tragedies of life is that men seldom bridge the gulf between practice and profession, between doing and saying ... On the one hand, we proudly profess certain sublime and noble principles, but on the other hand, we sadly practice the very antithesis of these principles ... We proclaim our devotion to democracy, but we sadly practice the very opposite of the democratic creed ... This strange dichotomy, this agonizing gulf between the ought and the is, represents the tragic theme of man's earthly pilgrimage.
>
> —Martin Luther King, Jr. [2]

It seems only fitting that this volume committed to action-oriented, reflexive, community-minded research, teaching, and service concludes with charges by two seminal historic figures who espoused key tenets featured in *Academics in Action: A Model for Community-Engaged Research, Teaching, and Service.* These two statements challenge readers to put into practice the lofty ideals many individuals espouse. Moreover, the epigraphs to this chapter suggest a process by which beliefs can become behavior, attitudes can become actions, and intellectualism can become praxis. Just as forward thinkers and activists such as Gandhi,

---

1. Dewey, John. 1944. *Democracy and education*, New York: Macmillan Company, p. 167.

2. The papers of Martin Luther King, Jr.: Advocate of the social gospel by Martin Luther King (Jr.), Clayborne Carson, Susan Carson, Ralph Luker, Penny A. Russell (Eds.). (2007). Los Angeles: University of California Press, p. 487.

Martin Luther King, Jr., Paolo Freire, Mary McCloud Bethune, and John Dewey endeavored to participate in societal transformation, this volume has endeavored to document efforts by a cadre of scholars, practitioners, and students to, in some small way, follow suit. Yet the desire to engage in cooperative problem solving for the common good is, by its very nature, an ongoing process.

This volume does not present our departmental paradigms, programs, and processes as panaceas; we don't presuppose to have all the answers. In fact, a core element of what this volume espouses is that particular actions must be informed by the intersecting contexts in which they take place; there are no singular solutions, but there are shared approaches. The writers here have attempted to provide a glimpse into a multidisciplinary academic space designed to promote reflexive student learning, equality, community partnerships, ethical involvement in society, and human empowerment. The Department of Human and Organizational Development and its programs (the undergraduate HOD program, HDC and CDA master's programs, and the CRA PhD program) reflect efforts to enliven and extend Dewey's legacy in contemporary spaces such that our students and faculty enhance the arenas they enter rather than diminish them. Participatory research, community engagement, counseling, and other efforts to enhance human development, broadly defined, can provide enriching experiences and a more holistic approach to teaching, learning, practice, and research. Moreover, academic structures that are rooted in a mission of social justice and human capacity–building, undergirded by similarly committed faculty and students, will engender multidisciplinary, integrative, action-oriented work that can transform individuals, communities, and society. After summarizing several key processes and best practices that emerged here, we conclude with two conceptual challenges for the future of academics in action!

Practical Implications for the Future

A primary goal of this endeavor has been to demonstrate the importance of contemplating and studying human and social development via a model that is inherently interdisciplinary because utilizing multiple lenses can lead to a more comprehensive understanding of the impact of the multiple ecological levels in which people and problems are situated. However, we acknowledge that to prepare individuals to successfully engage in such work, intensive and intentional training must occur in an environment that encourages critical awareness and queries that connect faculty and students to the world outside the ivory tower. Although we have addressed diverse topics, the following thematic imperatives provide common threads throughout the volume.

The Importance of Utilizing Multidimensional Theoretical Frameworks

Theoretical grounding often serves as the starting point for research and guides subsequent processes. As demonstrated in this volume, utilization of models that recognize the importance of both structure and agency and acknowledge the impact of multiple ecological levels on the lives and behavior of individuals is of utmost importance. Additionally, the ideological and theoretical influences of scholars such as Dewey can provide rubrics to transform traditional academic conceptualizations to address contemporary challenges, frame timely approaches, undergird the importance of context-specific methodologies, and serve as the foundation upon which present-day practices are built. However, these chapters also remind us how theoretical frameworks tied to structure versus agency, inequality in its many forms, organizational dynamics, human development, and macro- and micro-level relationships can influence teaching, research, coursework, internships, and the intellectual culture of an academic department. The results in this volume illustrate that the ability to understand and apply multidimensional theoretical frameworks can be transformative for faculty, students, and community members alike.

The Need for Community Input in Research Endeavors

One of the primary objectives of this volume is to demonstrate the need for community-based research and illustrate the benefits of tapping into community expertise throughout the process. Academic researchers who conduct their work solely from the confines of the ivory tower often fail to understand the lived reality in communities they may genuinely desire to learn about and assist. As demonstrated by many of the empirically oriented chapters here, research agendas that include community expertise and research members as *co-researchers* can uncover unexpected information, human capital, concerns, and research topics as well as participate in community transformations. This stance is based on the premise that persons directly affected by social concerns can and do want to be involved in developing corresponding solutions (Collins, 2009; Dewey, 1916, 1927/1954, 1938). Including and valuing differing types of expertise can ultimately lead to more comprehensive research agendas, relevant academic and applied work, context appropriate data collection, robust results, and more culturally sensitive strategies, social policy, and best practices (Collins, 2000). We contend that community partners can and should be integrated into the research agenda during each phase. Moreover, their involvement in early considerations of the research goals will help establish and strengthen collaboration and relationship building.

The Benefits of Partnerships

Intervention, research, and programmatic efforts that are fragmented can diminish the impact of community-based research. Cross-sector collaborations between various local, state, and national entities as well as interdisciplinary partnerships can be beneficial responses. Additionally, an ongoing need exists to consider the sensitive nature of multi-sector partnerships. Discussions about how to establish and sustain these partnerships must be an integral part of faculty and students' training. Relationships with diverse stakeholders require open-mindedness, consideration of multiple perspectives, patience, appreciation for diversity, as well as the desire and ability to reconcile numerous priorities. University-affiliated scholars must be aware of historical realities such as stereotypes, inequality, xenophobia, homophobia, and other beliefs and behavior that undermine the lived experiences of many communities in which we study and serve—and hope to establish partnerships. To negotiate complex contexts means embracing a respectful approach to partnerships that values alternative skills and expertise relevant to the community. Equally important, faculty and students must honestly and continuously reflect upon how these same systemic forces and beliefs influence their lives, values, research and teaching interests, and ability to engage in culturally sensitive research, teaching, and service. Neglecting to incorporate interdisciplinary scholarship, methods, and approaches or to consider the needs of different stakeholders can lead to research that is siloed, uninformed, and unable to address relevant issues.

Awareness of the Potential Benefits, Barriers, and Tensions of Research

This volume highlights the significance and potential benefits of non-traditional research approaches as well as barriers and tensions present when conducting research that is "outside of the box." Although expanding traditional notions of expertise and rigor creates multiple opportunities for high quality research, such efforts do not typically happen simply or seamlessly. Practitioners and researchers must be realistic about roadblocks that might be encountered (for example, IRB approval) and tensions to be navigated (for example, resistance and distrust from potential partners). Additionally, researchers are often expected to publish in peer-reviewed journals, but community-based partners may not consider such deliverables important. Furthermore, certain publishing outlets may be less interested in applied research. Given these types of potential conflicts, up-front communication is necessary to engage in research that is mutually beneficial for all partners. Moreover, students and faculty are challenged to honestly assess the professional and personal implications of engaging in non-traditional research.

Intentional Development of Training Practices for Students and Faculty

To engage in grounded, collaborative research and community involvement, undergraduate and graduate students must be trained to successfully and respectfully navigate the community of interest. Similar skills are needed for students interested during internships and practicums. The departmental mission as well as the pedagogical approach of faculty must inform student training and provide them with the theoretical and practical knowledge and skills to understand and engage in action-oriented work. Chapters in this volume help illustrate that via an interdisciplinary lens, students can acquire multiple perspectives on individual and community development throughout their core coursework. This type of expertise is necessary to both conduct sound community-based work in a variety of settings and to negotiate other professional spaces. Rigorous coursework, internships, field schools, and institutional structures can facilitate such learning.

Bridging the Gap Between Research, Teaching, and Service

Participatory learning and service-oriented activities inside and outside the classroom can foster real-life understanding of social issues for students and researchers. Collaborations that emphasize learning in action and create opportunities for hands-on involvement often only presented in textbooks can lead to transformations that enhance the lives of community residents, community partners, students, and faculty. Fieldwork that provides an opportunity for a glimpse into the lived experience of community members can stretch one's understanding of how to best design research projects and create opportunities for iterative and reflexive experiences.

Conceptual Challenges for the Future of *Academics in Action!*

Throughout this volume, the authors have presented theoretical frameworks, research findings and approaches, as well as academic structures, processes, and coursework that embody action-oriented work. They have provided many examples of how to engage in research and practice that is community-driven, social justice–oriented, and informed by creative perspectives. However, a myriad of additional queries emerge as a result of the information and insights presented here that challenge us to ask broader questions about the relationship between town and gown, publish or perish, and ultimately the ivory tower and communities it can serve. What are some of the next steps academicians, practitioners, and students might consider in the spirit of this volume? What might Deweyism look like in the twenty-first or even twenty-second century? How can we make action-oriented work more relevant, timely, and effective? What new societal changes and contexts can we anticipate that will require us to marry social justice work with academic inquiry? As we work for social justice and participatory democracy in the United States and beyond, will students, teachers, practitioners, and scholars resist the pitfalls of national consciousness as revolutionary philosopher Franz Fanon (1963/2005) entreated? How can we best leverage individual, group, community, and university strengths to make positive change in society? Several important themes and challenges emerge from this endeavor to hopefully undergird future work for readers. They revolve around continued efforts to adopt and adapt Deweyan prescriptions as we move toward what we are terming *transdisciplinary modes of inquiry*. Each concept and the related implications are detailed in the section that follows.

Extending Dewey into the Twenty-First Century

Many chapter writers suggest that their research, teaching, social action, and/or programs reflect an application and/or extension of Deweyism (1916, 1927/1954, 1938). A variety of exciting, novel, and timely work emerged. However, several suggestions should be considered for next steps for future application of his framework in creative, unexpected, and relevant ways. The chapters in this volume illuminate action-oriented work and its implications for contemporary society. Moreover, they illustrate how contemporary social injustices are often ensconced in micro-level attitudes and actions as well as macro-level structures and processes. The writers here posit that effective human development and community action are necessary to stem the tide of inequities as well as to better prepare college students to become global citizens. Extending Deweyism acknowledges that rigorous scholarship is impotent without complementary applied work and social policies that address social problems in the United States and abroad. Oftentimes, as university-affiliated scholars, we are restricted in making these real-world connections, but we believe that they are central to efforts to span the research-practice gap. Next steps for the usage of Dewey's ideology mean that proponents must proactively endeavor to bridge the gap between structural inequities that disproportionately impact vulnerable groups. In this volume, we illustrate that such efforts must consider multiple disciplines, methods, and analytical approaches. Extending Deweyism will thoughtfully reflect the spirit and rigor of his original work—made relevant for the current global context.

For example, in order to foster more active dialogue and collaborative problem solving between academia and the public, well-resourced institutions and organizations as well as similarly resourced individuals must do more to address social ills for the common good. This call to action means that such institutions must acknowledge their relative positions of privilege, not from a place of guilt, but based on the reality that they may have access to certain resources and can become involved in participatory democracy in ways that are often difficult and/or impossible for their less-resourced counterparts. Applying Dewey more constructively means refusing to place the onus of social activism on the shoulders of disenfranchised groups or specific collectives and institutions historically responsive to social justice issues. Furthermore, extending Dewey in contemporary spaces means acknowledging and identifying untapped resources that historically disenfranchised groups have to offer as organic intellectuals.

Action-oriented teaching, research, and community service must also focus on the nuances of global complexities that will require group-based solutions as well as recognize emergent new challenges and realities such as color-blind discrimination, intra-ethnic inequity, trends in global immigration, and spatial discrimination that now share the stage with preexisting social issues such as poverty, sexism, and ageism. For example, what might the college matriculation process "look like" if more curricula incorporated reading and activities designed to promote the common good, prepared students to become reflexive practitioners, emphasized constructivist skills, married intellectualism and professional development, informed theory and practice, and concertedly focused on global issues, citizenship, and critical thinking? We further posit that cultivating such a classroom culture will require teachers to expect more from students than proficiency on exams, term papers, and oral presentations but will rather intentionally create teaching/learning dynamics that impact students affectively, cognitively, and behaviorally. Coursework must also include processes to foster problem-solving, consensus building, conflict management skills, as well as a thirst for service learning. To accomplish such tasks, professors, other teachers, and practitioners may need to be trained and re-trained (as well as to become transdisciplinary thinkers as described in the following paragraphs). Ultimately, to accomplish these goals means to first cultivate classrooms that are "safe spaces" where all issues and topics can be questioned, followed by "brave spaces" where such queries result in intellectual, emotional, social, and psychological transformations for students and faculty alike.

Each person involved in the academic experience must prepare and expect to create new knowledge—useful knowledge—that will reflect the current demographic mosaic in society. Appropriating and re-appropriating Dewey means believing that to concertedly strive to promote human development, community improvement, and social justice is *worth doing* (Dewey, 1916, 1927/1954, 1938; Freire, 1970). It means being more cognizant about how we frame problems and solutions as well as thinking systemically because we realize that micro-level remedies are needed, but they are insufficient without systemic change. Moreover, espousing Dewey means preparing for possible tensions and conflict from citizens who may embrace differing views.

Transdisciplinary Modes of Inquiry

The chapters here reflect interdisciplinary/multidisciplinary work that is informed by academic arenas such as social psychology, community psychology, sociology, ecology, and cultural studies. Each piece illustrates some of the benefits of employing several lenses when addressing social issues for more comprehensive work and possible solutions. Informative in their own rights, these findings suggest an imperative to *push* academic inquiry—and the boundaries of the academy, more generally—further into unchartered physical and theoretical territories that lend themselves to original, imaginative, cutting-edge scholarship and teaching. We broadly refer to this process and framing approach as *transdisciplinary modes of inquiry* because, rather than synergize information from existing disciplines, it reflects the actual development of new disciplines from which new ideas, theories, praxis, approaches, and designs would emerge to address both the human condition and human development. Moreover, we posit that transdisciplinary inquiry would illustrate extending Deweyism at its best!

Moving from interdisciplinary/multidisciplinary inquiry to a transdisciplinary frame is more than a buzz word or moniker, but a new frame of reference that positions academic work to move into new arenas. Negotiating a society that is becoming increasingly more complex means questioning reductionist views about social problems and centering the lives and experiences of other groups, especially historically disenfranchised groups. Although we may not find answers to all of our concerns and questions, the process of inquiry should seek out many voices, views, and vantage points, particularly around decision-making tables, with the belief that certain solutions are only yet to be discovered. This frame welcomes new insight from other disciplines, while continually challenging the appropriateness and relevance of prevailing disciplines for addressing certain issues. A transdisciplinary frame requires us to consider the possible influence and benefits of inquiry that is informed by disciplines other than the arts and sciences and humanities, broadly defined. For example, what might scholars and students from biology, chemistry, criminology, computer science, and medicine have to offer research on human and community development? How can such disciplines become more concertedly part of this academic process? What benefits, challenges, and learning curves should be anticipated? This academic frame acknowledges and appreciates existing scholarship and instructional processes such as positivism, but seeks out and welcomes other approaches for data gathering and analysis that can capture experiences.

By extension, transdisciplinary modes of inquiry must acknowledge that multiculturalism will give way to transcultural influences as a result of heterogeneity and intersectionality around lived experiences linked to ethnicity, nationality, race, sexual orientation, gender, and other statuses or profiles. Individuals that embrace this frame are comfortable thinking in new and exacting ways as well as forging inter-institutional allies, networks, and friendships across universities, colleges, and grassroots groups here and abroad. This frame also recognizes that students as well as community members, regardless of their profiles and histories, are the best source of knowledge and insight about themselves and their lives. Thus, as organic intellectuals, such persons can be powerful purveyors of ideas and solutions. Although less familiar with academic jargon, they often possess unique expertise and subjugated knowledges that can be both individually and collectively transformative (Collins, 2000, 2009).

Additionally, transdisciplinary teachers, practitioners, students, and scholars must expand their abilities to create and develop new understandings, concepts, and paradigms about what constitutes the common good, power, privilege, and social redress now and for the future. This means revitalizing inquiry using lenses that more concertedly uncover social structures in which chronic and contemporary social ills are embedded as well as groups that have historically benefited or experienced hardship as a result. The proposed mode of inquiry is inherently reflexive, collaborative, creative, culturally sensitive, curious, and holistic in its theoretical, methodological, analytical, and practical approaches. Holistic research and subsequent teaching and community engagement must include case studies, large-scale studies, and theoretical projects to illumine voices in all their manifestations. Scholars suggest that transdisciplinary work centers the organization of knowledge around complex, varied domains rather than around disciplines such that participants welcome a thoughtful fusion of diverse sources of knowledge, collaborative approaches, as well as individuals with formal and informal expertise. This means that transdisciplinary research ultimately transcends borders tied to disciplines, science and practice, scientific and practical knowledge, scientific results, and systemic changes (Schweizer-Ries & Perkins, 2012).

The outcomes in this volume reflect research, teaching, and community engagement from a multidisciplinary perspective informed by disciplines such as sociology, community psychology, education, psychology, and cultural studies. These results also provide a glimpse of a theoretical/practical framework, coined here as *transdisciplinary modes of inquiry*, that we suggest reflects the evolution of a multidisciplinary (or interdisciplinary) framework. A multidisciplinary lens creates a teaching/learning environment that does not elevate any particular discipline, methodology, analytical process, or individual over another. Moreover, it acknowledges that students, teachers, and community members are better prepared to understand, study, and address complex real-world problems when a varied group of thinkers are "sitting around the table." Collaborative efforts are essential and increase more equitable processes and outcomes. Our use of the term "transdisciplinary" does not suggest that multidisciplinary efforts are passé and will be replaced, but rather that, like any intellectual process, scholars should anticipate the continual evolution of how we perform research, instruct students, and interact with communities. Society is constantly changing; academe must similarly change and prepare to meet this challenge.

In addition to creating and illuming new knowledge that emerges during academic encounters, transdisciplinarity suggests ever-increasing intentionality to cultivate genuinely collaborative teams; students, teachers, and community members that are genuinely open to perspectives beyond their own; innovative capacity-building at each phase of a project; and thoughtfully incorporating new approaches to respond to complex questions and social issues. However, we posit that the feature that most readily distinguishes transdisciplinarity from multidisciplinarity is the potential for the emergence of entirely new disciplines, paradigms, methods, analytical approaches, and collaborative teams that are more than mere combinations of their predecessors. Such outcomes would reflect genuine syntheses that are typically difficult to accomplish due to differentials associated with power, resources, organizational capacities, time, and human foils. A transdisciplinary approach also means that individuals engage in research and teaching driven by a desire for the *greater good* and expect that community-based work will actually help answer questions and combat problems that continue to plague society such as racial and ethnic divisiveness, class conflict, immigration challenges, and other issues that undermine human development, trust, and relationships.

Proponents of a transdisciplinary perspective also agree to share power, more proactively work to dismantle power structures and processes as they become evident, and acknowledge and attempt to diminish personal and collective forms of entitlement. The concept means extending a Deweyan model further *as an idealized paradigm* to be pursued in the real world. This concept reflects a work in progress; by design, it is fluid and calls into question static ways of instruction and study. For example, dimensions of transdisciplinarity are evident in the spirit of Donna Haraway's (1991) "Cyborg Manifesto" as a specific model to promote inclusivity. Moreover, groundbreaking work by Du Bois (1903/1996), Collins (2000), and Fine (2009) have made inroads as well. At its best, a transdisciplinary mode of inquiry would reflect a transformative paradigm for academic and applied work, community interaction and enhancement, interpersonal behavior, and human development to proactively cultivate democracy in society in general and in higher education in particular. A plethora of challenges, opportunities, unknowns, and tensions should be anticipated as this mode of inquiry is championed. These two broad themes—twenty-first century Deweyism and transdisciplinary modes of inquiry—are not mutually exclusive but rather should inform and nurture each other in academe and ultimately move outside the ivory tower to be most effective. Readers are encouraged to consider these proposed emerging frames of reference for future research, teaching, and community action.

References

Collins, P. H. (2000). *Black feminist thought: Knowledge, consciousness and the politics of empowerment* (2nd edition). New York: Routledge.

Collins, P. H. (2009). *Another kind of public education: Race, schools, the media and democratic possibilities.* Boston: Beacon Press.

Dewey, J. (1916). *Democracy and education.* New York: Simon & Schuster.

Dewey, J. (1927/1954). *The public and its problems.* Chicago: The Swallow Press.

Dewey, J. (1938). *Education and experience.* New York: Touchstone, Simon & Schuster.

Du Bois, W. E. B. (1903/1996). *The souls of black folk.* New York: The Modern Library.

Fanon, F. (1963/2005). *The wretched of the earth.* New York: Grove Press.

Fine, M. (2009). Postcards from metro America: Reflections on youth participatory action research for urban justice. *The Urban Review, 41*(1), 1–6.

Freire, P. (1970). Pedagogy of the oppressed. New York: Herder & Herder.

Schweizer-Ries, P., & Perkins, D. D. (2012). Sustainability science: Transdisciplinarity, transepistemology, and action research. *Umweltpsychologie (Environmental Psychology), 16,* 6–11.

About the Editors

SANDRA L. BARNES is a joint appointed Sociology Professor in the Department of Human and Organizational Development in Peabody College of Education and Human Development and the School of Divinity at Vanderbilt University in Nashville. Her research and teaching areas include urban sociology, sociology of religion, inequality, statistics, and African American studies. Her publications include *Live Long and Prosper: How Black Megachurches Address HIV/AIDS and Poverty in the Age of Prosperity Theology* (Fordham, 2012); *Black Megachurch Culture: Models for Education and Empowerment* (Peter Lang, 2010); *Subverting the Power of Prejudice: Resources for Individual and Social Change* (InterVarsity, 2006); and *The Costs of Being Poor: A Comparative Study of Life in Poor Urban Neighborhoods in Gary, Indiana* (SUNY, 2005). Her articles have been included in *SOCIAL FORCES*, *Social Problems*, *Journal of African American Studies*, and *Sociological Spectrum*.

LAUREN BRINKLEY-RUBINSTEIN recently completed her Ph.D. in Community Research and Action (CRA) in Peabody College of Education and Human Development at Vanderbilt University. Her research interests include health disparities, the social determinants of health, and the intersection of HIV and incarceration. Lauren has published fourteen peer-reviewed journal articles, the most recent of which centers on the experience of intersectional stigma among HIV-positive, recently incarcerated African American men.

BERNADETTE DOYKOS is a doctoral student in the Community Research and Action (CRA) program at Peabody College of Education and Human Development at Vanderbilt University and a Research Associate at the Center for Education Policy, Applied Research, and Evaluation at the University of Southern Maine. She is the author of several policy briefs about educational equity issues in the state of Maine. She has also contributed to a number of published articles appearing in *Journal of Community Practice*, *Journal of Community Psychology*, *Social Work and Public Health*, and *Teachers College Record*.

NINA C. MARTIN is an Associate Clinical Professor in the Department of Human Development and Psychology and Department of Human and Organizational Development in Peabody College of Education and Human Development at Vanderbilt University. Her research interests include adolescent depression, longitudinal research methods, and the design and application of school- and community-based intervention and prevention efforts to enhance the well-being of children, adolescents, and families. Some of her articles include "Predictors of youths' post-traumatic stress symptoms following a natural disaster: The 2010 Nashville Tennessee flood," *Journal of Clinical Child and Adolescent Psychology* (Martin et al., forthcoming); "Peer victimization (and harsh parenting) as developmental correlates of cognitive reactivity, a diathesis for depression," *Journal of Abnormal Psychology*, 123(2), 336–49 (Cole, Martin et al., 2014); and "A randomized controlled trial of a cognitive-behavioral program for the prevention of depression in adolescents compared with nonspecific and no-intervention control conditions," *Journal of Counseling Psychology*, 60(3), 432–38 (Possel, Martin et al., 2013).

ALLISON PATTEN McGUIRE is a Lecturer in the Department of Human and Organizational Development in Peabody College of Education and Human Development at Vanderbilt University. She has worked as a teacher in several contexts with students ranging from seventh grade through graduate school. Her doctoral training is in Community Psychology, focused on adolescent development in the context of community, specifically young people's meaning-making processes about their involvement in community service. Her research interest is identifying and creating contexts that scaffold the development of core competencies of group and community participation, including critical and reflective thinking and conflict management. Dr. McGuire teaches lifespan human development, emphasizing the role of context and culture on human development; small group behavior and development; and community and organizational interventions focusing on changes at the group level of analysis.

Index

academic programs: caring in, 60–61; generativity in, 60–61; policy-oriented, 90–92
Accountable Talk, 40
AES (Alignment Enhanced Services), 72; ecological theory and, 108–9; youth development and, 103–5
American Pragmatism, 28
American Recovery and Reinvestment Act, 89–90
application, CRA approach to health, 131–32

Barnes, Sandra L., 18
Benbow, Camilla, 18
Bess, Kimberly, 19
Bethune, Magaela, 19
Boyer, Ernest, 73, 124; scholarship types, 126–27
Buber, Martin, 193

caring, 60; academic programs and, 60–61
Caring and Competent Society, 49
CBPR (community-based participatory research), 143; field school and, 179–80; NPN case study, 148–57
CDA (Community Development and Action), 142–43, 238–39; curriculum, 246–48; pedagogy, 242–46; philosophy, 241; practice model, 242; program model, 239–41; program theory, 241–42; reflective-generative practitioners, 242
Chadwick, Caleb, 19
Chatman, Vera, 2n3
China field school, 176
CITI (Collaborative Institutional Training Initiative), 154–55

civic education, ISL and, 171
classroom communication patterns, 40–41
client-professional relationships: Freud's arrow, 53–54; power, 52; prophetic pragmatism, 55; reflective-generative practice, 63–64; reflective practice, 61–63. *See also* professions as practice
CNA (community needs assessment), NPN case study, 148–57
collaborative community research, 109–12, 263–64; benefits, 112–15; interfaith project, 207–9; ISL and, 171
Collins, Patricia Hill, 9
communities of inquiry, 39–42
community: constructivism and, 31–32; individuals and, 33–34
community-based rapid re-housing, 78
community development research: CBPR and, 143; CRA and, 142–43; democratization of, 144–45; NPN case study, 148–57; obstacles, 146–47; PAR and, 143–44; residents' expertise, 145; rigor, 147–48, 155–56
community research: benefits, 112–15; collaborative, 109–12
community service, 4
complementarity, 100
constructivism, 30–31; community and, 31–32; engaged communication and, 34; HDC M. Ed., 214; HOD UGCI, 214
contextualism, 100
CRA (Community Research and Action), 142–43; approach to public health, 126–38; case studies, 133–38; degree, 73n2

critical race theory, 3
cross-cultural adjustment, ISL and, 171
cultural barriers, dialogic communication, 38

Democratic Century, 44
Dewey, John, 3, 9, 13; CRA and, 142–43; current reading, 266–68; democratic society and, 7–8; *Experiences and Education*, 215; higher education reform and, 28–29; holistic education, 125; on learning, 30–32; naturalistic worldview, 33–34; *The Public and Its Problems*, 29–30; on teaching, 30–32
dialogic communication: Accountable Talk, 40; cultural barriers, 38; learning communities, 39–42; Obama, Barack, 40; participatory democracy and, 37–38
discovery, CRA approach to health, 129–30
diversity of belief systems, 34, 191–92
Dokecki, Paul, 2n3, 18
Doykos, Bernadette, 19

ecological theory of human development, 3, 99–100; youth development and, 107–9
education: caring in, 60–61; generativity in, 60–61; holistic, 125; preexisting ideas and, 35
educational architects, 11
EHDC (Ethics of Human Development and Community), 49–50; decision-making framework, 64–66; participatory research and, 50; professions as practice, 55–59
ELL (English Language Learner) programs, 105
ethics, 50–51; client-professional relationships, 52; community development, 66; EHDC and, 49–55; ethical tasks, 54–55; human development, 66; virtue ethics, 59–60
Experiences and Education (Dewey), 215

experiential learning, 163, 213–15; Kolb's model, 216–18; professions as practice, 58–59; youth development and, 99. *See also* internships (HOD)

Family Options experiment, 77–78
family processes, homelessness and, 79–81
feminist theory, 3
Field School in Intercultural Education, 167–68; academic partners, 184–85; CBPR, 179–80; China, 176; cultural outsiders' challenges, 180–81; design, 168–70; distinctions, 169–70; expectations management, 175–77, 182–84; facilitating, 185–87; history, 172–74; ISL and, 170–71; New Mexico, 176; South Africa, 177; student buy-in, 181–82; sustainability, 177–78; teams, 169; theoretical foundations, 170–72; university-community partnerships, 174–75
Freire, Paulo, 30–31
Freud's arrow, 53–54
Frieden, Gina, 2n3, 18, 173
Fromm, Erich, *The Sane Society*, 51–52

Gardenia Valley: collaborative research, 111–12; youth development and, 105–7
generative narratives, 58–59
generativity, academic programs and, 60–61
goods internal/external to practice, 57–58
Green, Judith, prophetic pragmatism, 55
Griffin, Brian, 2n3

Habermas, Jurgen, 9
HDC (Human Development Counseling) M.Ed., 214, 238–39, 249–51; accreditation, 214n2; compared with other programs, 251–52; Dewey and, 255–56; internship, 216–24, 254–55; philosophy, 252–53; practicum, 254–55; program structure, 253–54

health, influences, 124–25
higher education reform, Dewey and, 28–29
Hobbs, Nicholas, 49
HOD (Dept. of Human and Organizational Development), 1–2; educational philosophy, 214; field schools, history, 172–74; intellectual focus, 9–10; interdisciplinary inquiry, 6–10; internships, 214; mission, 4, 100. *See also* EHDC
HOD UGCI (HOD Undergraduate Capstone Internships), 214, 224–27; benefits, 227–33
HomeBase, 88–89
homelessness, 72; community-based rapid re-housing, 78; Family Options experiment, 77–78; family processes and, 79–81; family separation, 85–87; family support networks, 82–83; housing services and, 79–87; housing subsidies and, 77–78; HUD (Dept. of Housing and Urban Development), 78–79; income inequality and, 76–77; prevention services, 87–90; social exclusion and, 76–77; social services and, 78
Horton, Cheryl, 19
Housing Choice Vouchers, 77–78
housing services, homelessness and, 79–87
HPRP (Homelessness Prevention and Rapid Re-housing Program), 78, 89–90
HUD (Dept. of Housing and Urban Development), 78–79
human development, ecological theory of, 3

I and Thou (Buber), 193
ICT (information and communication) revolution, 44
individuals, community and, 33–34
inert knowledge, 31
Innes, Robert, 2n3, 18
inquiry: communities of inquiry, 39–42; knowledge and, 33–34; as social activity, 35–38; transdisciplinary, 268–71

integration, CRA approach to health, 130–31
integrative learning, 216, 218–19
interdisciplinarity, 6–10
Interfaith and Community Service Campus Challenge, 191–92
interfaith conflict, 192–93
interfaith initiatives, 193–94; language, 200–1
interfaith project, 195–96; activities, 198–200; collaboration, 207–9; competence and, 200–3; participant observation, 196–97; participatory research, 196–202, 207–9; reflexive knowledge, 205–7; relational knowledge, 203–5; representational knowledge, 200–3; research team, 196–98
Interfaith Youth Core, 191–92
intergroup research, 193
internships (HOD), 214; HDC M.Ed., 216–24; HOD UGCI, 214, 224–33
interviews, videos, 18–20
ISL (international service-learning), 170–71
Islamic Society of North America's Office for Interfaith and Community Alliances, 192

James, Williams, 71

Karakos, Holly, 19
King, Martin Luther, 9
Kinghorn, Ben, 20
knowledge: inert, 31; inquiry and, 33–34; prior knowledge and learning, 35; relational, 203–5

League for Industrial Democracy, 29–30
learning: constructivism, 30–31; Dewey on, 30–32; experiential, 163, 213–15; integrative, 216, 218–19; Kolb's experiential learning model, 216–18; preexisting ideas and, 35; prior knowledge and, 35; registrative, 218; theory, ISL and, 171
learning communities, dialogic communication, 39–42
legitimate peripheral participants, 37

life narratives, 58
Lippmann, Walter, 29
Locke, Alain, 9

marginalized groups, learning communities and, 37–38
McCormack, Mark, 19
multidimensional theoretical frameworks, 262
Muslims, othering and, 193–94

narratives, 58
Nation, Maury, 173
naturalistic worldview of Dewey, 33–34
New Mexico field school, 176; sustainability and, 177–78
Newbrough, Bob, 2n3
NICHD (National Institute of Child Health and Human Development), 79
Nixon, Carol, 20
Nossett, Caitlin, 19
NPN (Nashville Promise Neighborhood) case study, 148–57
Nwosu, Oluchi, 19

Occupy Wall Street, 27n1; participatory democracy and, 27–28
organizational theory, 3
othering, 193–94

PAR (Participatory Action Research), 143–44
participant observation, interfaith project, 196–97
participatory democracy: dialogic communication and, 37–38; Occupy Wall Street movement and, 27–28; *The Public and Its Problems* (Dewey), 29–30; sustained peripheral participation, 38; Tea Party Movement and, 27–28
participatory research, 11–12, 36–37; EHDC and, 50; interfaith project, 196–202, 207–9; ISL and, 171; legitimate peripheral participants and, 37. *See also* community development research

Partridge, William, 168, 172
Patel, Eboo, 192
Peabody College, 9n4; Hobbs, Nicholas, 49
Perkins, Doug, 18, 173
postmodernism, in academia, 50–51
power: client-professional relationships, 52; coercive, 52–53; degree, 53–54; Freud's arrow, 53–54; kind of, 53–54; synergic, 53–55
practice, professions as, 55–59
praxis, theory and, 23–24
preexisting ideas, 35
Prilleltensky, Isaac, 172–73
privilege, 4–6
problematic situations, inquiry and, 35–38
professions as practice, 55–59; reflective-generative practice and, 59–60. *See also* client-professional relationships
prophetic pragmatism, 55
The Public and Its Problems (Dewey), 29–30
public health, 124–25; case studies, 133–38; CRA approach, 126–38; disciplinary divides, 126; health of incarcerated men, HIV positive, 134–36; refugee health, 136–38; scholarship, early, 125–26; traditional approaches, 125–26

reflection, constructivism and, 32
reflective-generative practice, 3; CDA program, 242; client-professional relationships, 63–64; synergic power and, 53; virtue ethics and, 59–60
reflective practice, client-professional relationships, 61–63
reflexive knowledge, interfaith project and, 205–7
registrative learning, 218
relational knowledge, interfaith project, 203–5
religious diversity, 191–92; interfaith conflict, 192–94
research: CBPR, 143; community-based, 4; community development,

73–74; community input need, 262–63; democratization of, 144–45; participatory, 11–12, 36–37; rigor, 147–48, 155–56; team-based, 11–12; university support, 92–94; youth development, 72

SAAF (Strong African American Families), 72; ecological theory and, 108; youth development and, 101–2
Sagor, Richard, 11–12
Sandler, Howard, 2n3
The Sane Society (Fromm), 51–52
scholarship (Boyer), 73, 126–27; public health and, 129–33
SDS (Students for Democratic Society), 30
service-learning, ISL and, 171–72
Shields, Sharon, 2n3, 18, 20, 173
Shinn, Marybeth, 19
simultaneity, 100
Smith, Ashley, 19
Smith, Heather, 19
social action, 100
social capital, 6
Social Darwinism, 44
social services, homelessness and, 78
societal magnet, 54
socioeconomic background: faculty, 4–6; students, 4–6
South African Field School, 72, 177; CBPR, 179; sustainability and, 178; youth development and, 105–7

stereotype confirmation, 35
sustainability, field schools, 177–78
sustained peripheral participation, 38
synergic power, 53–54; power distribution and, 54–55

teaching: community-based, 4; CRA approach to health, 132–33; Dewey on, 30–32; Freire, Paulo, 30–31
team-based research, 11–12
Tea Party Movement, participatory democracy and, 27–28
theoretical frameworks, 262
theory, praxis and, 23–24
Tift, Jay, 19
town/gown separation, 4–5
training practice development, 264–65
transdisciplinary modes of inquiry, 268–71
Turner, Susie, 19

Veenstra-VanderWeele, Robin, 19
videos of interviews, 18–20
virtue ethics, 59–60

West, Cornel, 9

youth development, 72; AES and, 103–5; ecological systems theory, 99–100; ecological theory in, 107–9; Gardenia Valley, 105–7; intervention programs, 98–99; SAAF and, 101–2; variable experiences, 99

www.ingramcontent.com/pod-product-compliance
Ingram Content Group UK Ltd.
Pitfield, Milton Keynes, MK11 3LW, UK
UKHW040425270326
469305UK00005BA/23